Introduction

The photographs in this book were all taken i ... 2 and 1992. It was a very difficult time for the city as its traditional industries experienced a catast ... great hardship as a result.

By the end of the period the first signs were ... t-industrial city. Sheffield still makes steel, of course, but more people now work in commerce an...

That story has been told well elsewhere. This ... nsition in terms of the city's landscape and buildings. Most of the scenes depicted have changed although a few, mostly featuring nineteenth century listed buildings, remain little altered. I have kept the captions as brief as possible but sufficient, I hope, to orientate the reader in terms of the city's geography and recent history.

On a personal level this is also a record of my own decade as a citizen, a photographer and as a roofer in the local building trade, an occupation that did on occasion provide me with an unusual, if precarious, camera position.

If you would like to see more of my work or contact me about these pictures then please visit www.adrianwynn.com.

ISBN 1-905278-17-9

Published & Printed by Pickard Communication,

11 Riverside Park, Sheaf Gardens, Sheffield S2 4BB

Telephone 0114 275 7222 or 275 7444

email info@pickardcommunication.co.uk

www.pickardcommunication.co.uk

The Rivelin Valley viewed
from Crookes, 1982.
Looking towards Stannington

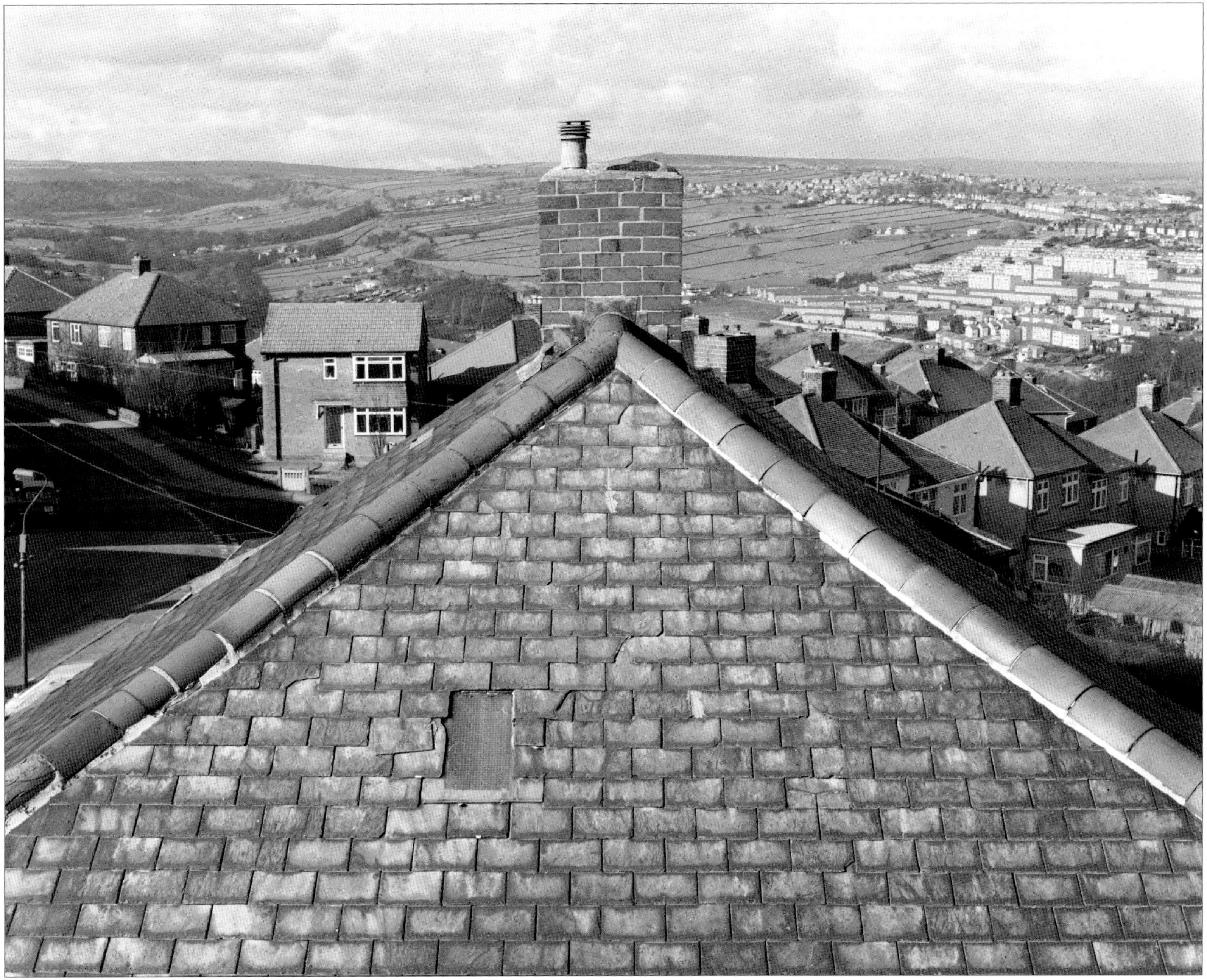

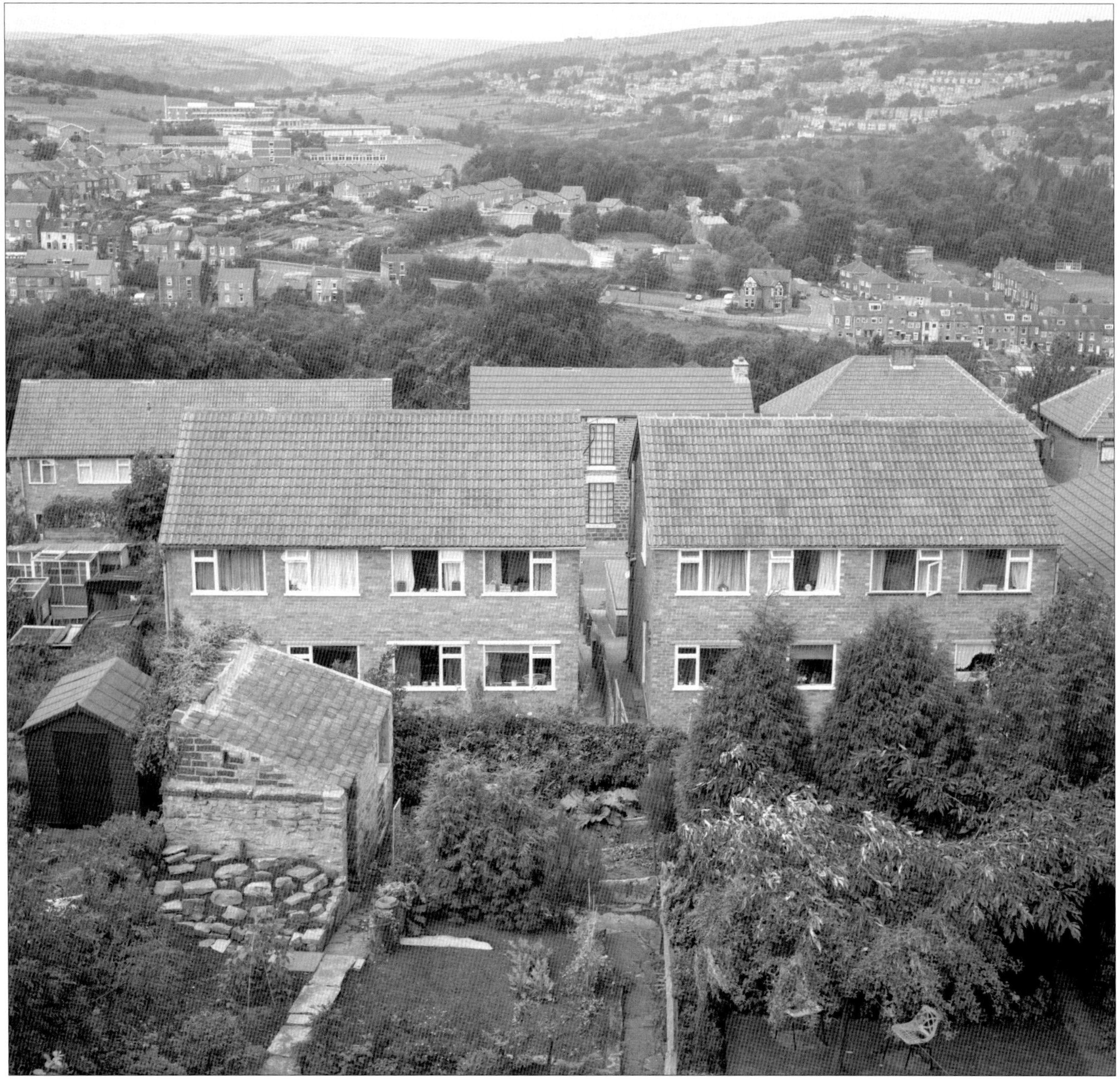

The Loxley valley from Walkley, 1982.
Myers Grove school is in the middle distance

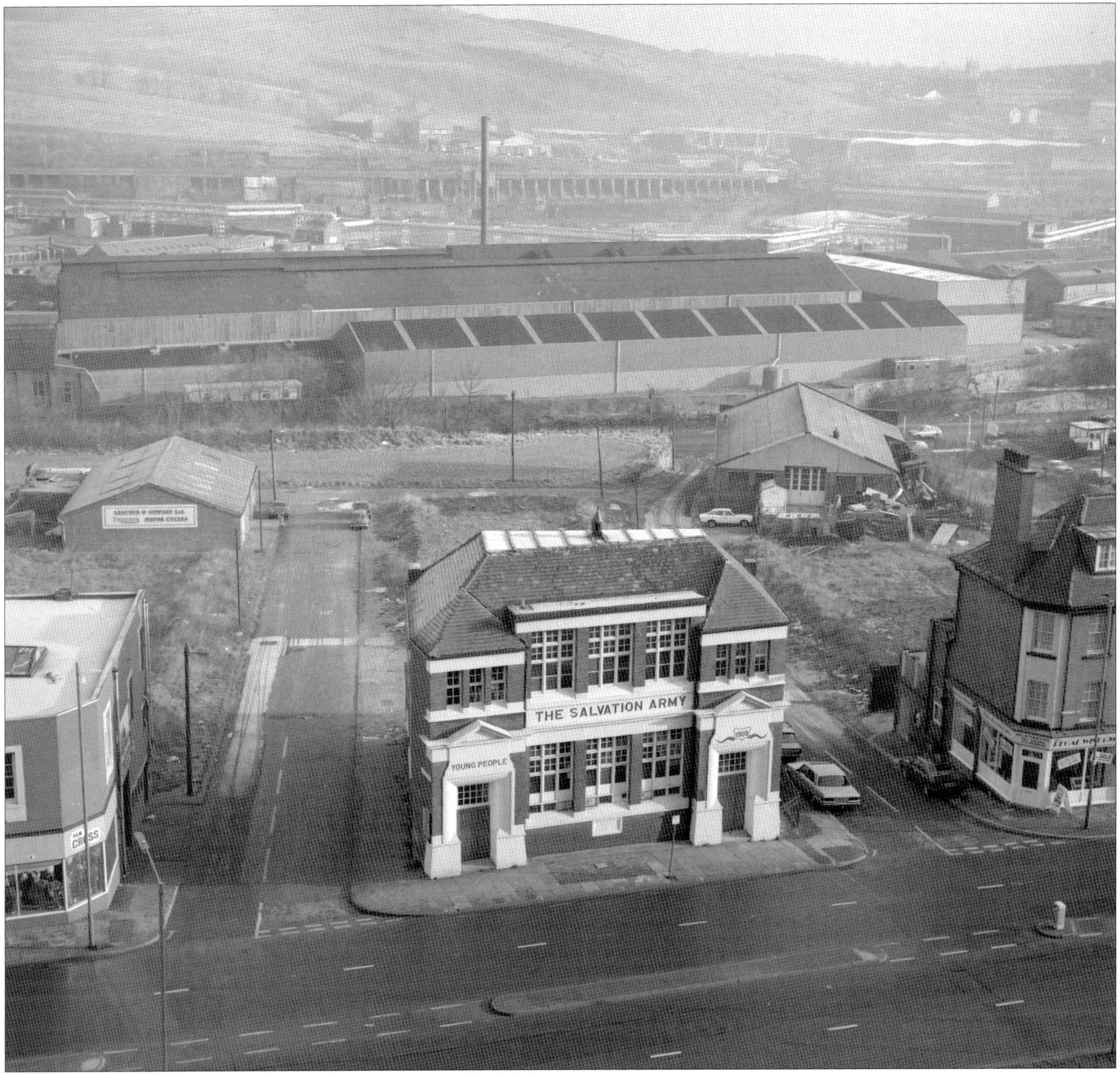

The Upper Don valley
at Neepsend, 1983.

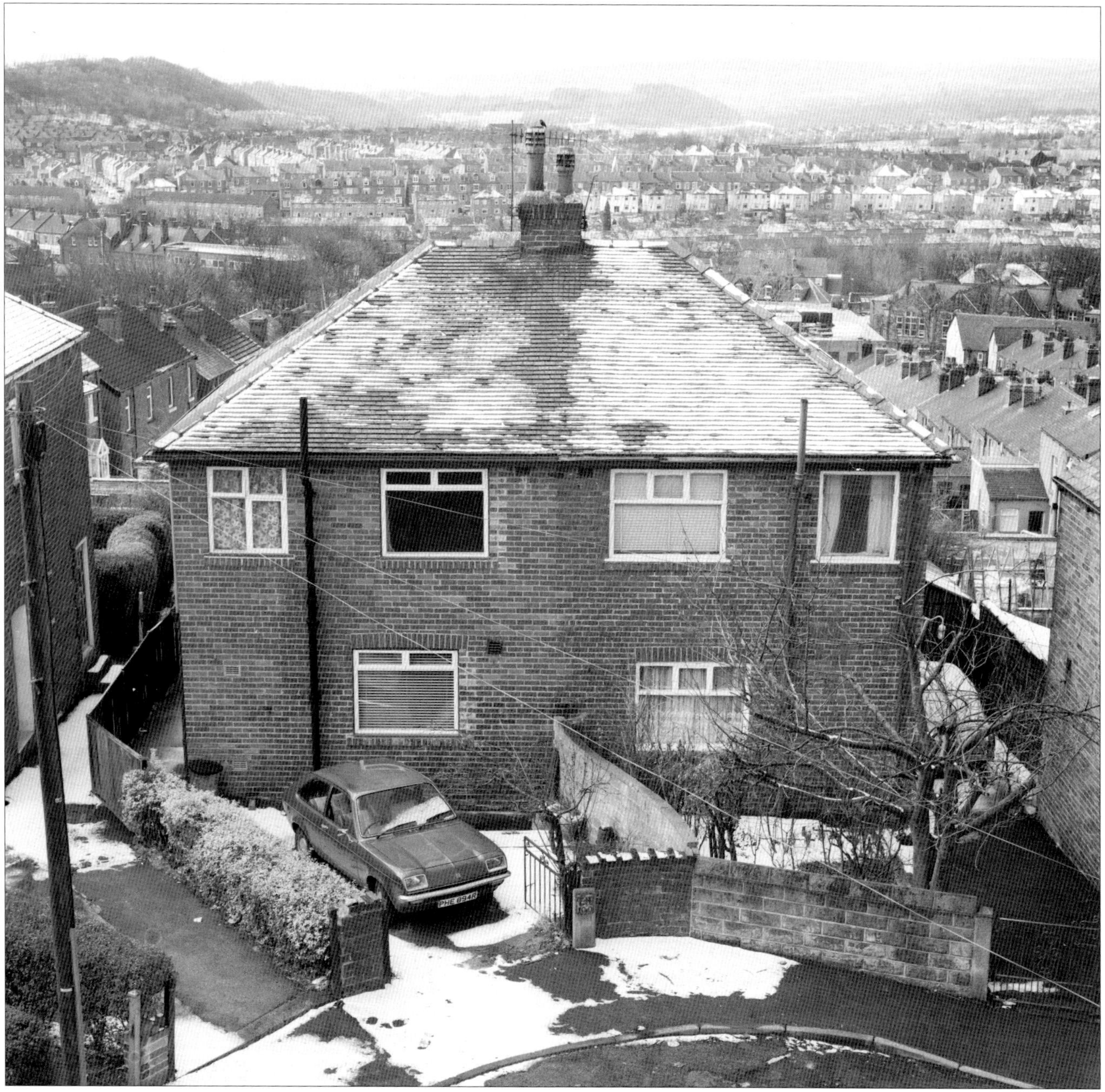

The valley of the Sheaf from Woodseats, 1985. Towards Abbeydale.

The Porter Brook valley, 1983.
From Banner Cross looking to
the city centre.

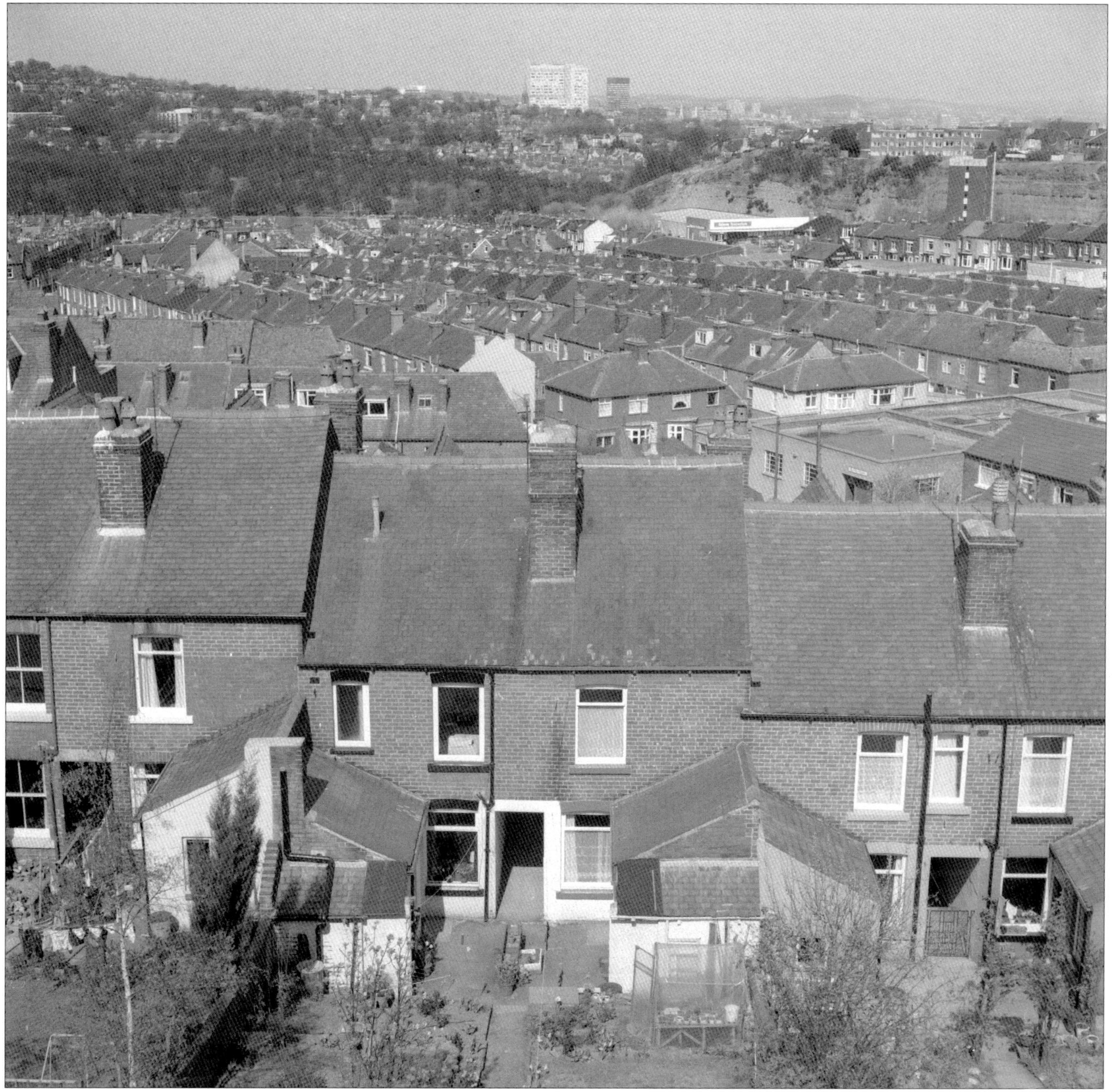

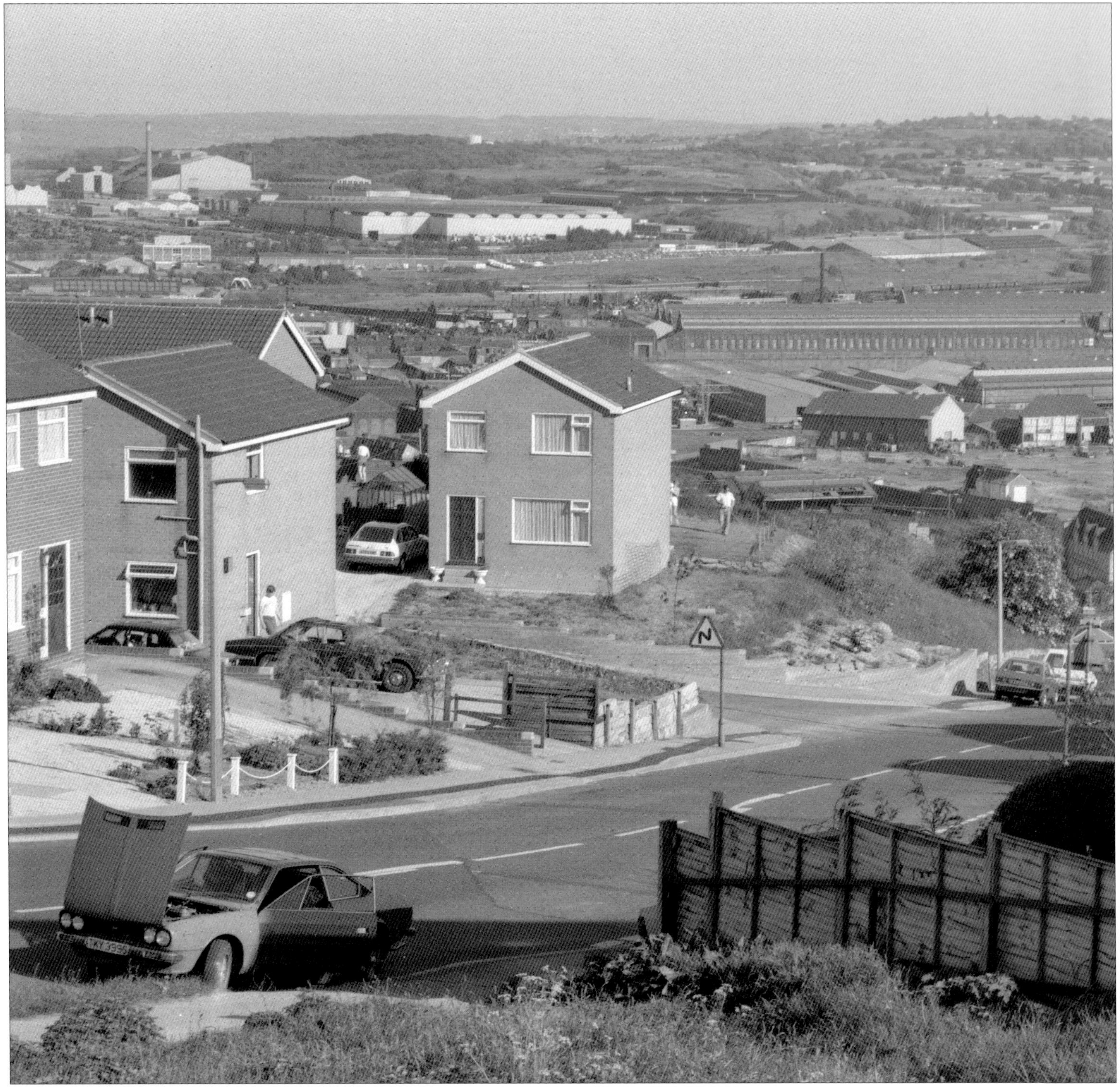

The Lower Don valley at
Brightside, 1986.
From Jenkin Road.

The Blackburn valley, 1983 looking across the valley of the Don from Tinsley

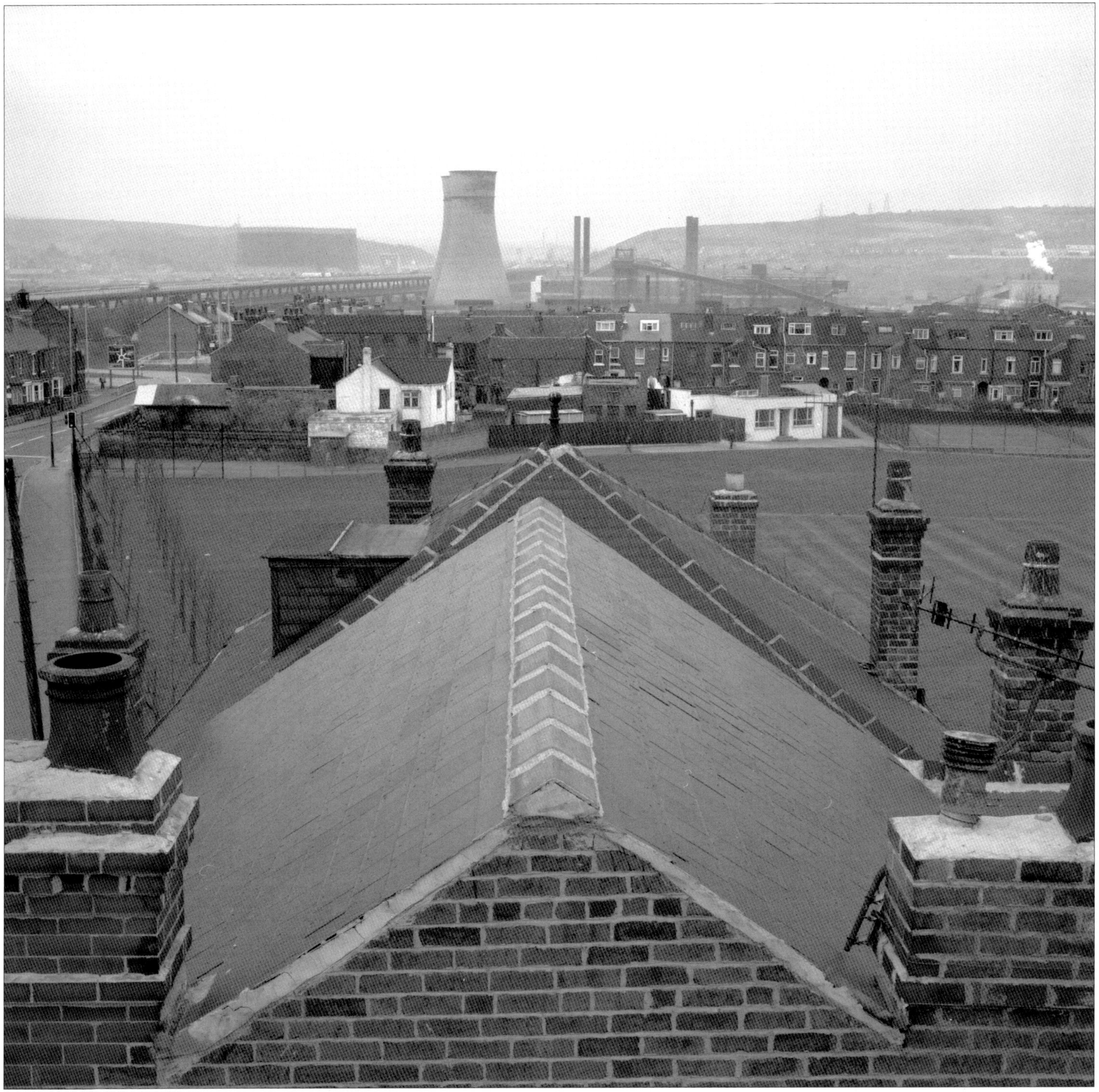

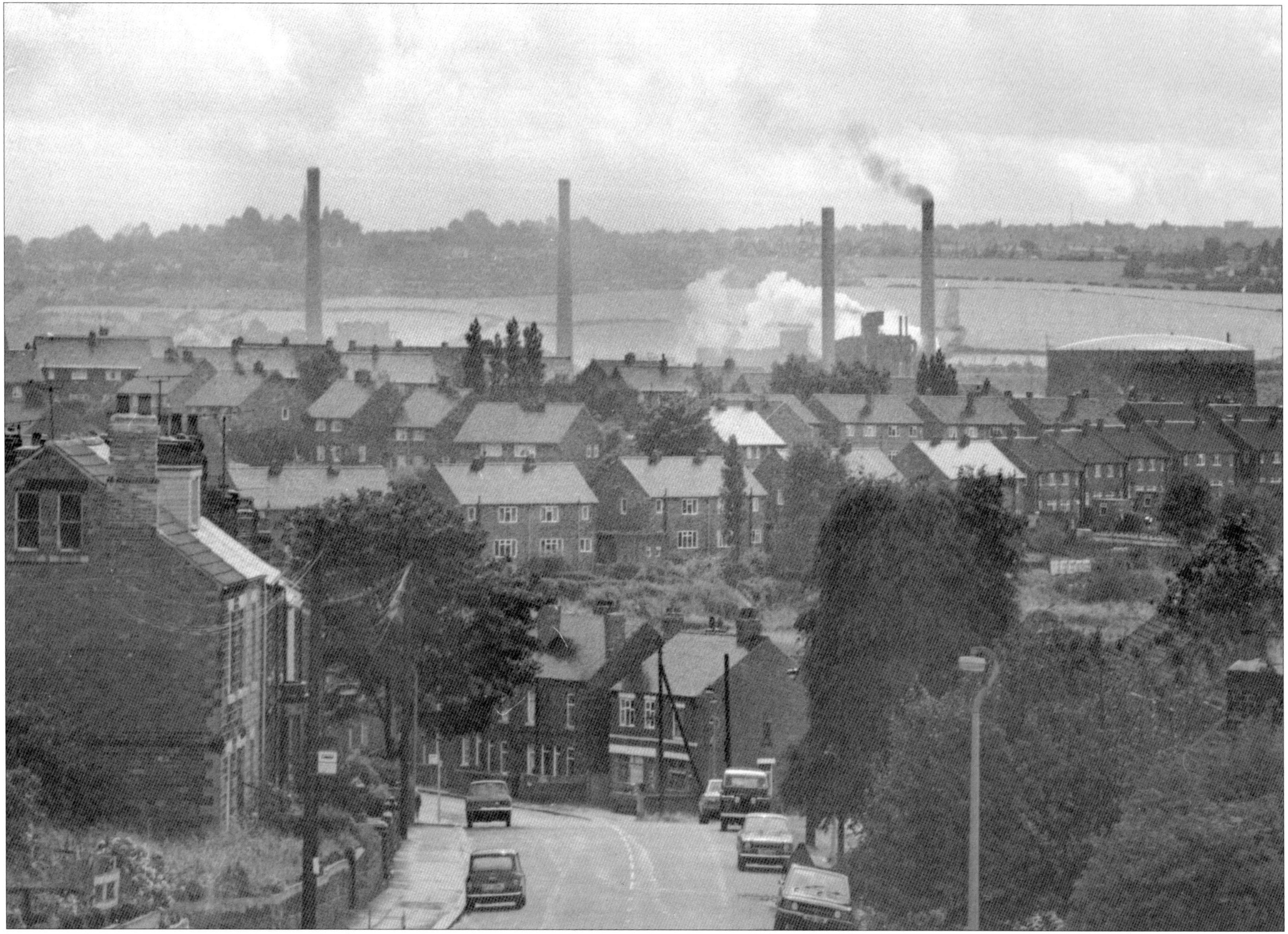

Treeton village, 1983. On the eastern edge of the city, Treeton was dominated by the Orgreave coking plant which became the scene of bitter conflict during the miners' strike of 1984-5.

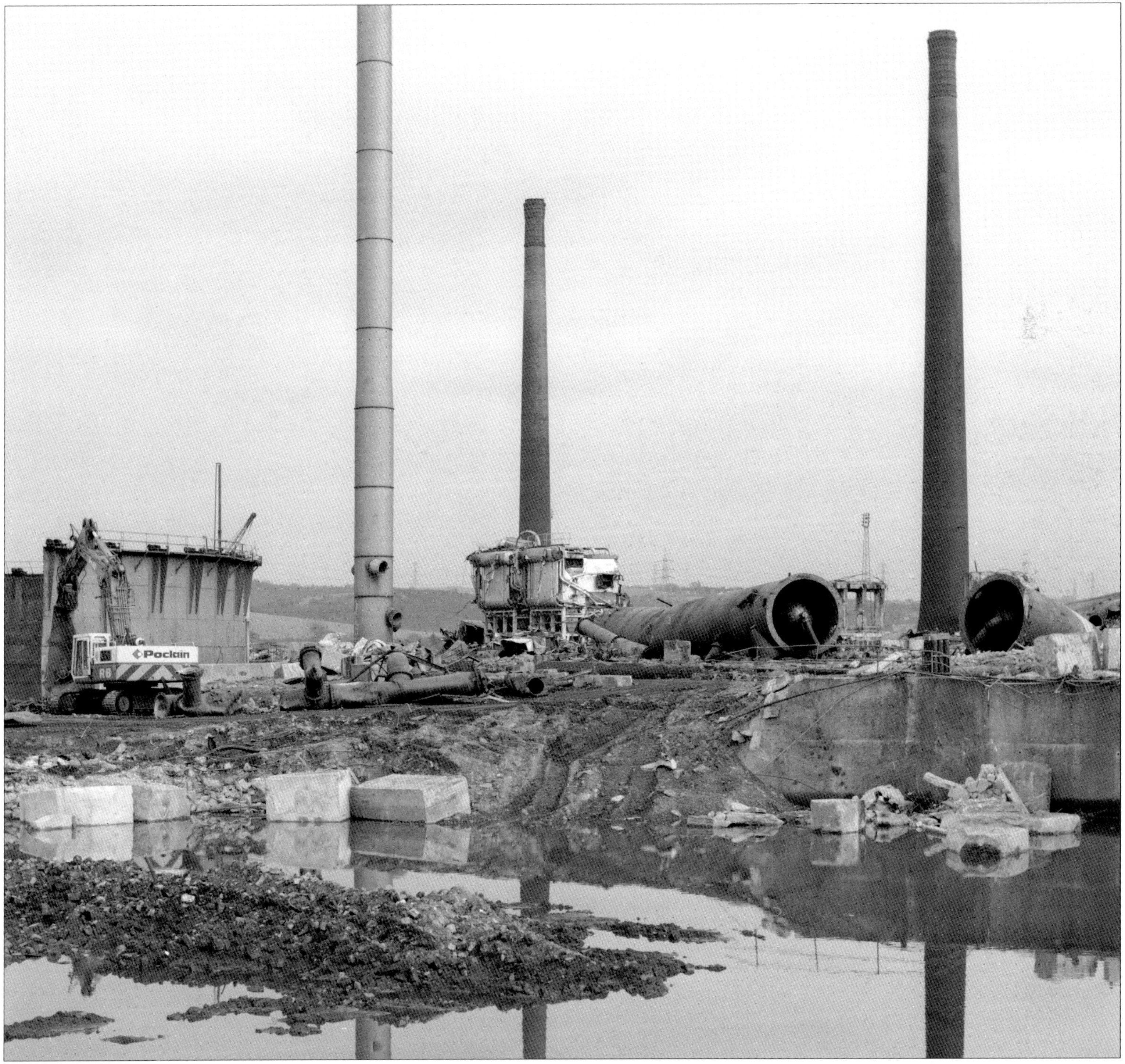

Orgreave coking plant, 1992.

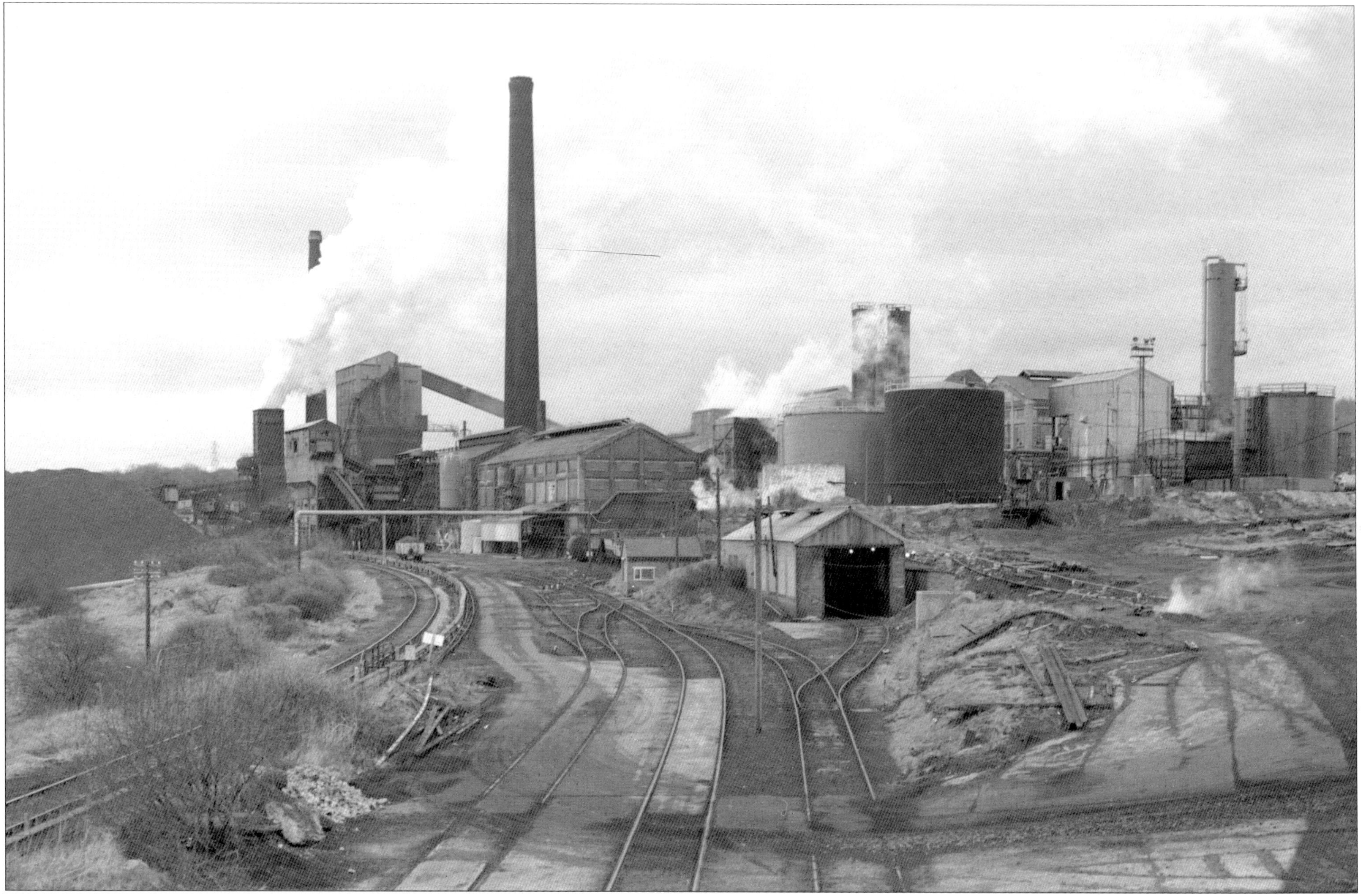

Smithywood coking plant, 1982.

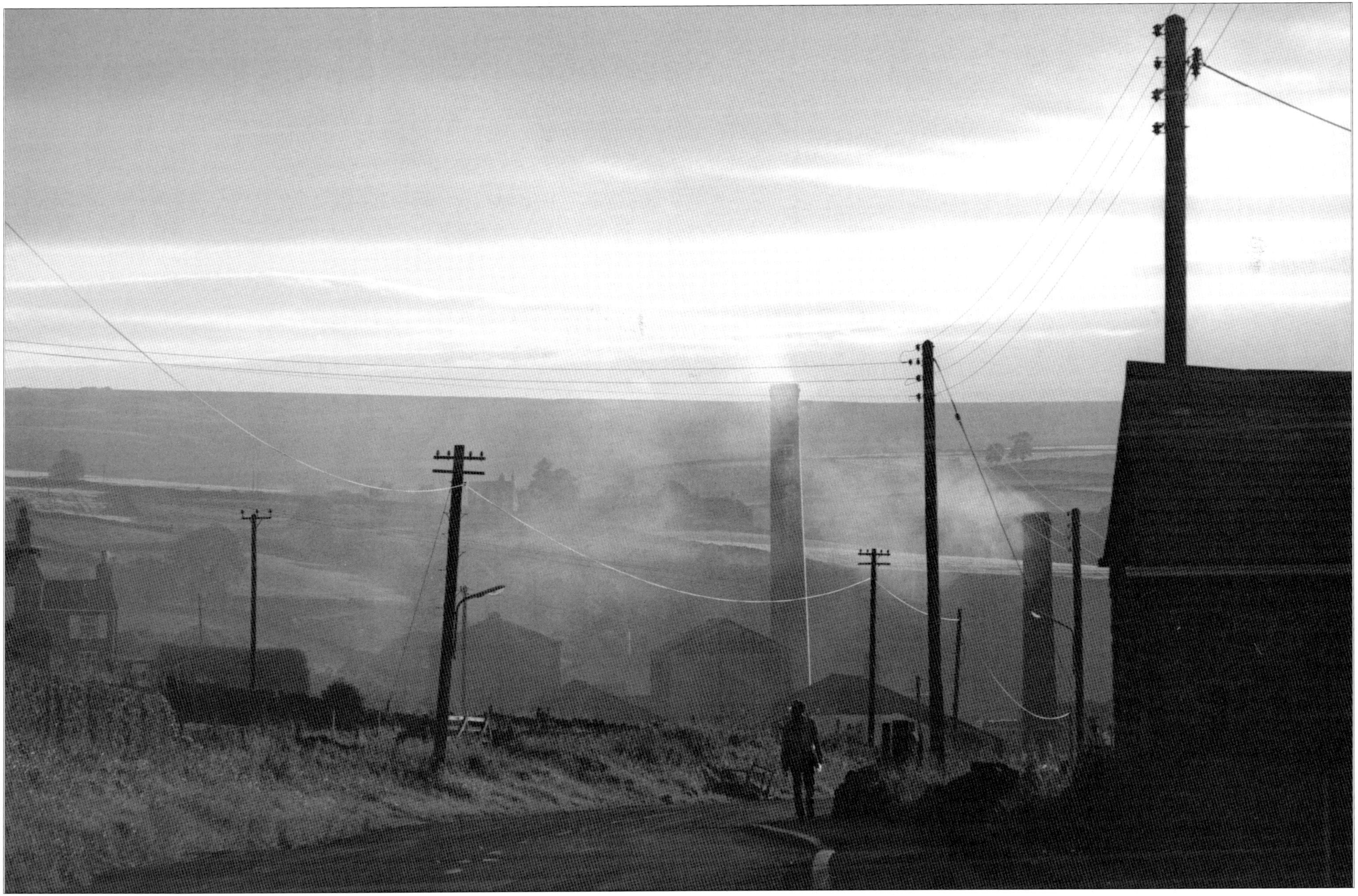
Refractory industry, Loxley Valley, 1982

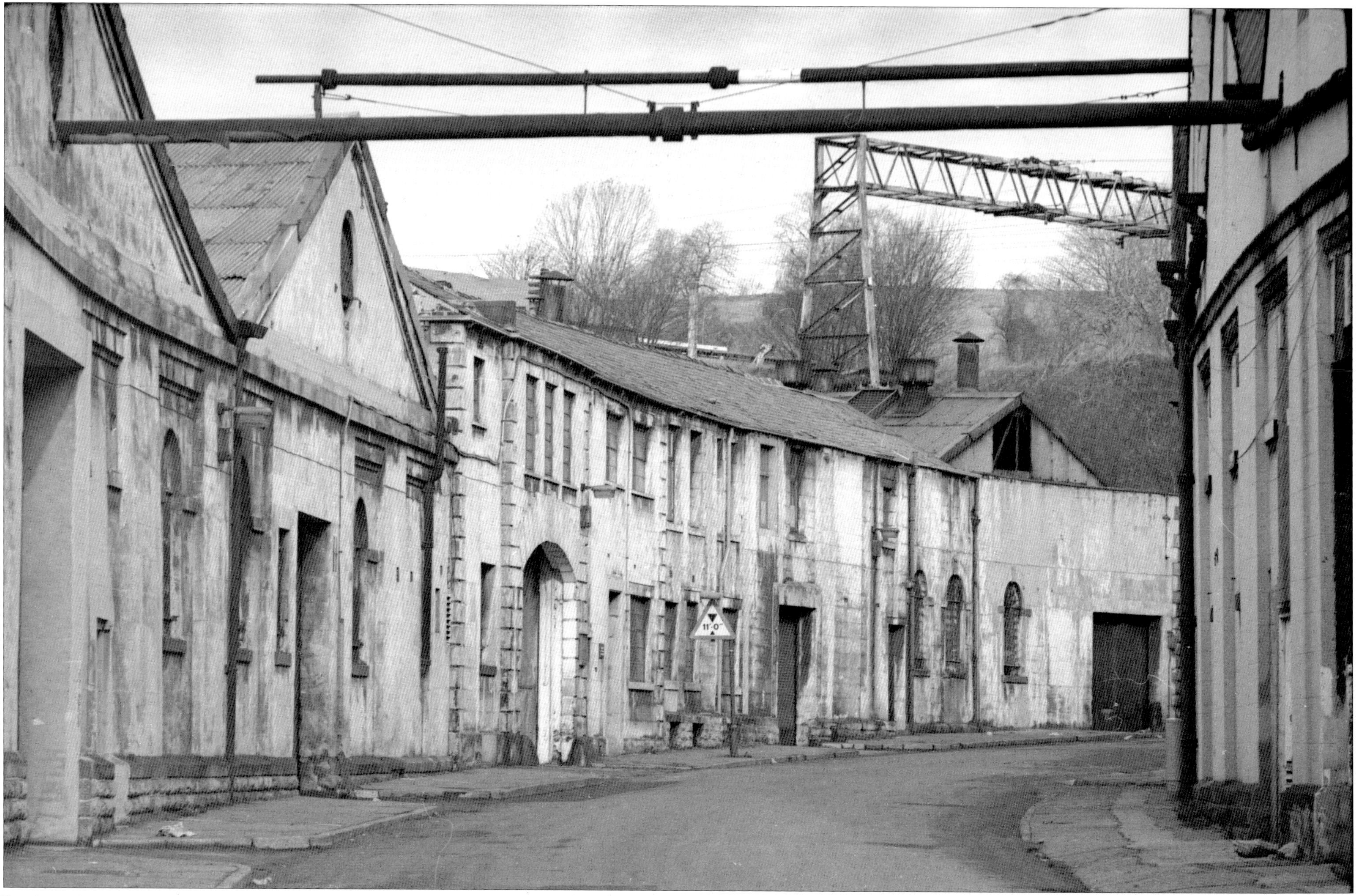

Bardwell Street, Neepsend, 1982.

Bardwell Street, 1987

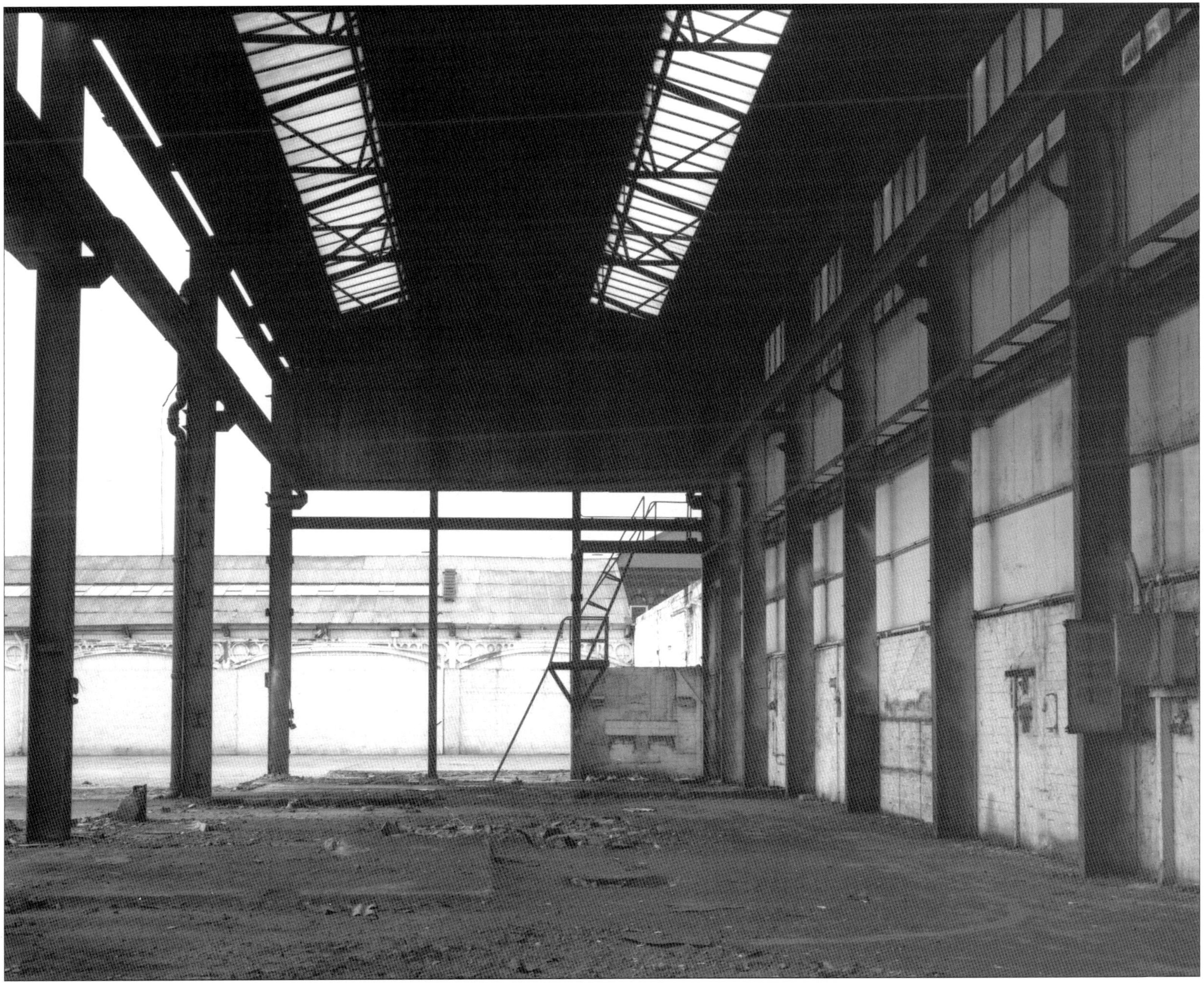

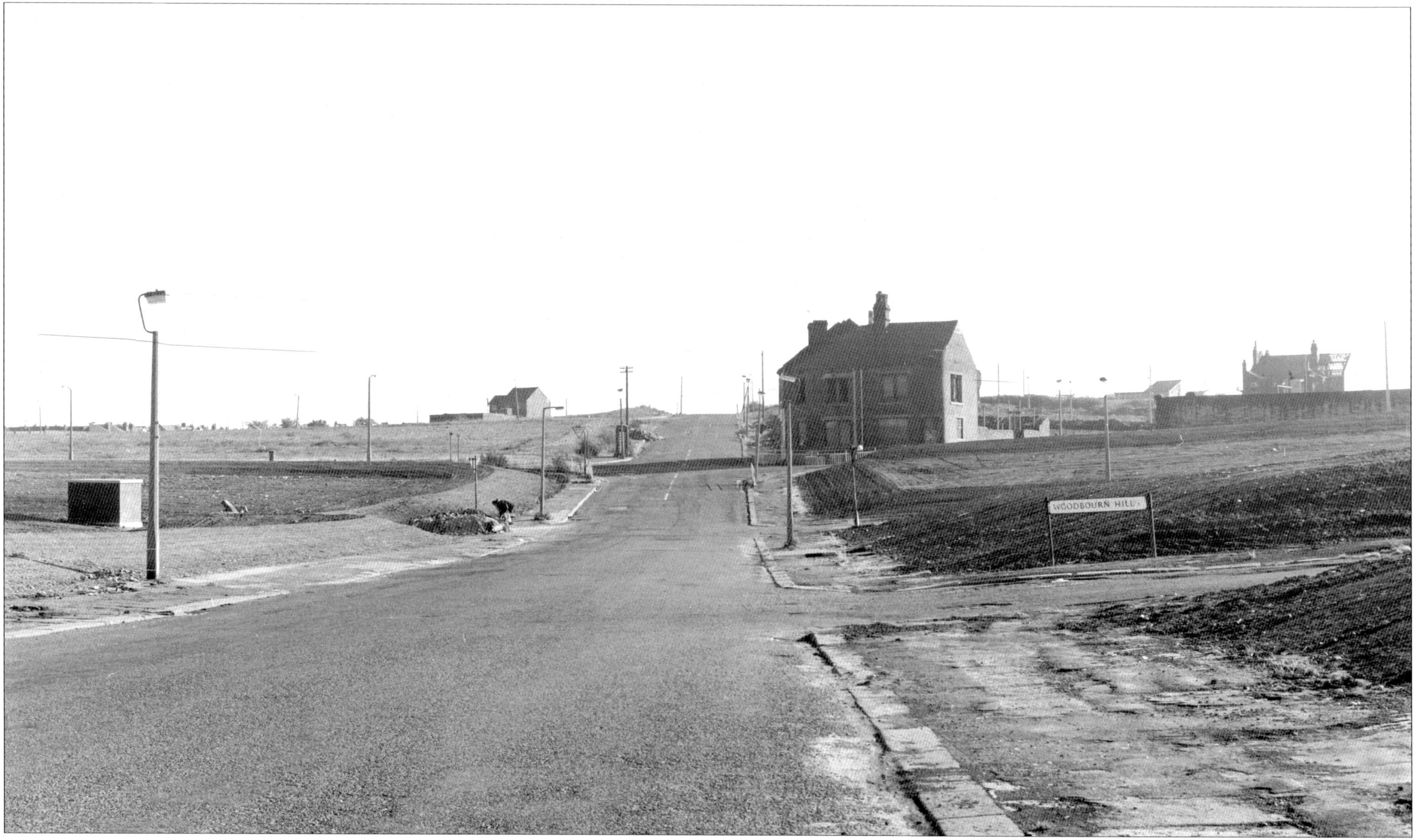

Worthing Road, Attercliffe. 1982.

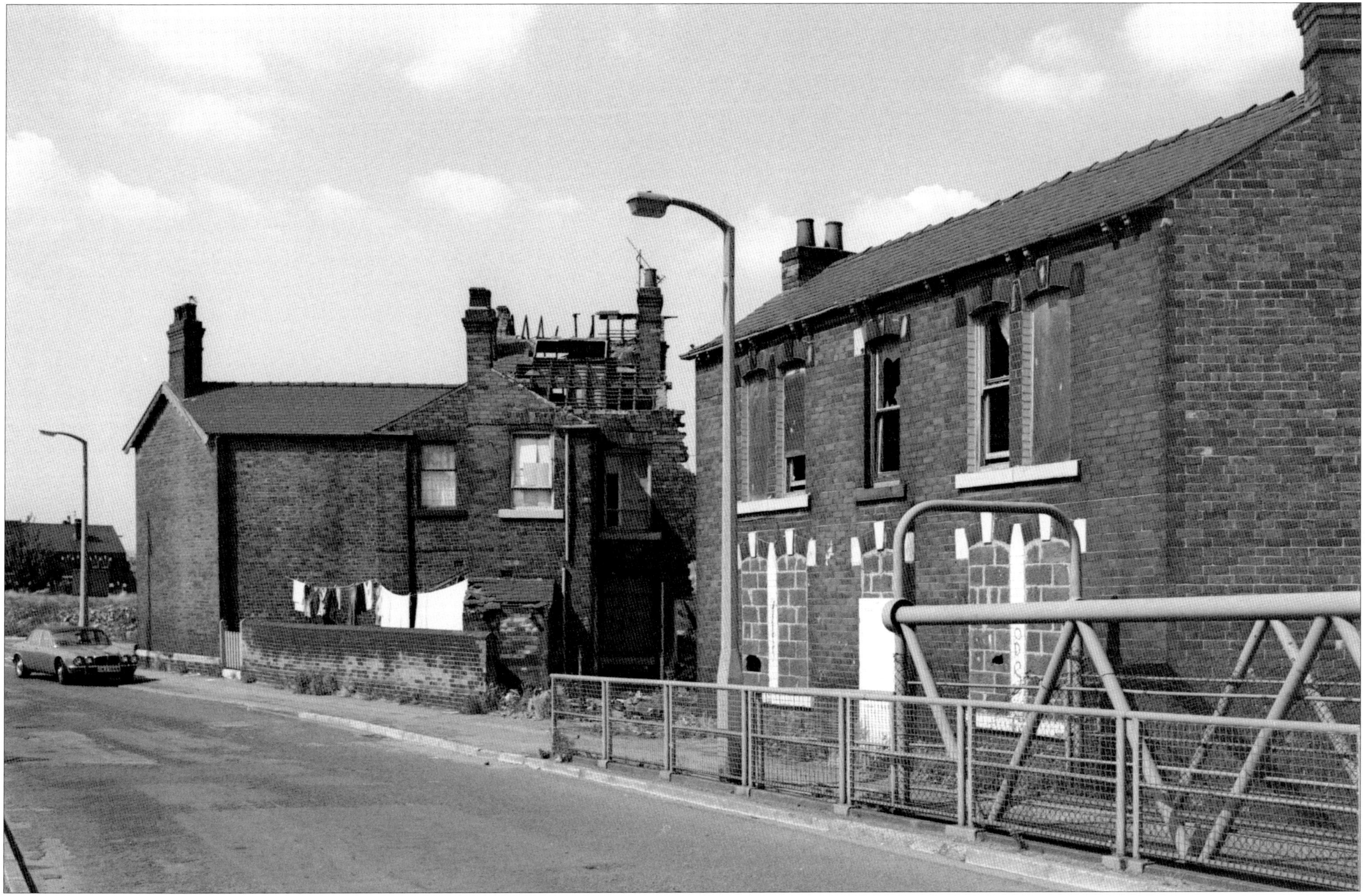

Shirland Lane, Attercliffe. 1983.

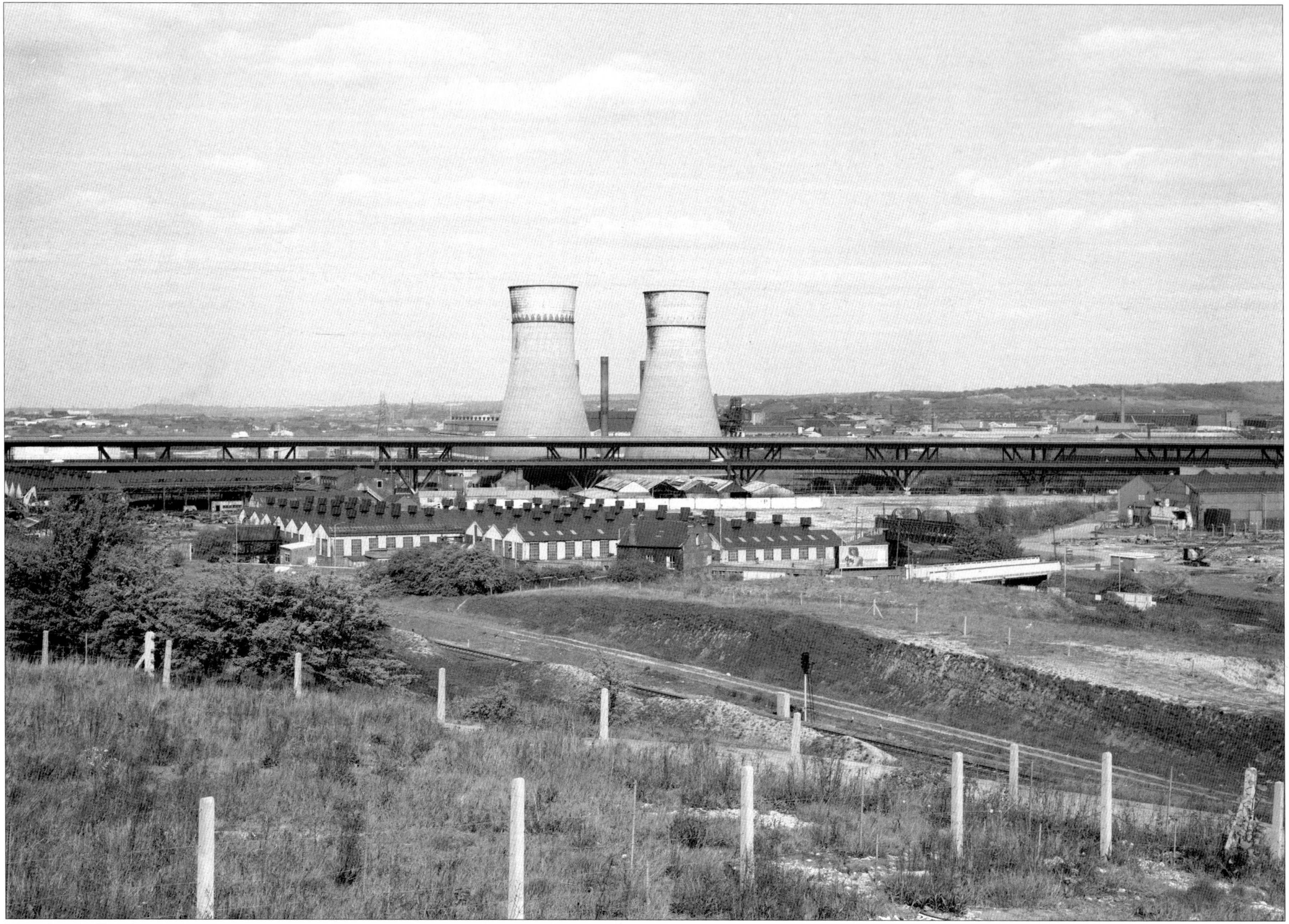
Meadowhall, 1984. The works site was later cleared for the Meadowhall shopping centre.

The Lower Don valley,
from Wincobank, 1986.

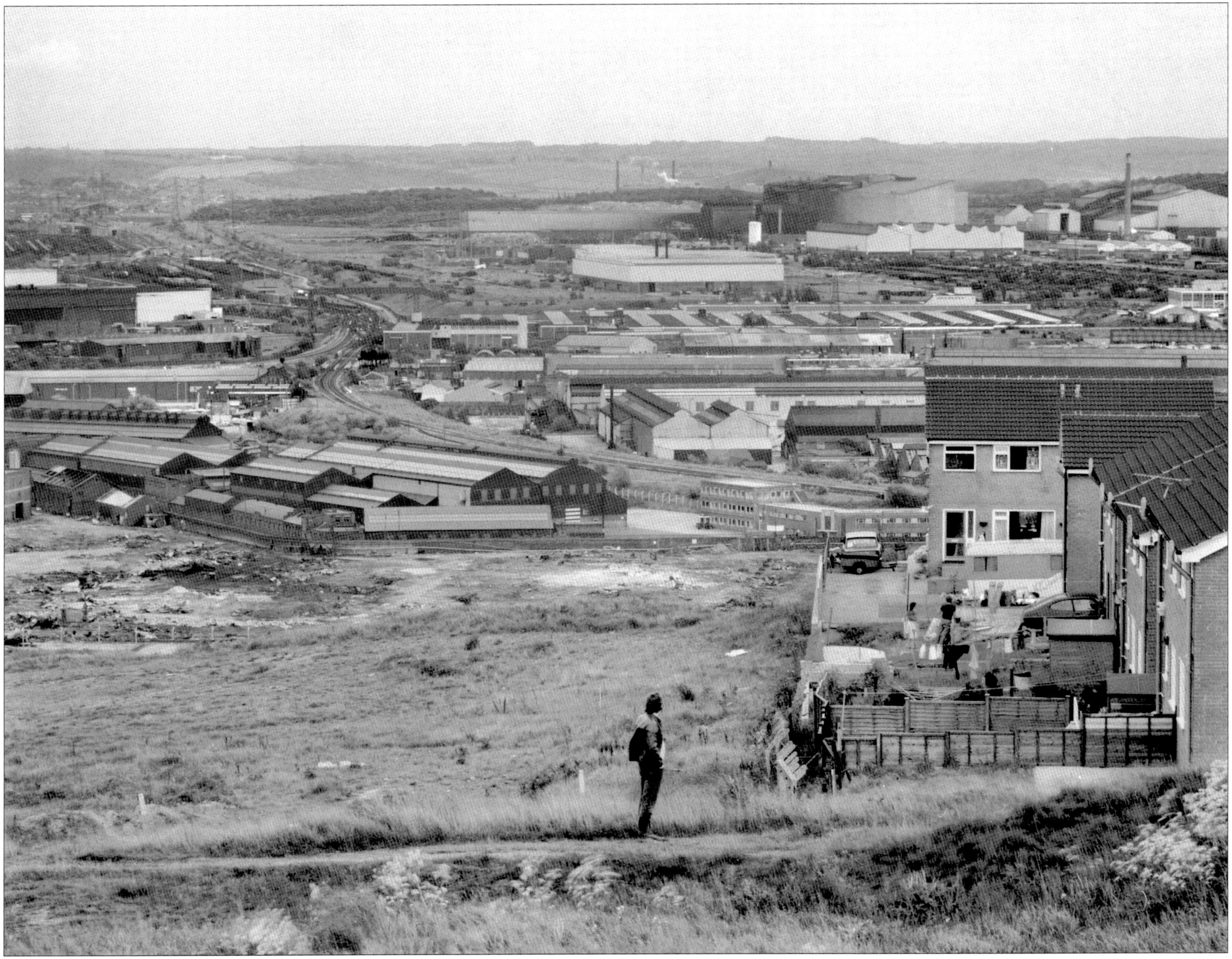

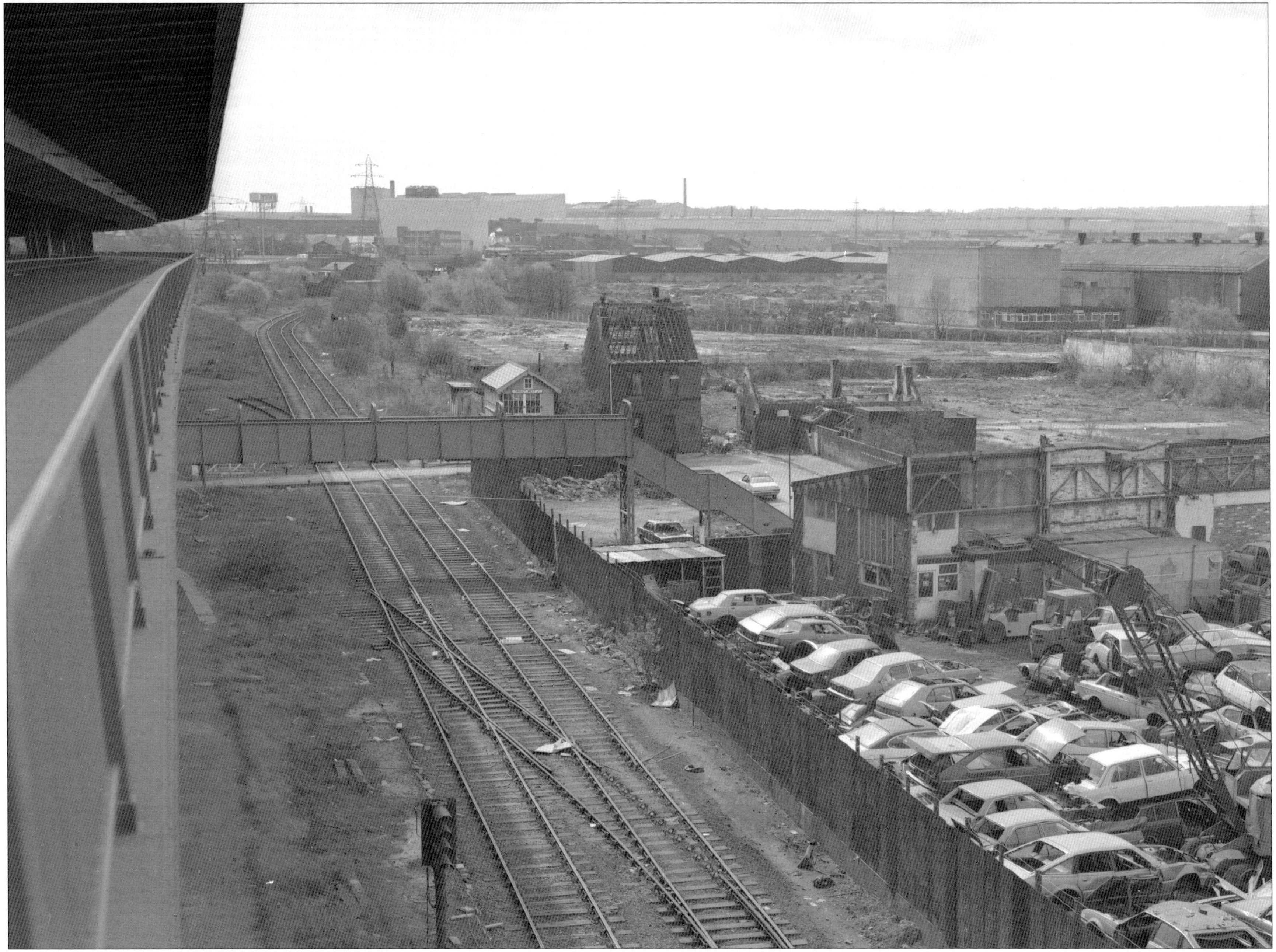

From the Tinsley viaduct, 1988. The railway lines ran to the coking plant at Smithywood and the trackbed is now occupied by the tramline that runs to the Meadowhall shopping centre.

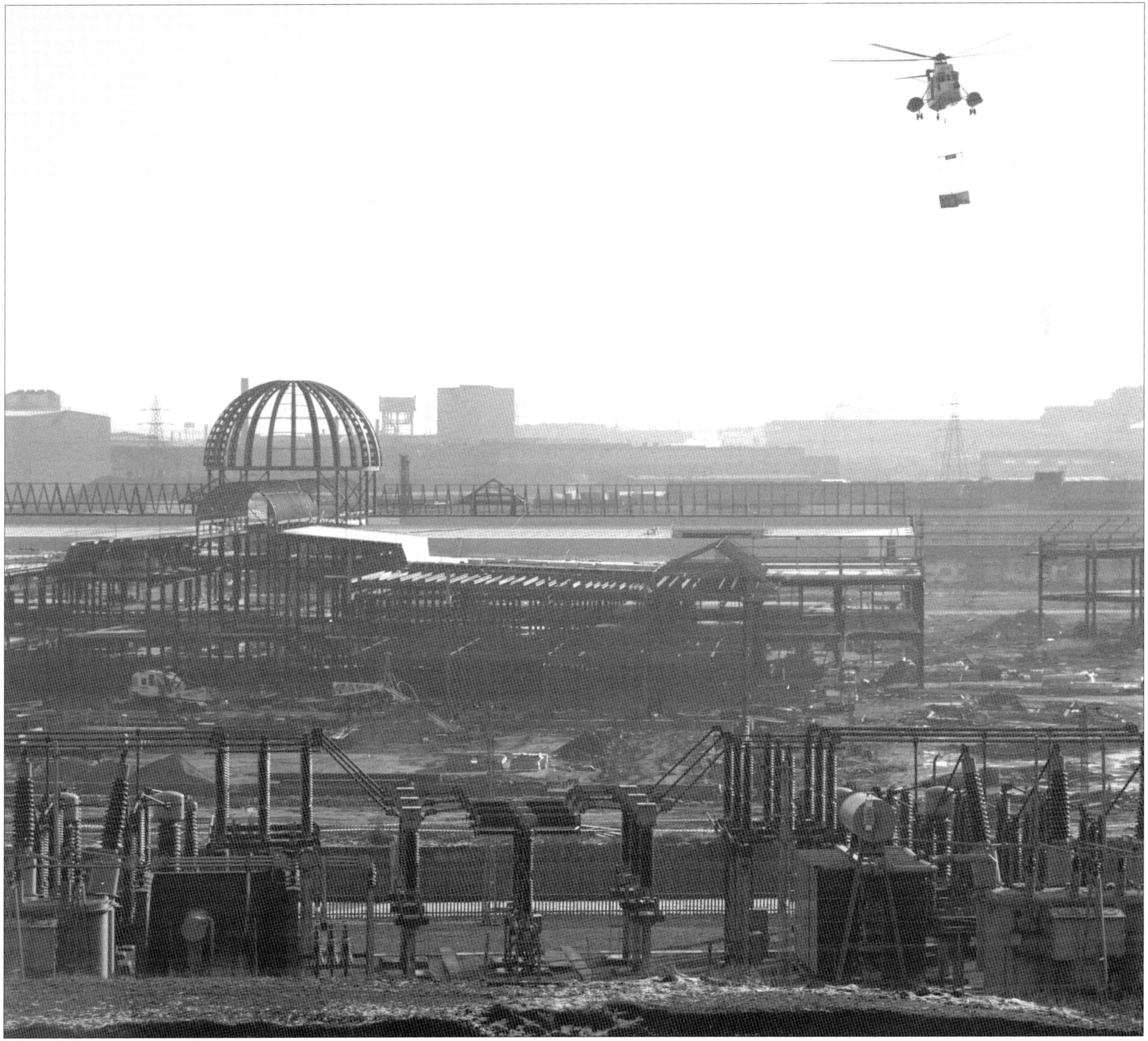

Construction of the Meadowhall shopping centre, 1988.

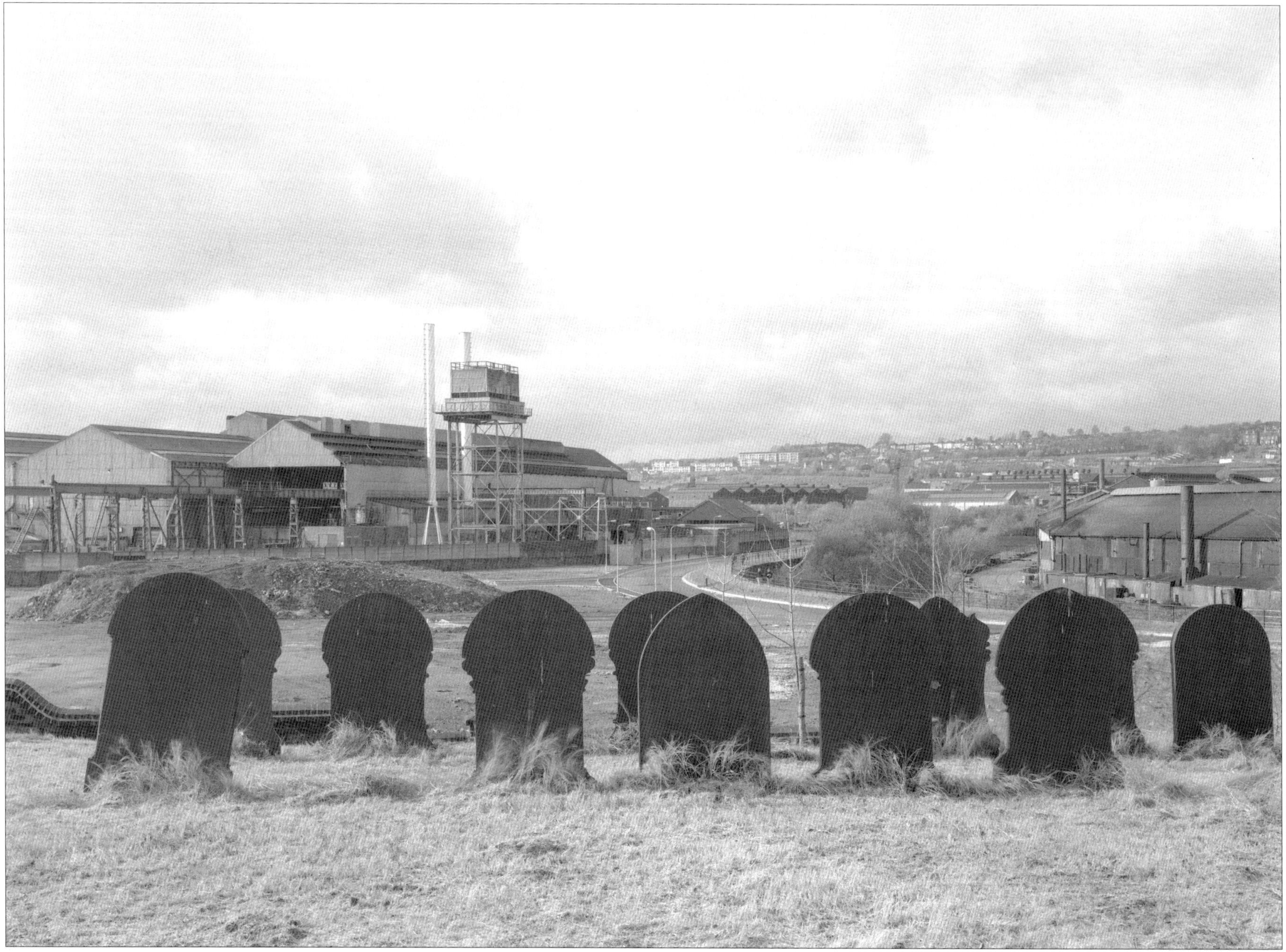

Attercliffe cemetery, 1992.

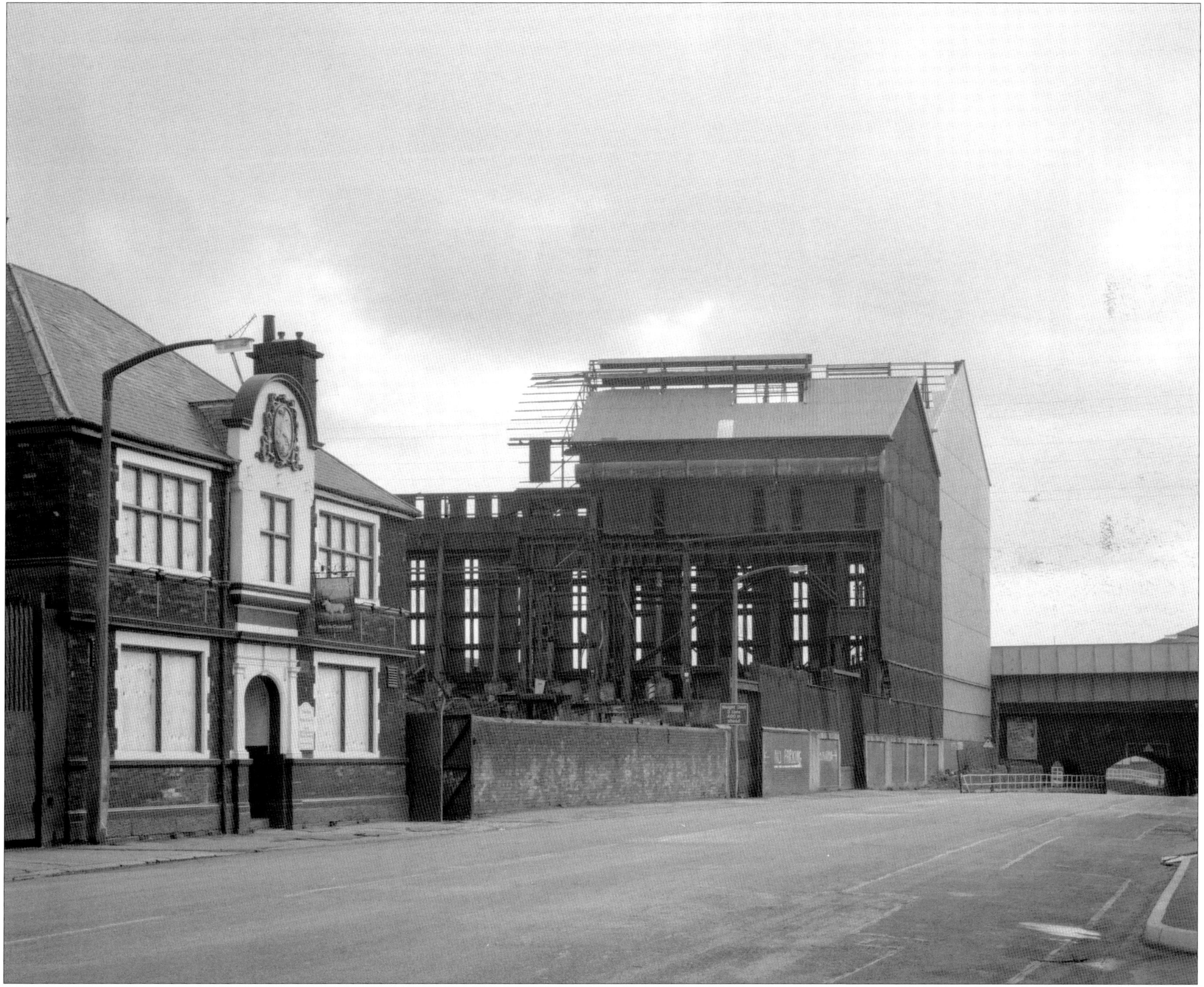

Worksop Road, 1985. Demolition of the Brown Bayleys steelworks. Also to the left of the photograph is the White Hart public house.

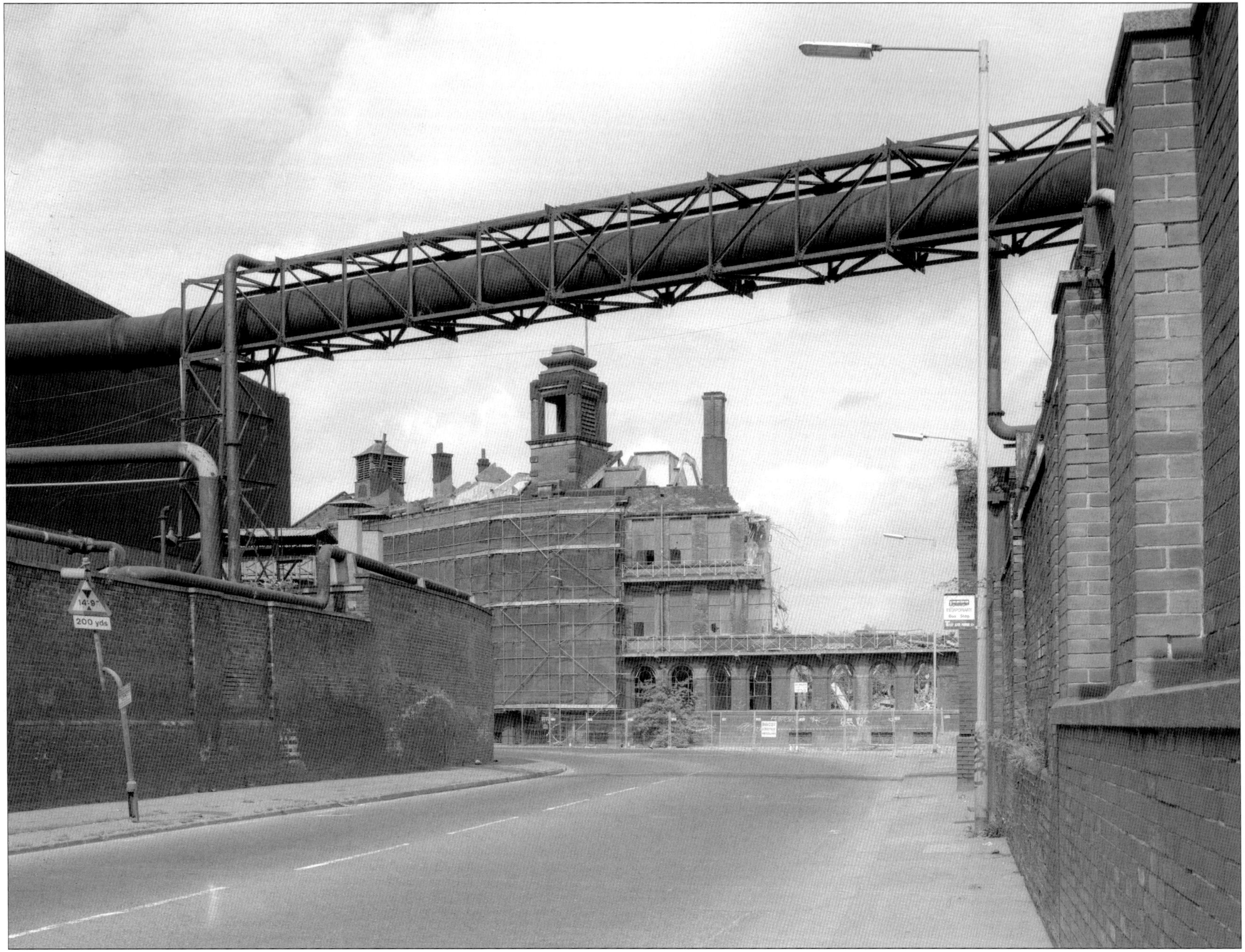

Brightside Lane, 1991. Demolition of the Jessop-Savile building.

Savile Street East, 1988.
Looking toward the city.

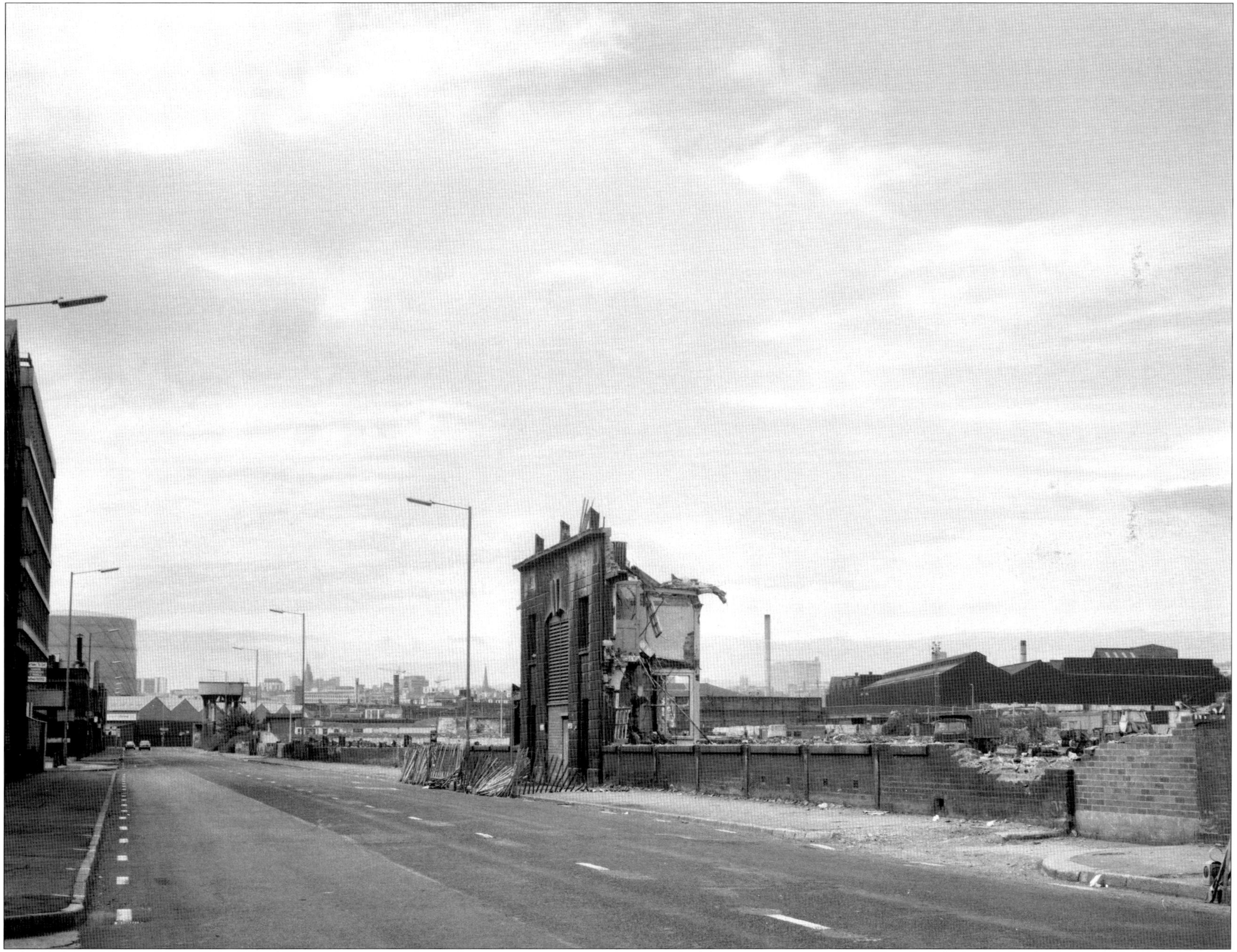

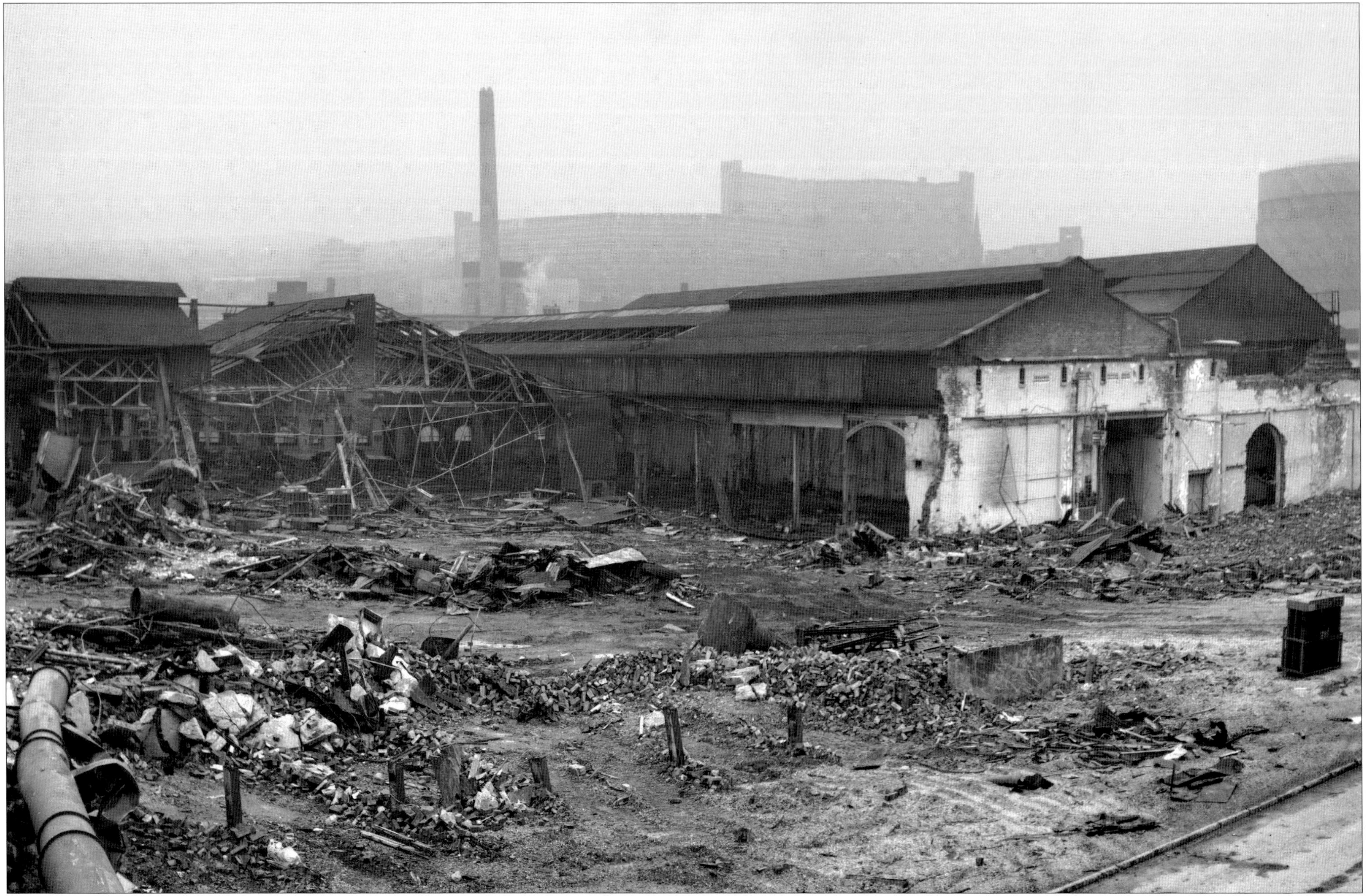

Cyclops Works, Savile Street, 1988. From Sutherland Road.

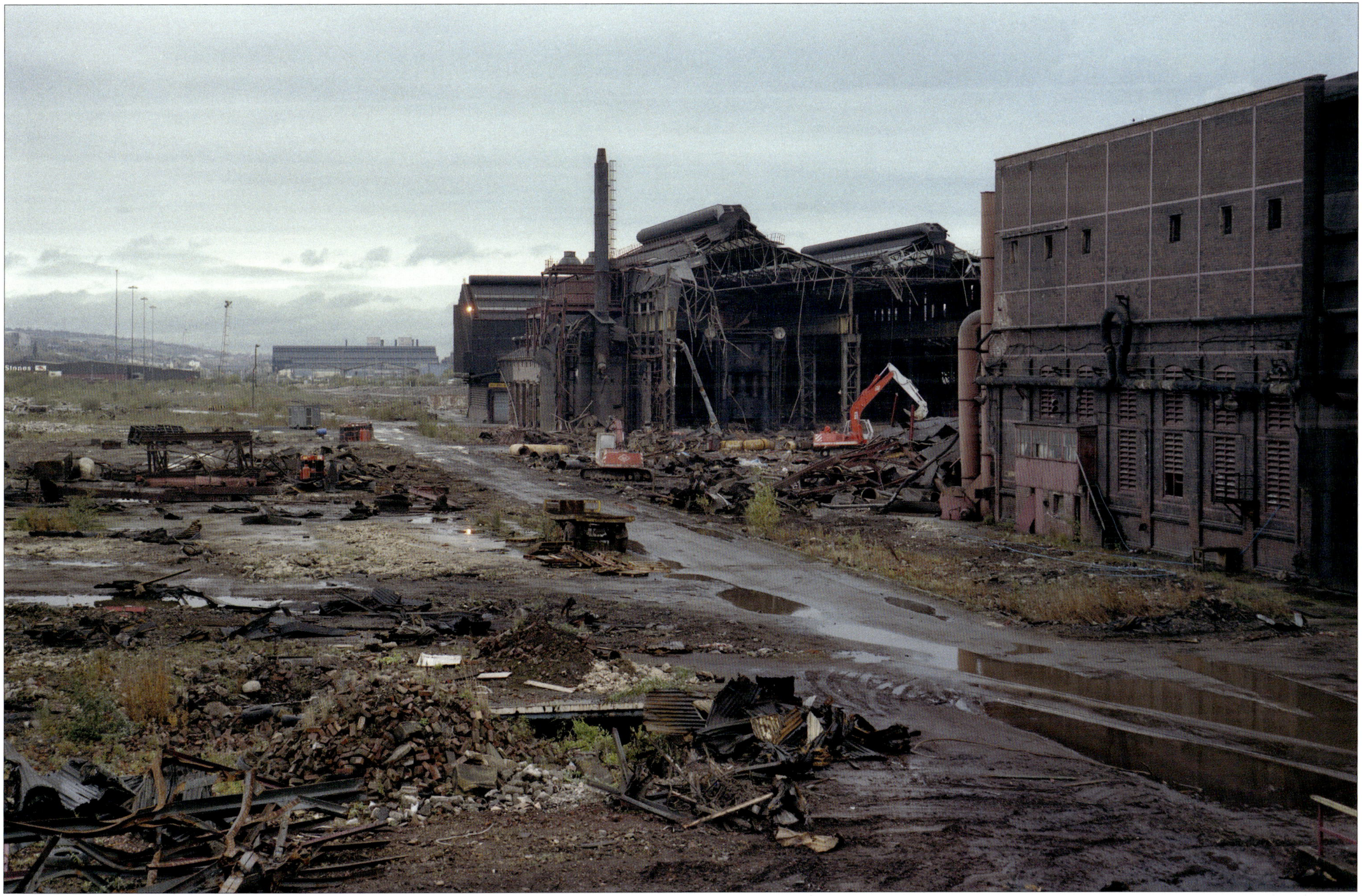

Atlas works, 1989

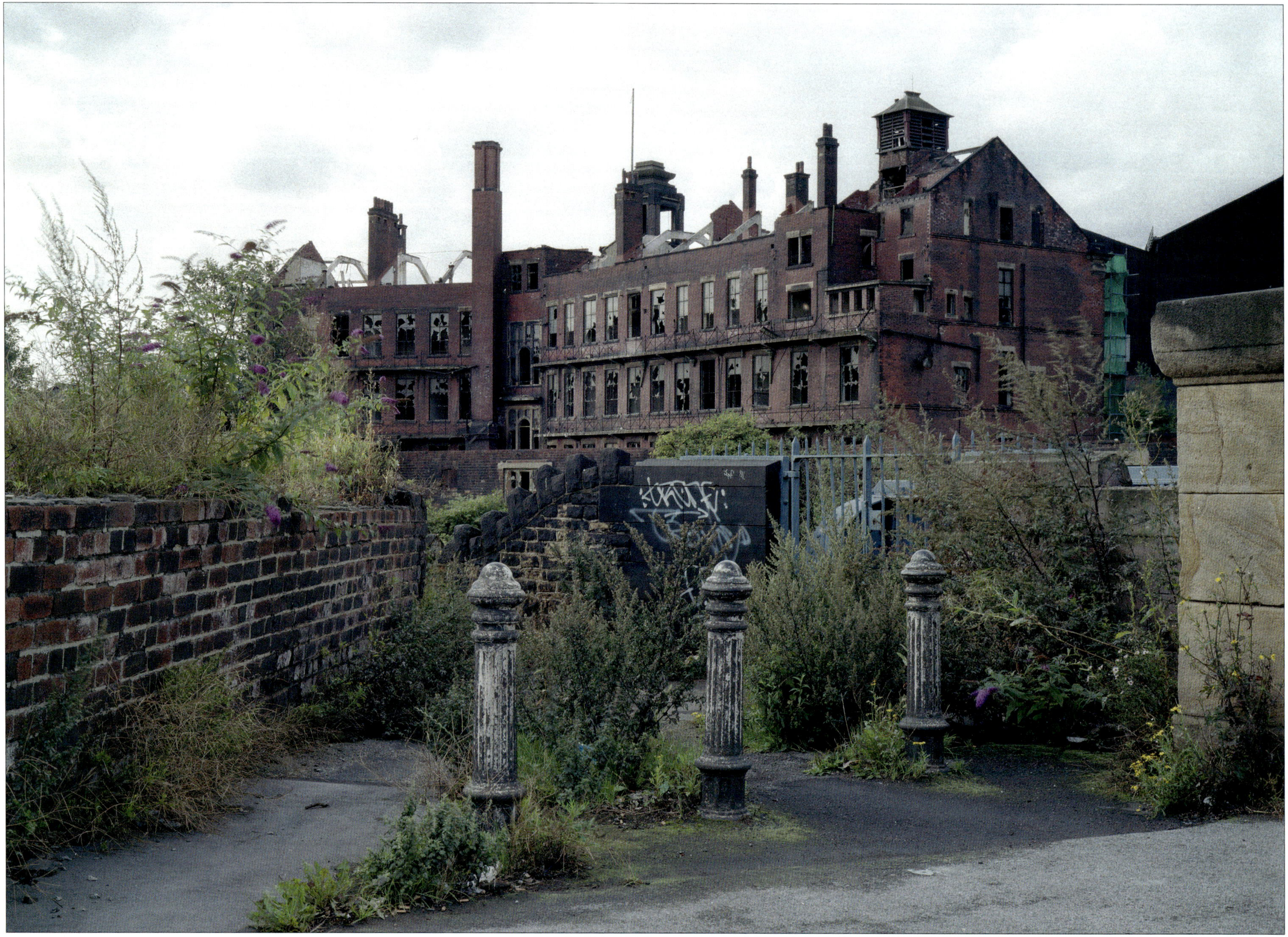

Jessop-Savile building, 1992.

Britannia Works, 1992.

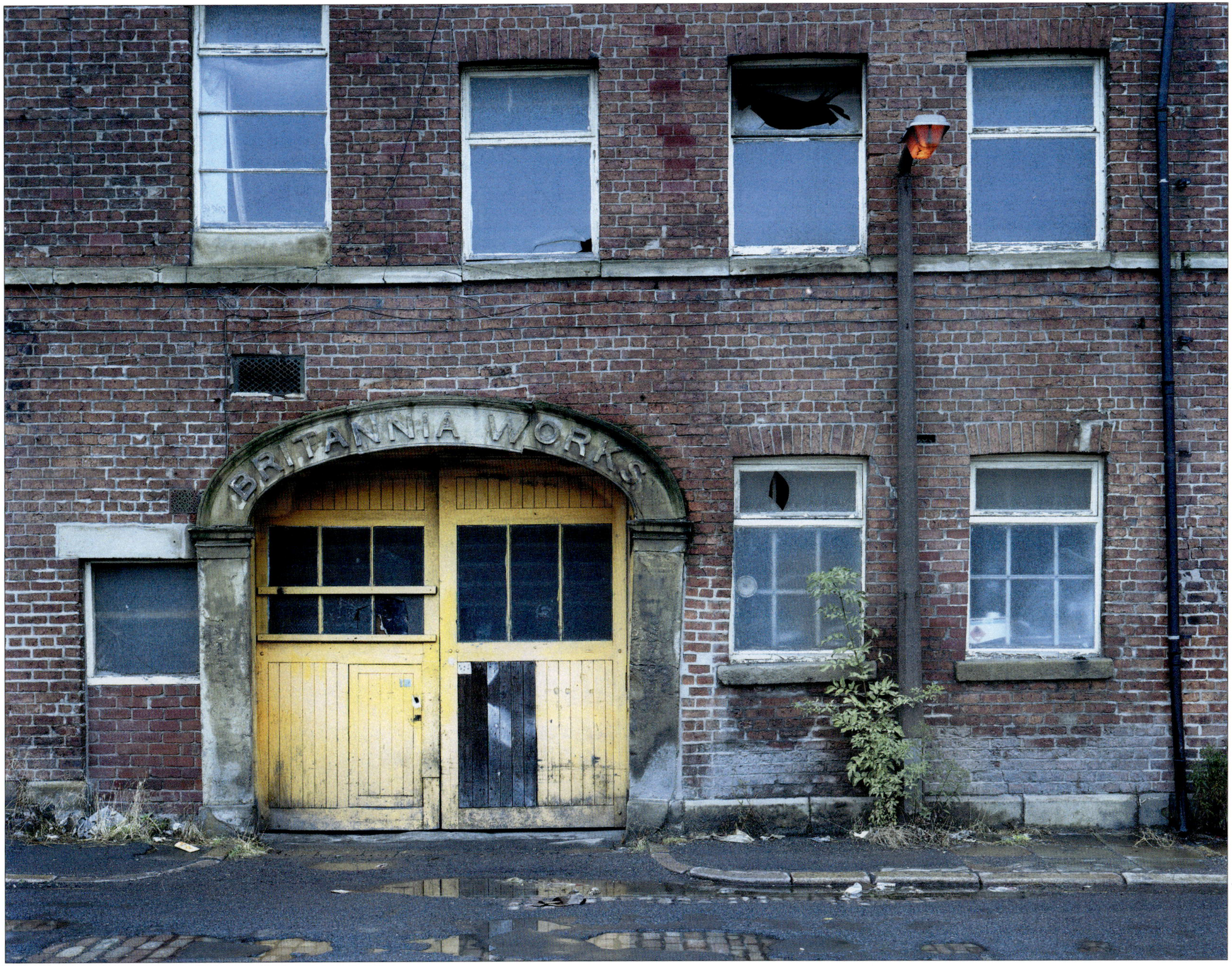

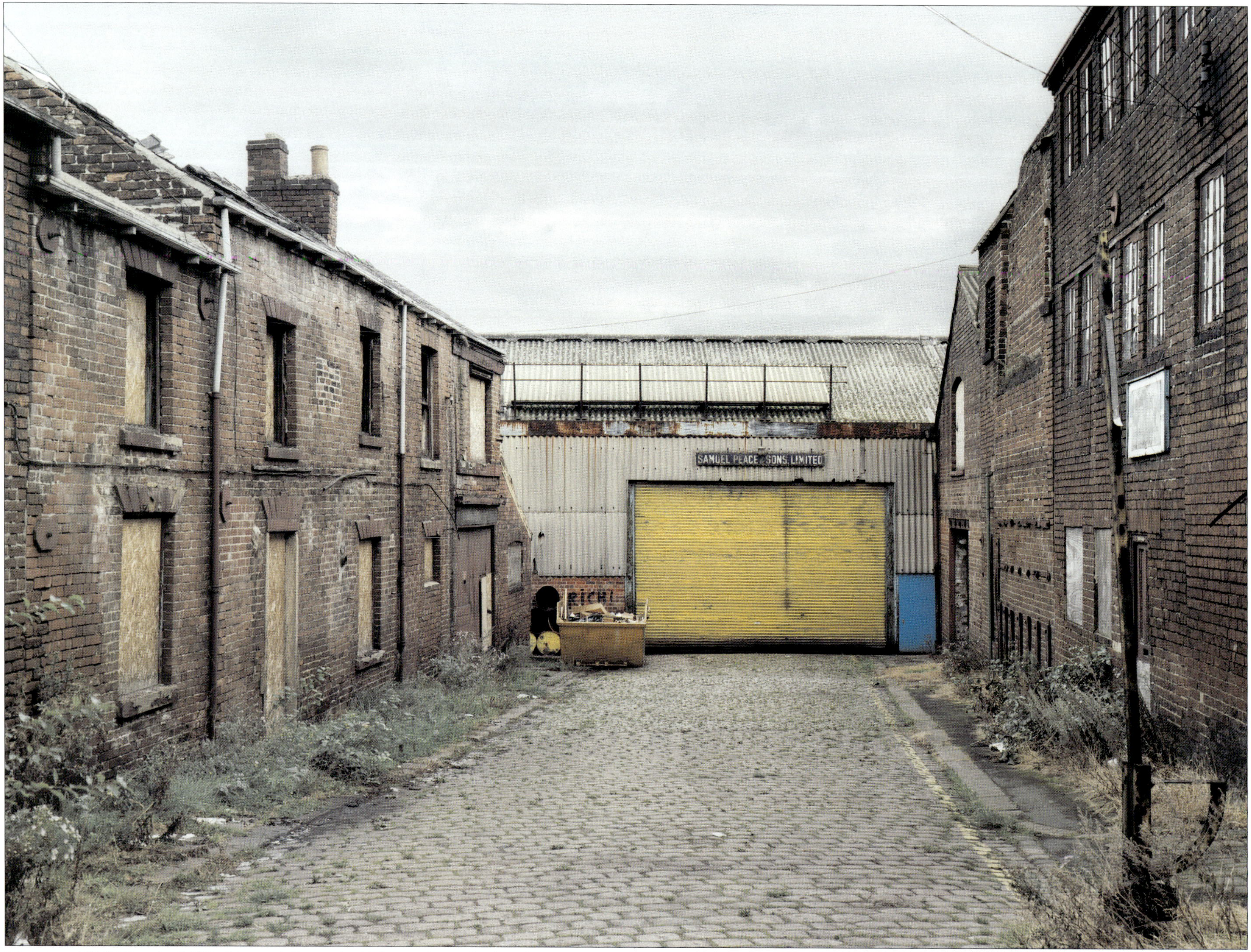

Meadow Well Street, 1992. Samuel Peace's 19th century steelworks.

Portobello,1990.

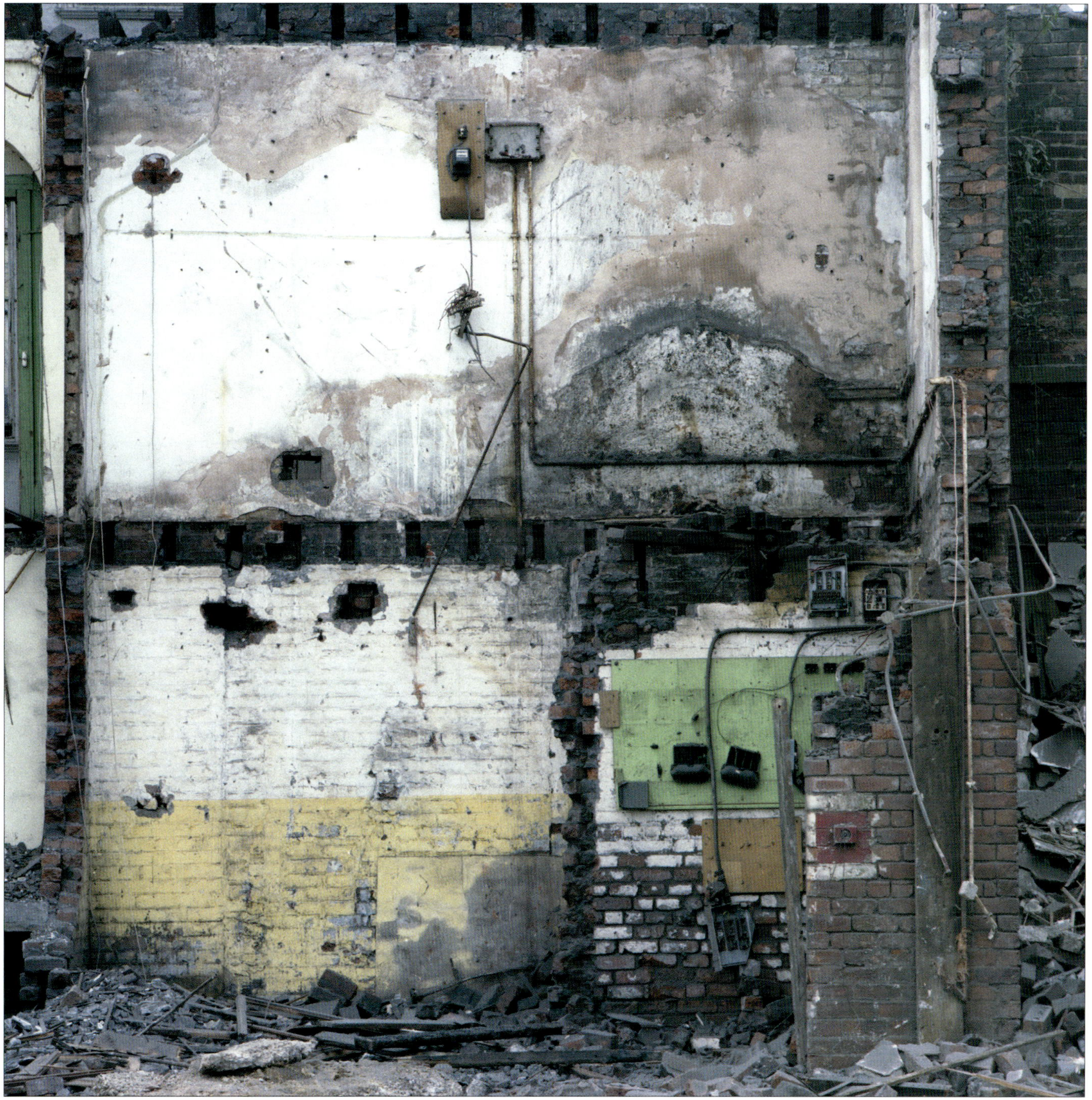

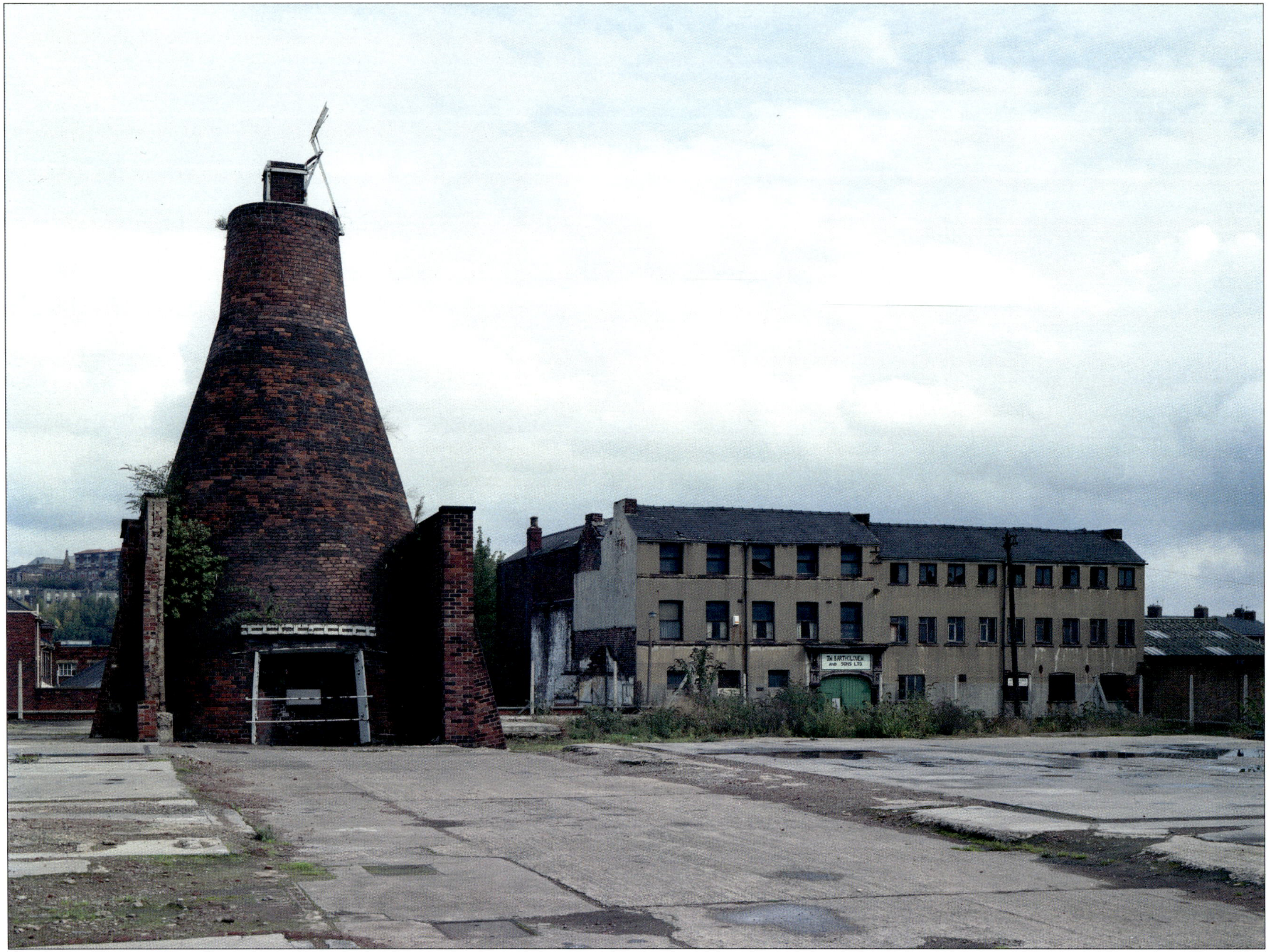

Doncaster Street, 1992.
Daniel Doncaster's
cementation furnace
built in 1830.

Blast Lane, 1993. Part completed arch of the tramway viaduct.

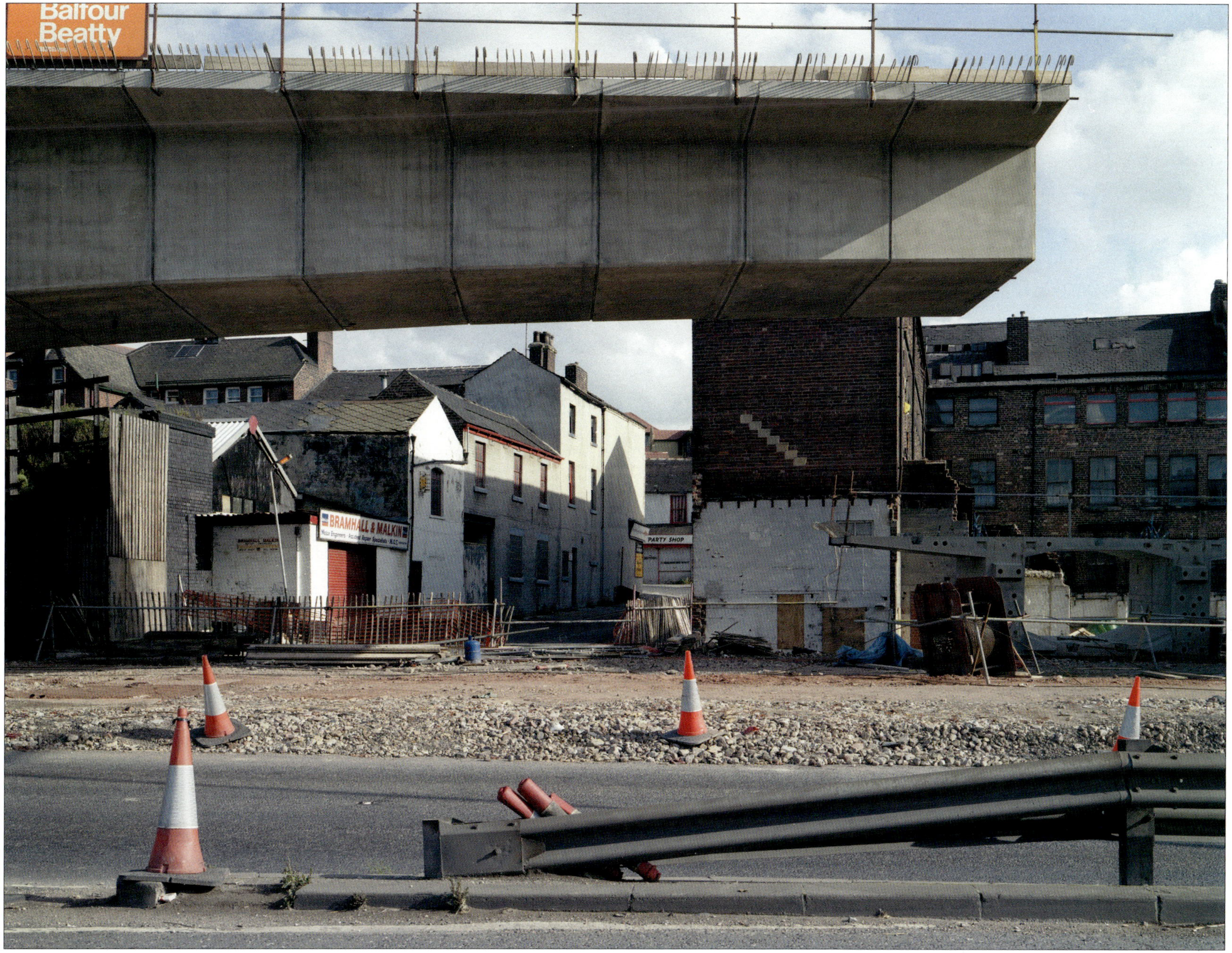

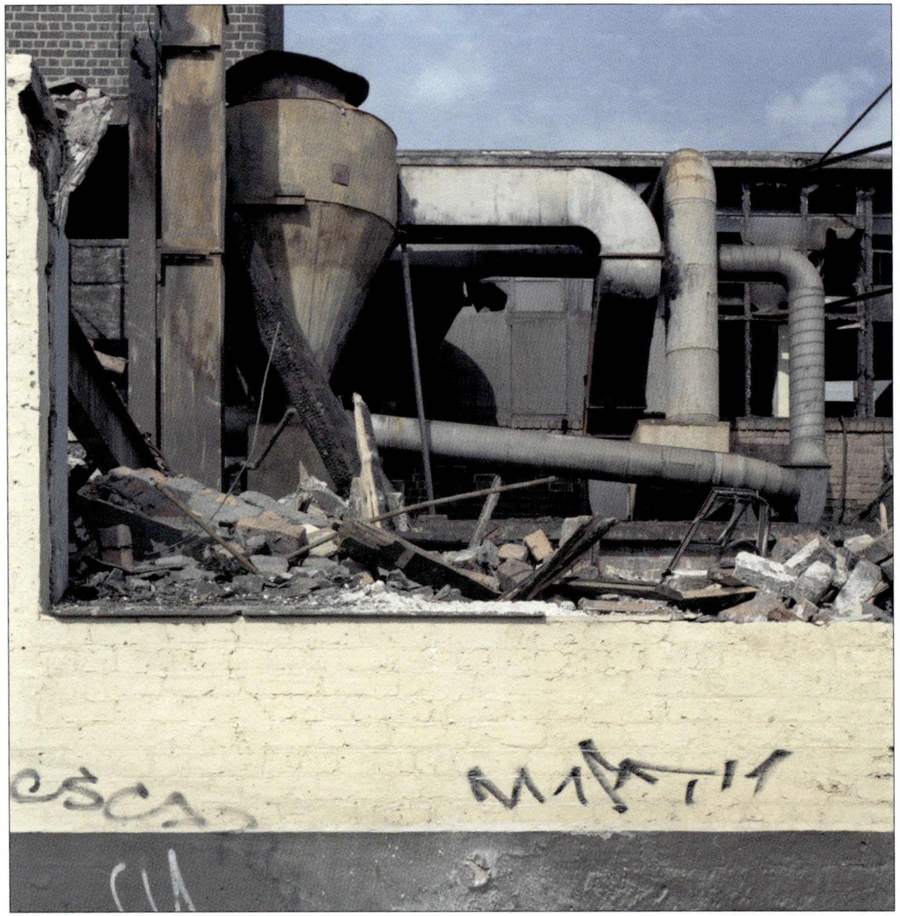

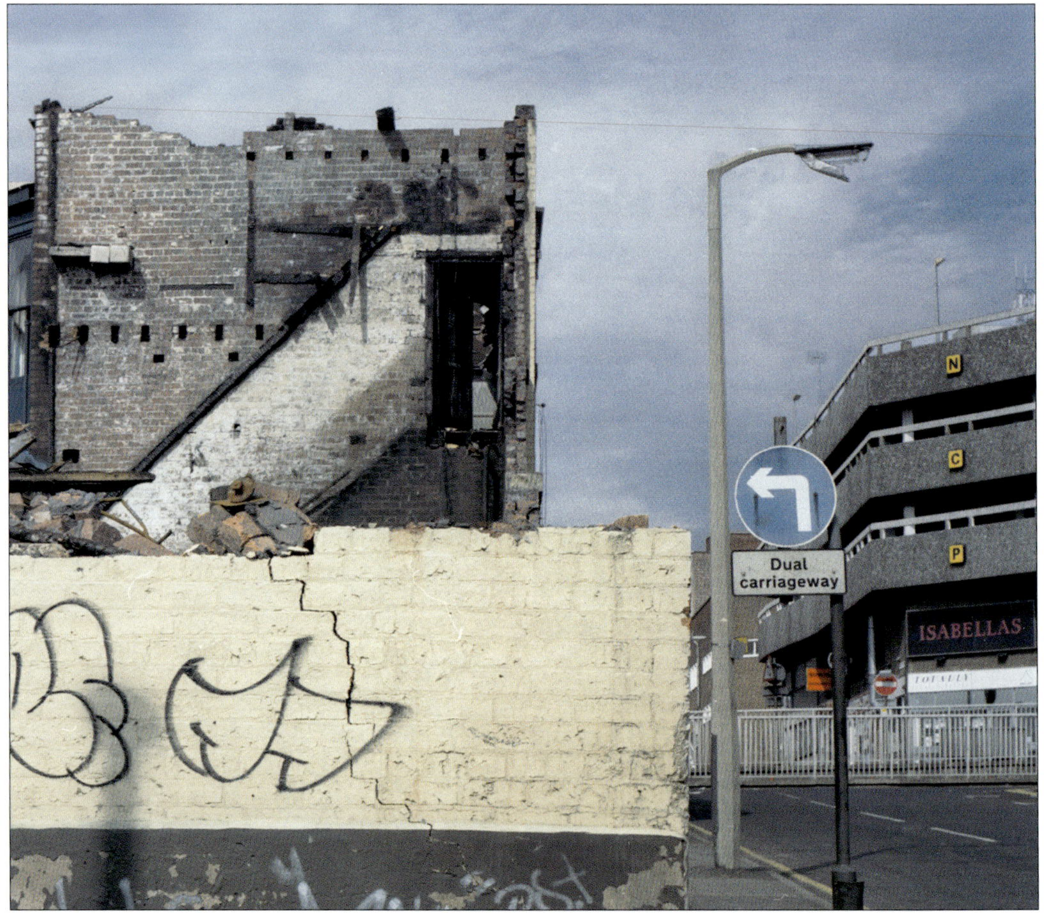

Eyre Lane, 1989.

Backfields, 1987. The large building in the background is the Cole Brothers department store on Barkers Pool.

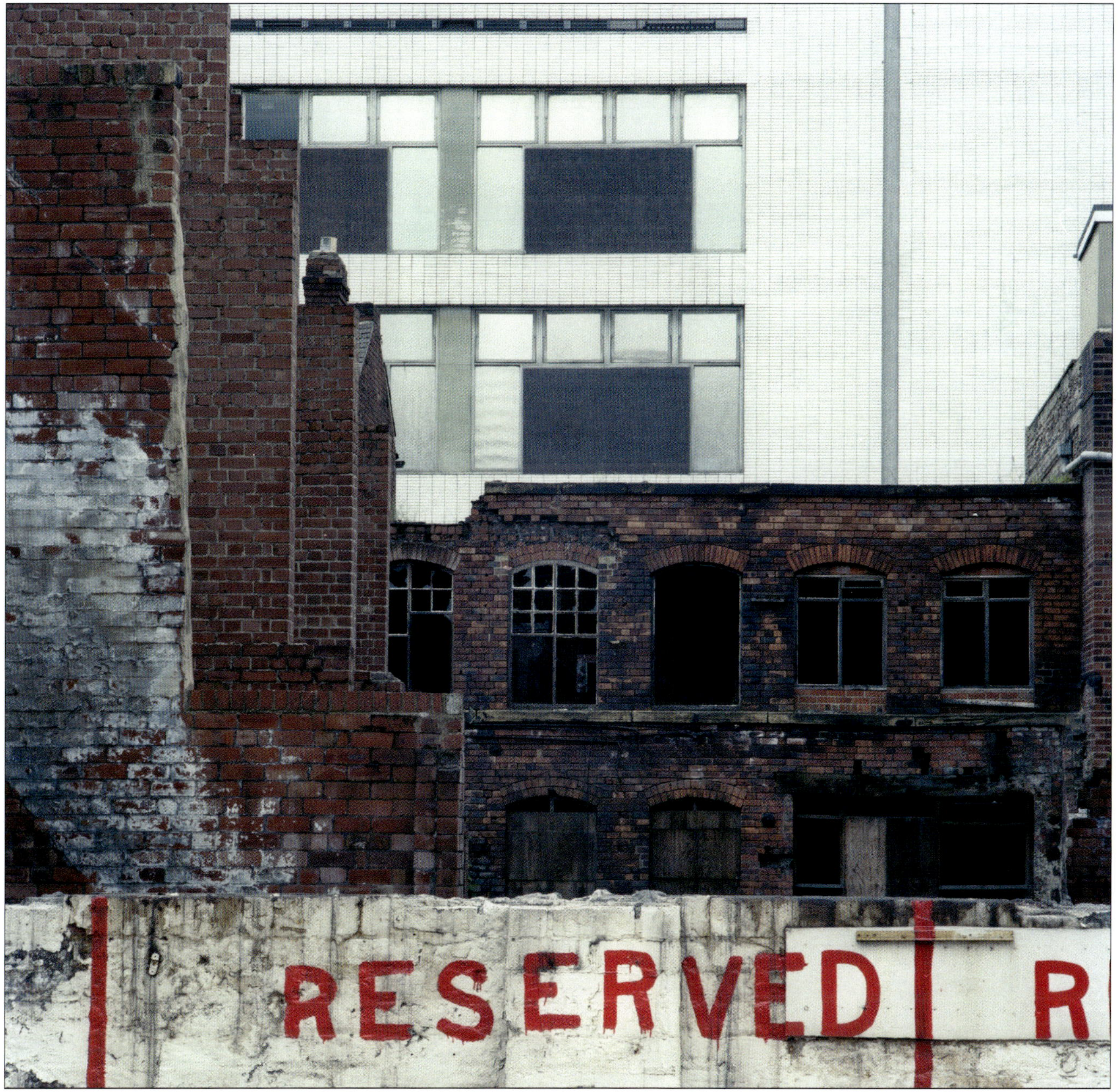

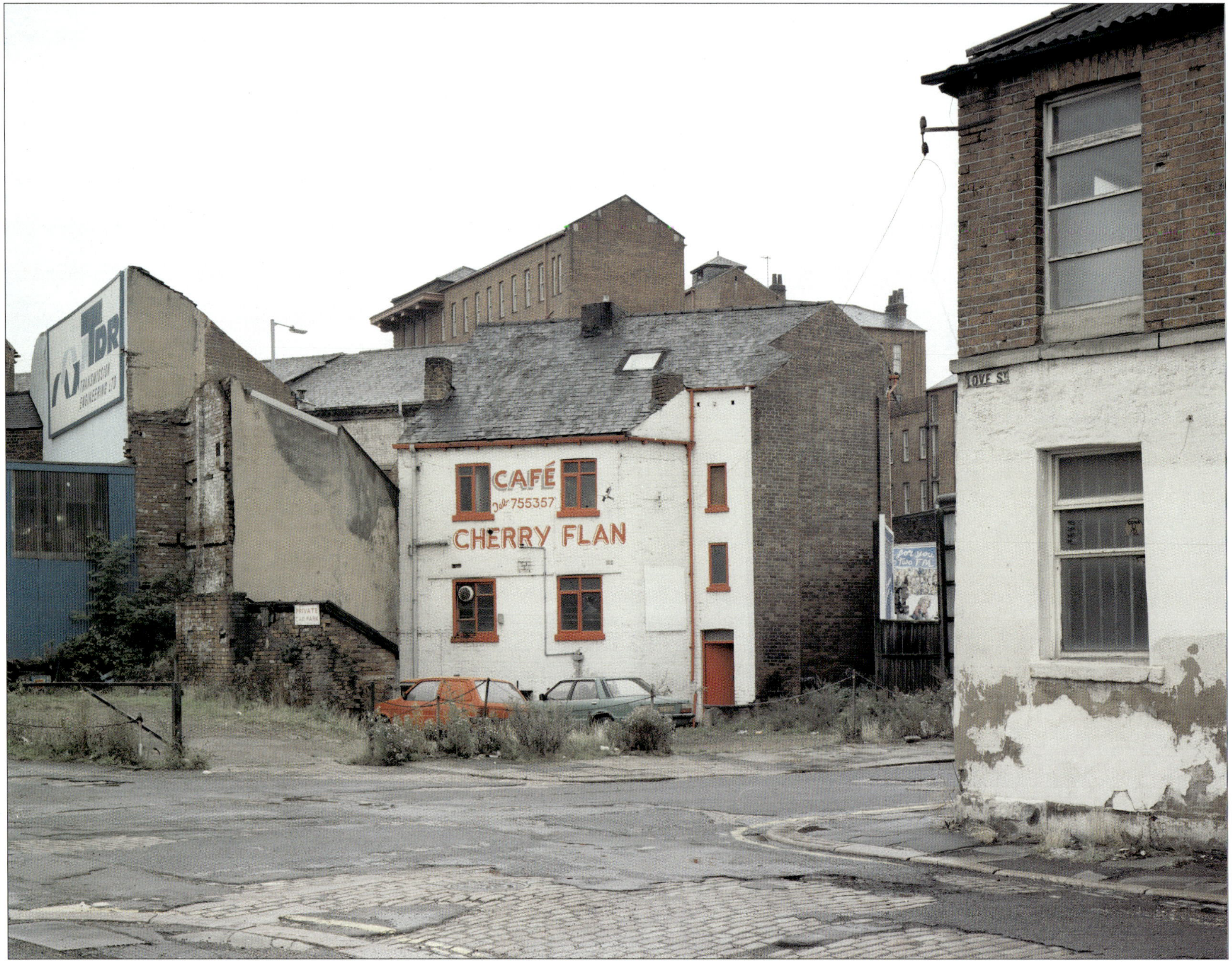

Love Street, 1992.

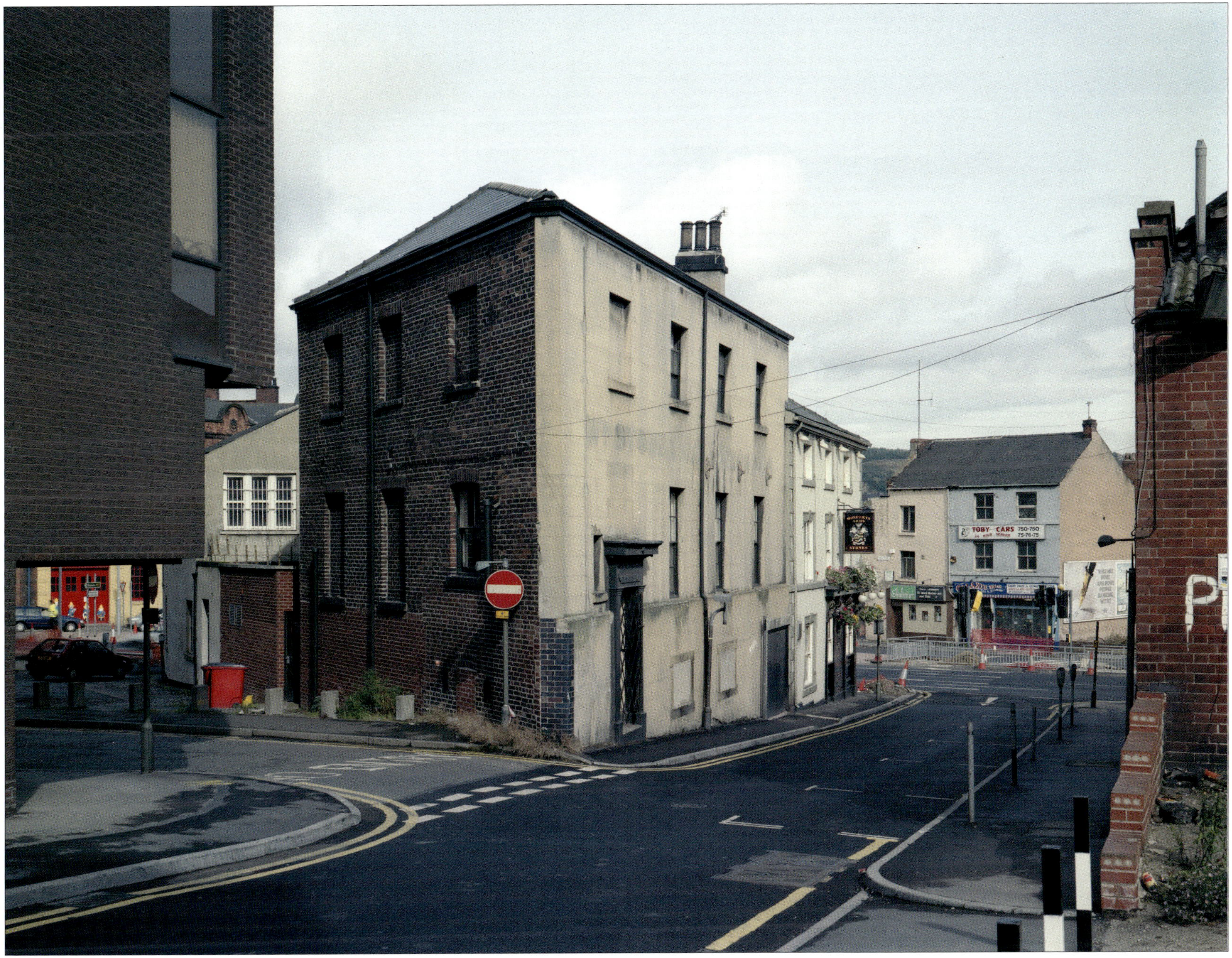

Paradise Street,
1992.
The now defunct
Moseley Arms
stands at the
bottom.

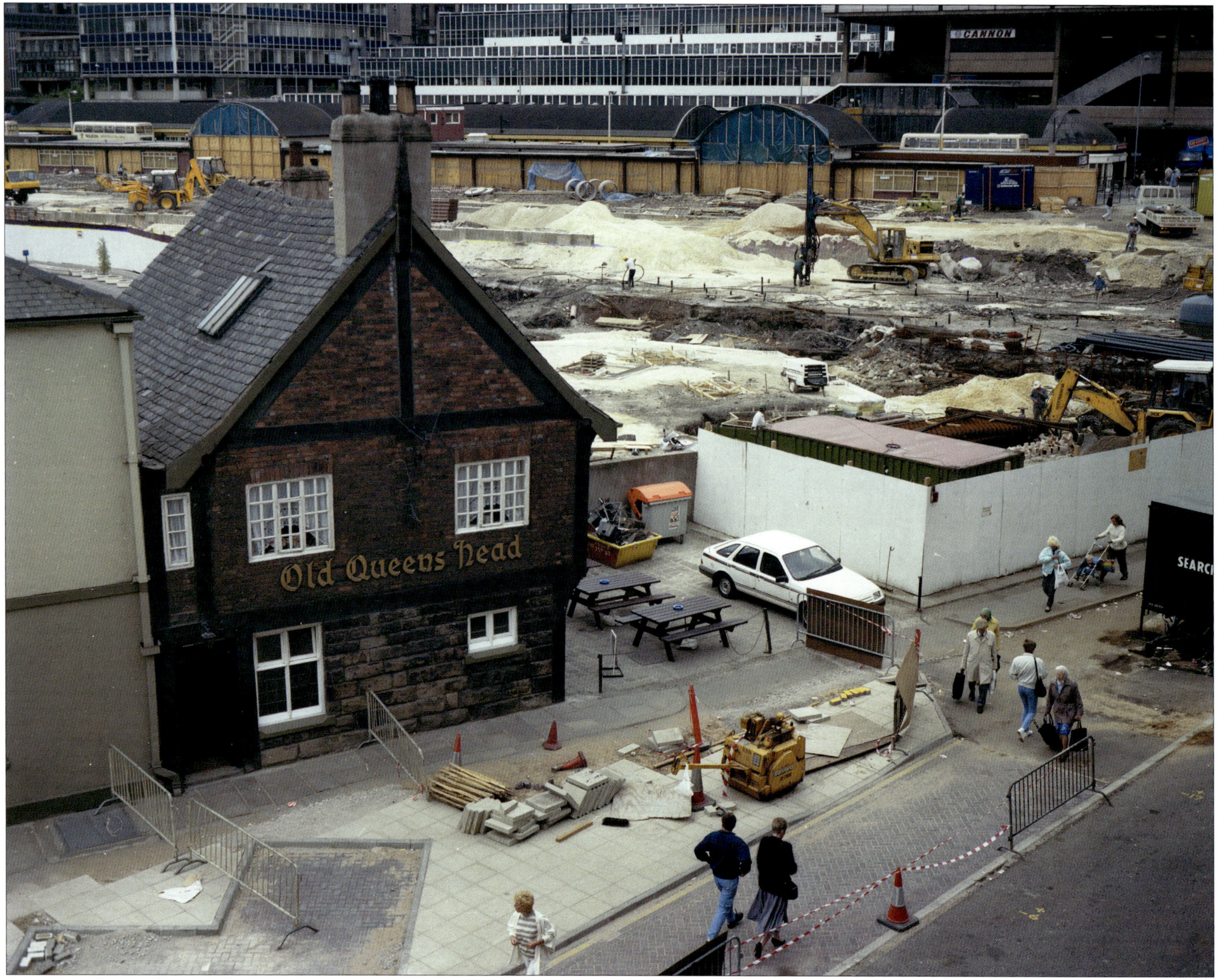

The "Queen's Head",
Pond Hill 1989.

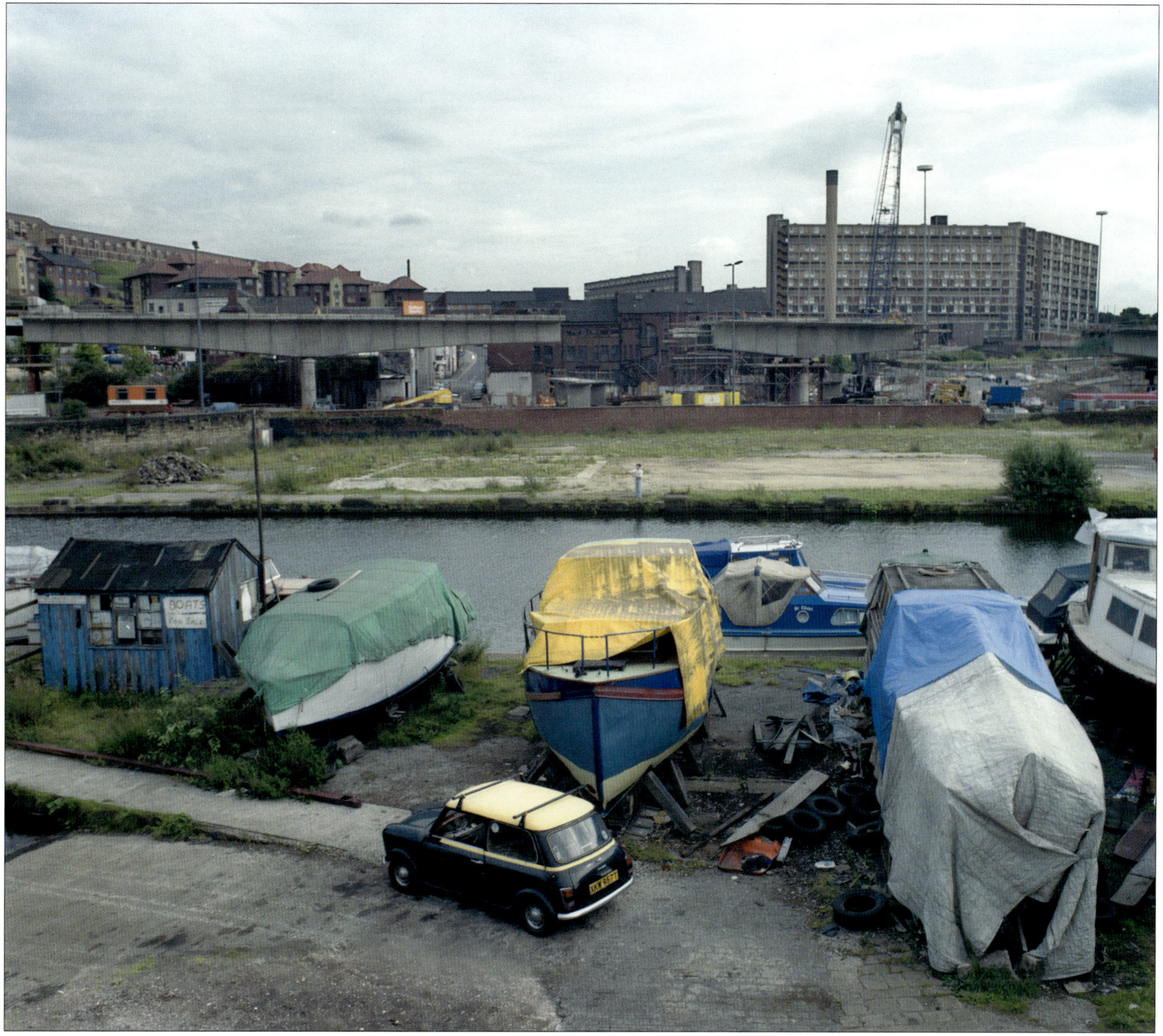

The canal basin, 1992.

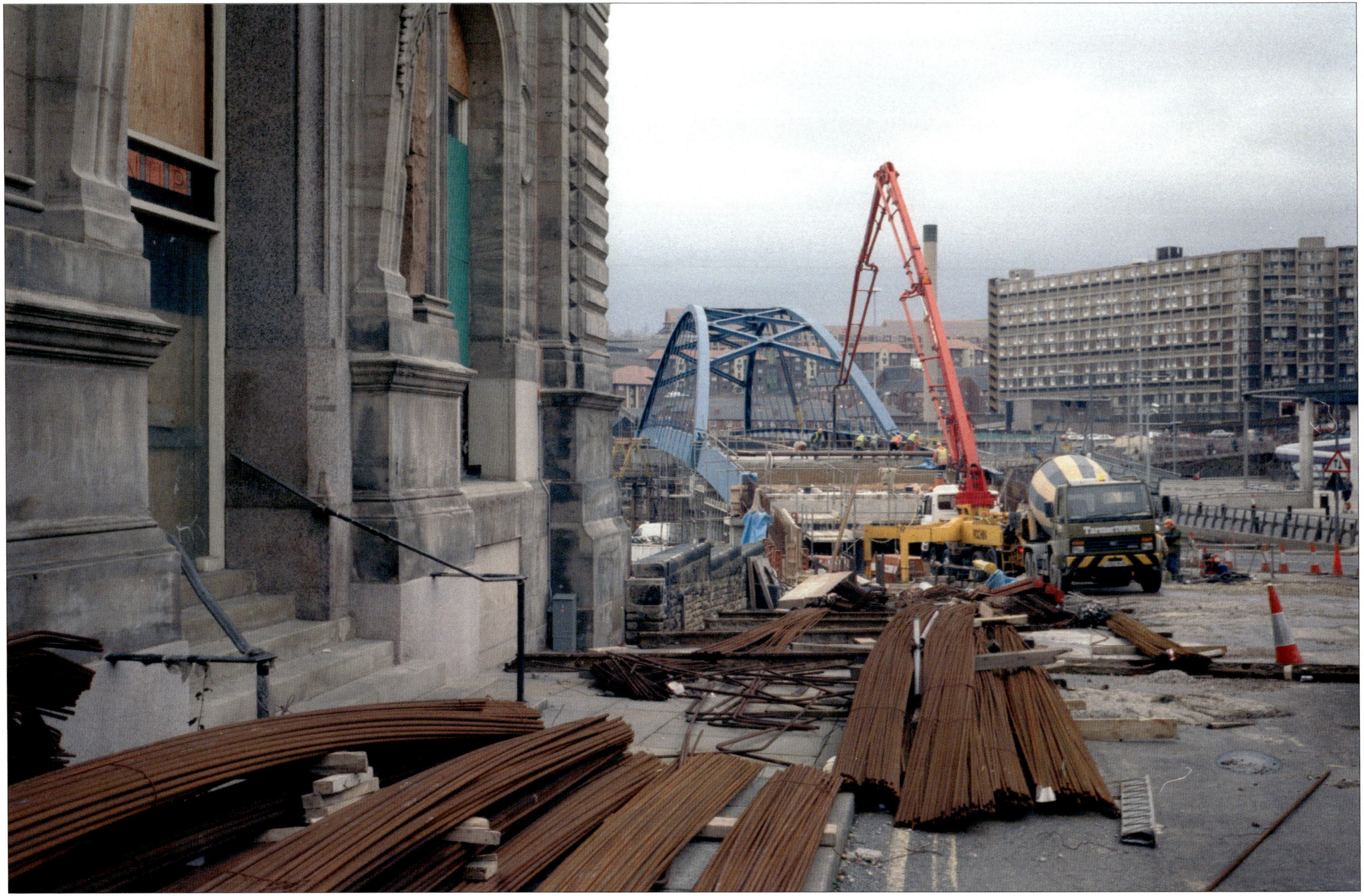

Commercial Street, 1992. Tramway construction underway.

Pond's Forge, 1989.
The arch was later
incorporated into the
pool building.

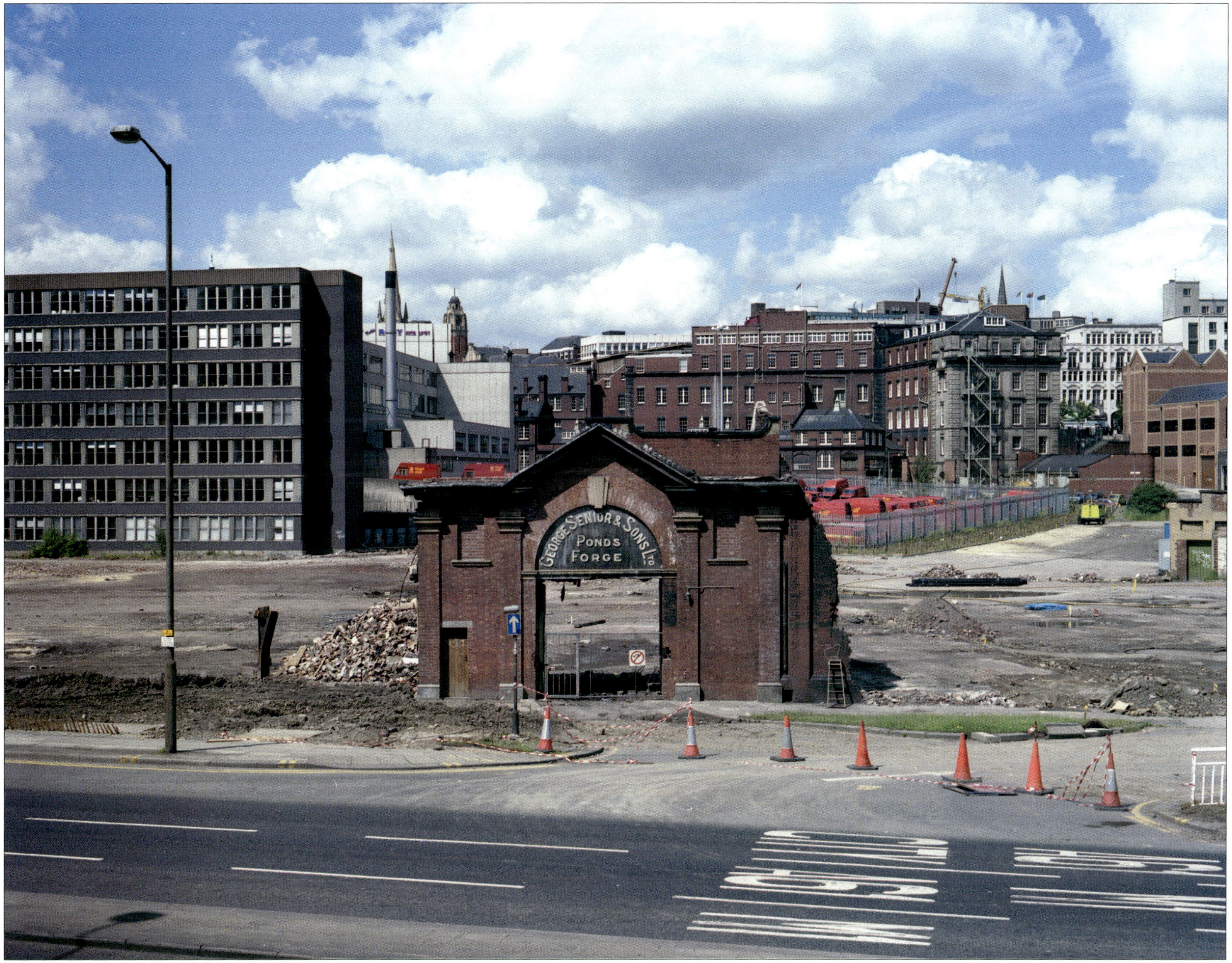

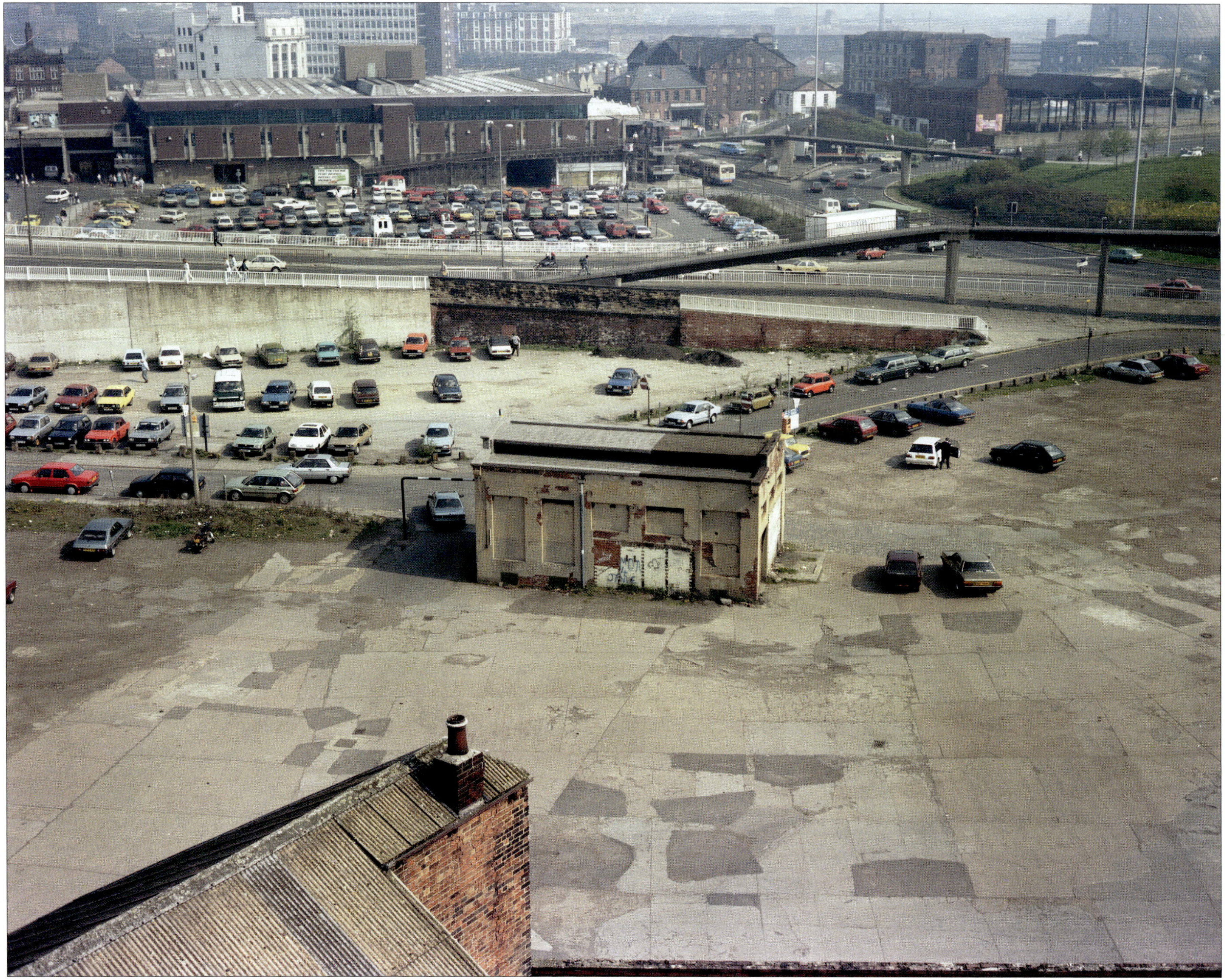

Park Square and Commercial Street, 1988. The foreground is now occupied by the Ponds Forge swimming pool that was built for the World Student Games of 1991.

Roof structure, Pond's Forge, 1989. Hyde Park and Parkhill flats in the background.

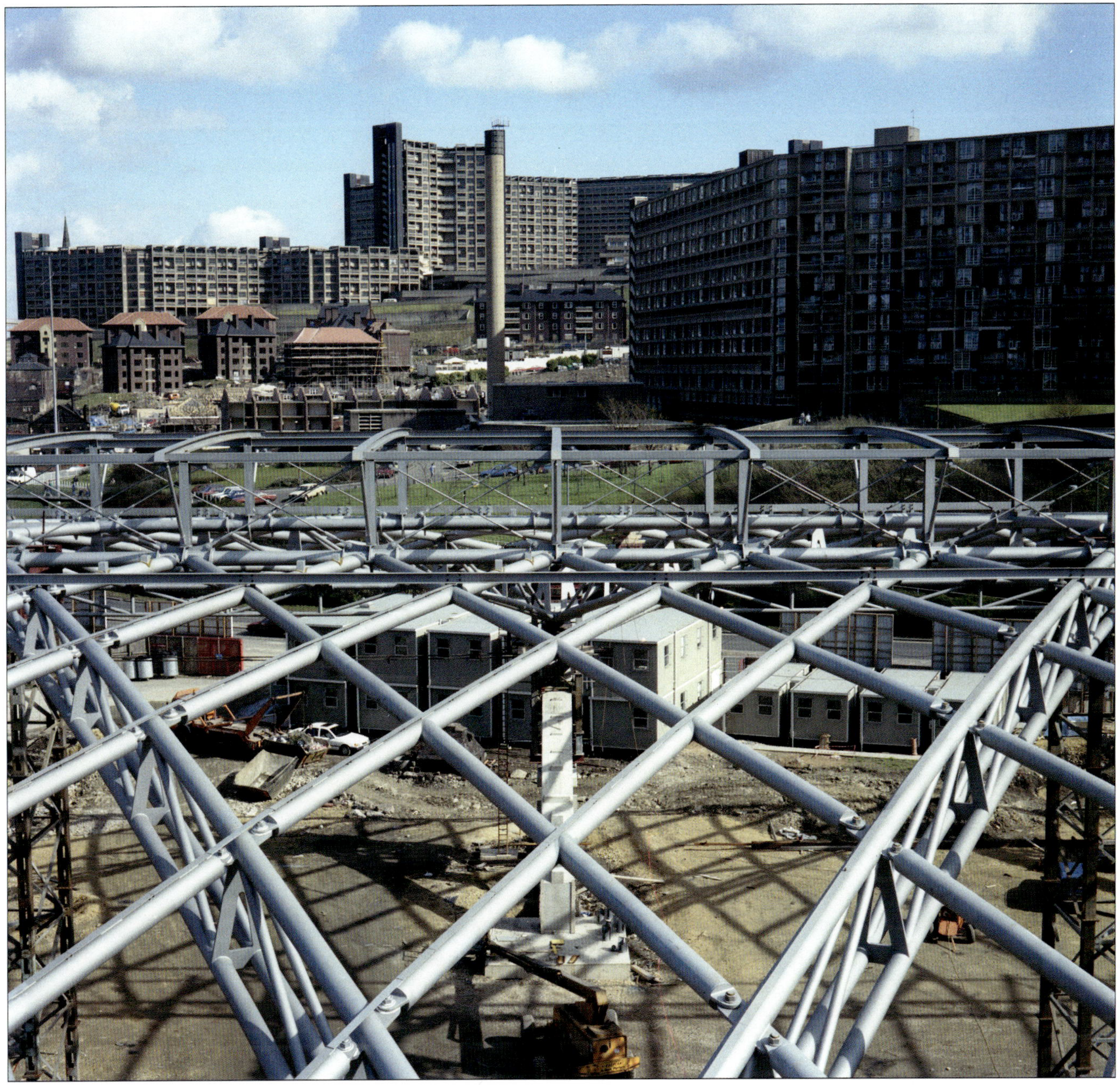

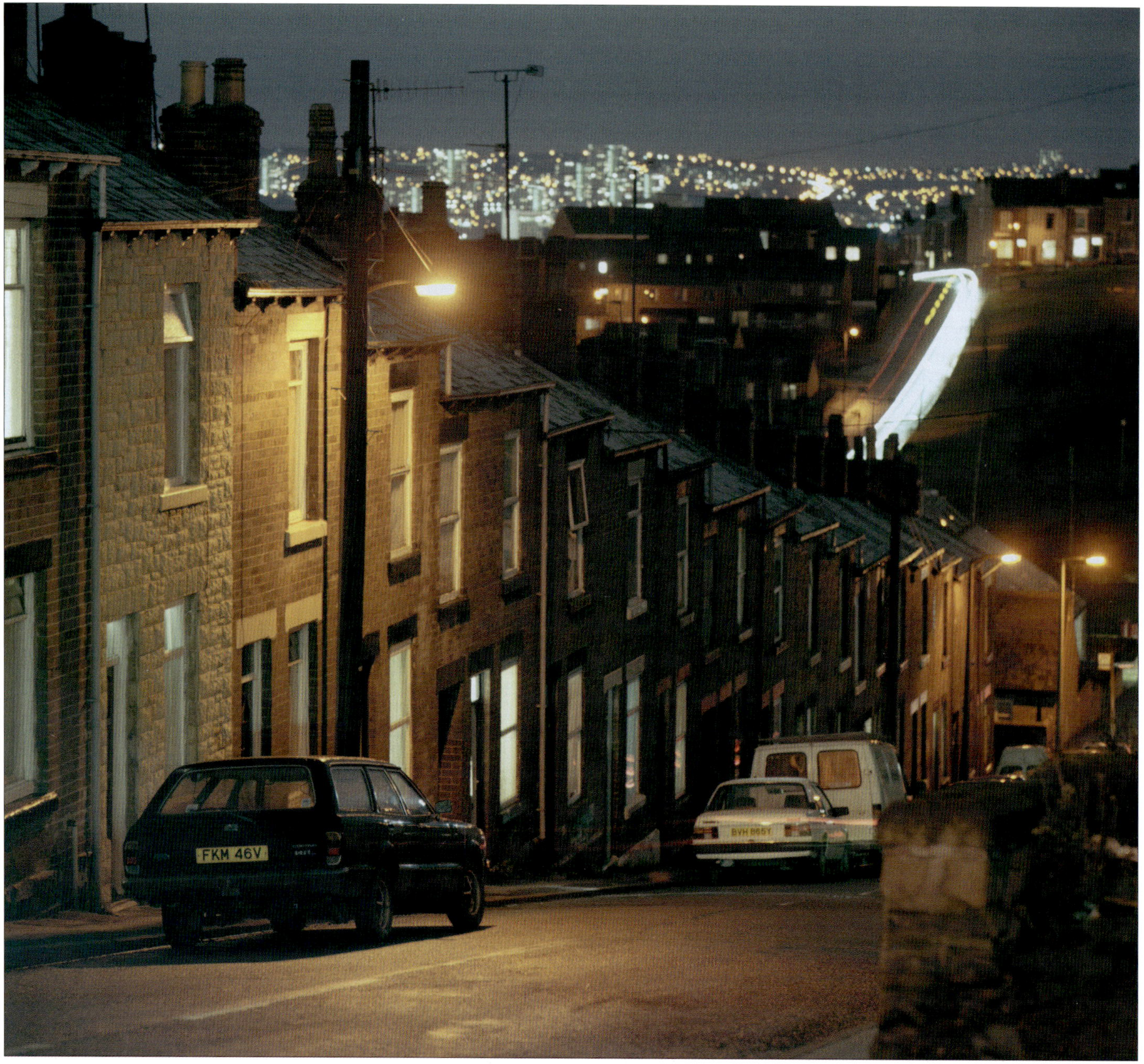

Whitehouse Road, Walkley, 1990.

Main Post Office,
Fitzalan Square,
1990.

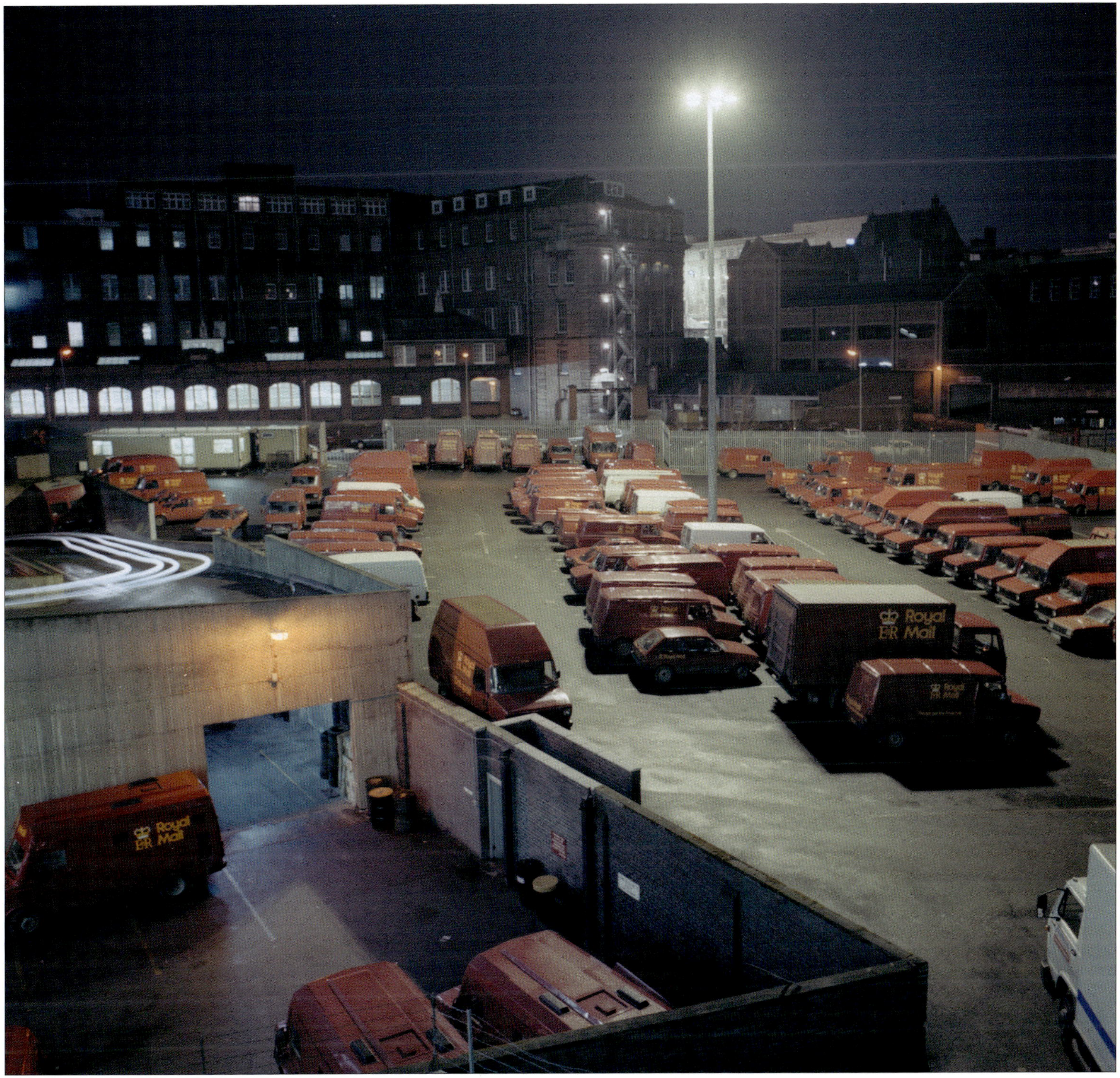

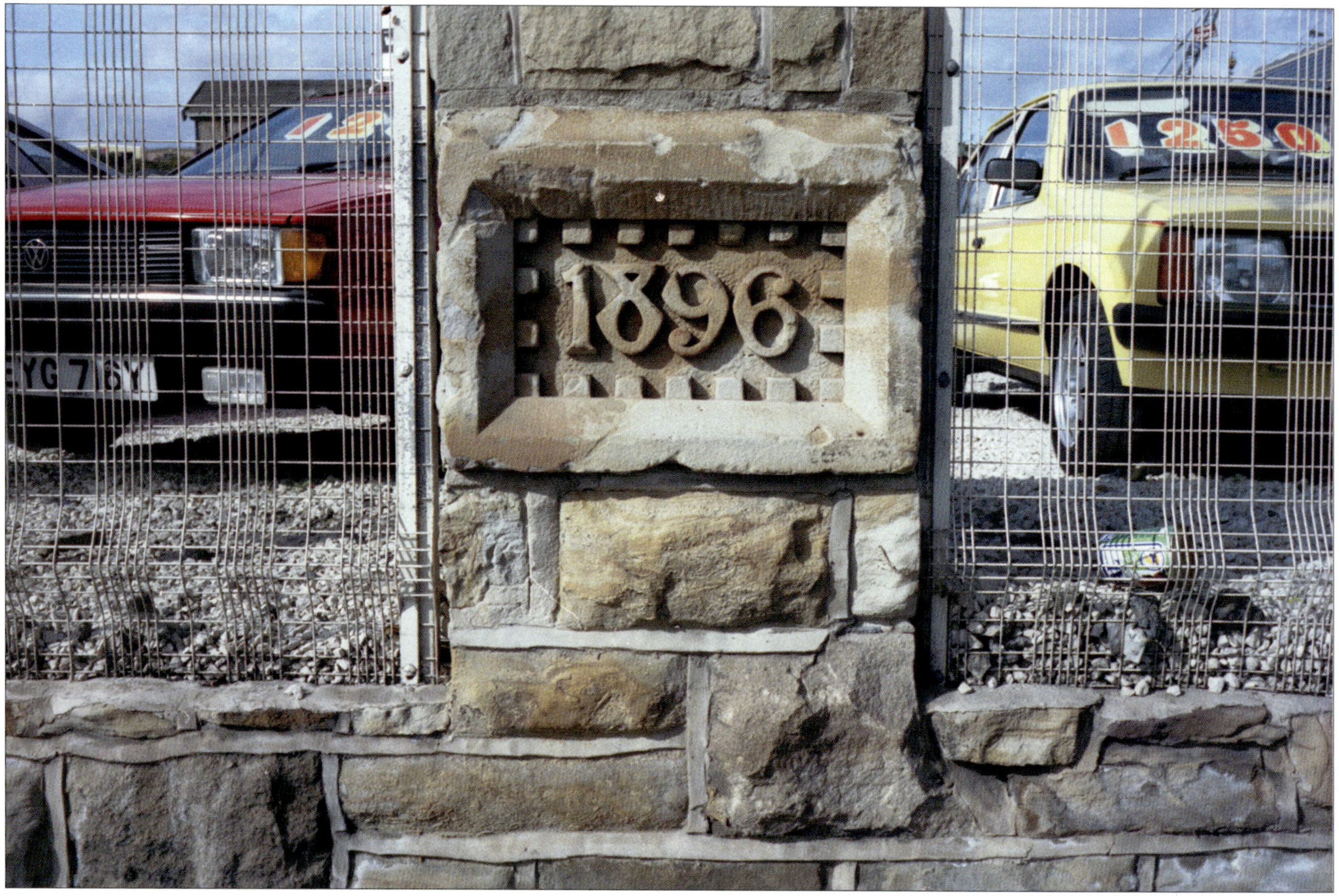

Meadowhall Road 1989.

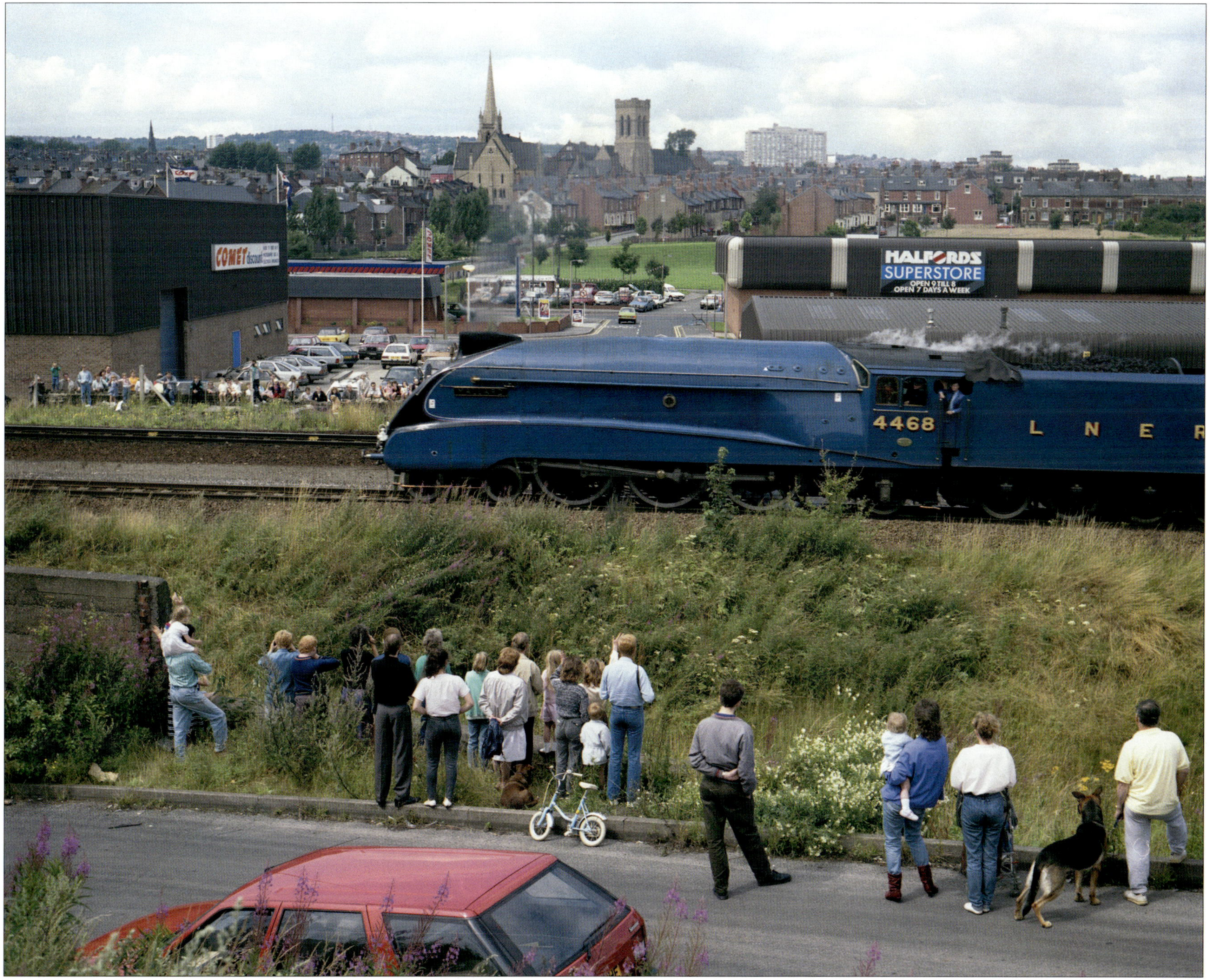

Guernsey Road, Heeley, 1987. The National Railway Museum's world record holder "Mallard" on a special train.

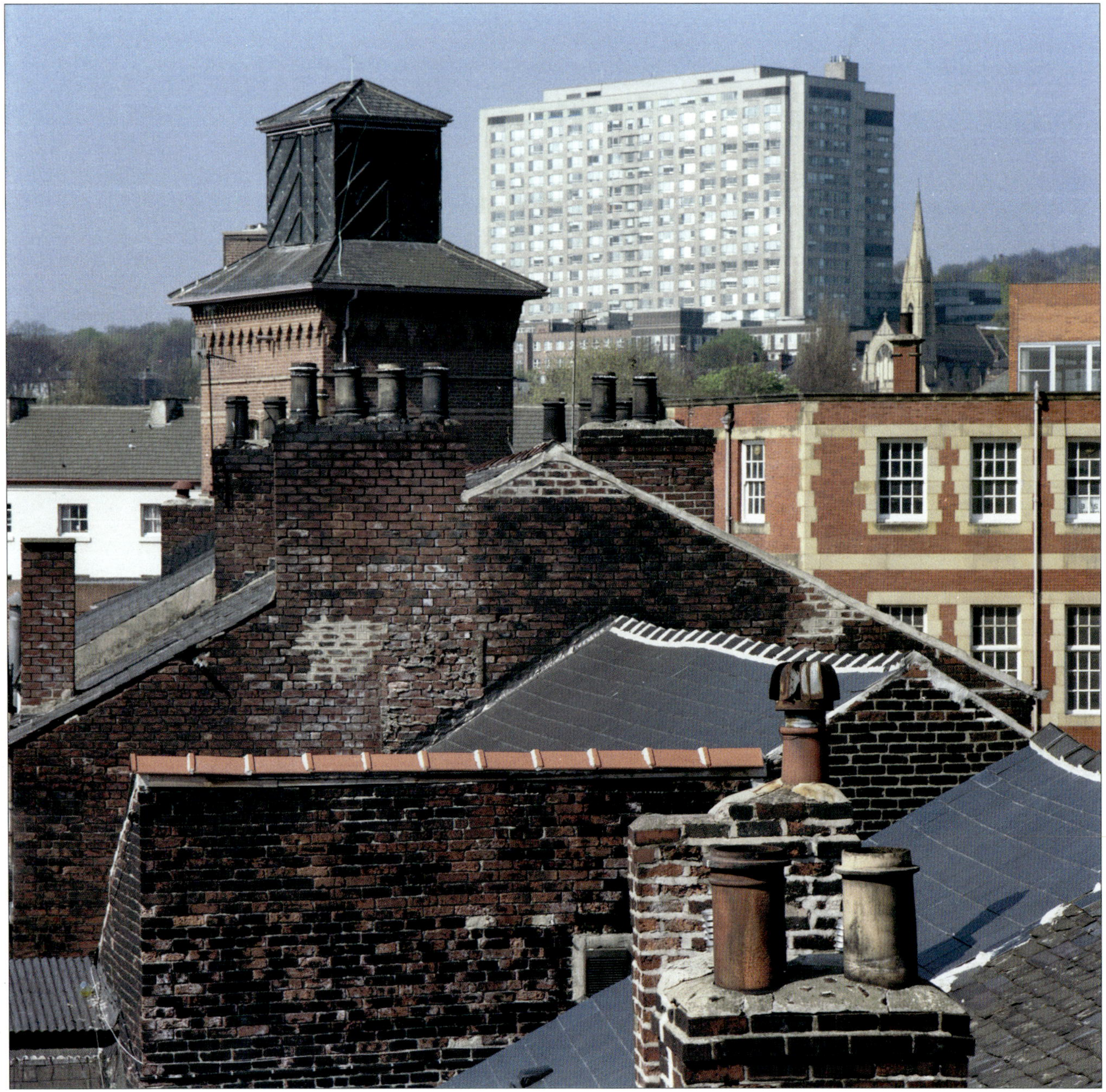

The Hallamshire hospital, 1989. From Fitzwilliam Street; the complex roof to the left of the picture belongs to the Turkish baths built in 1877.

The University Arts Tower, 1988. The boating lake at Crookes Valley Park is a survivor of the 19th century reservoir system.

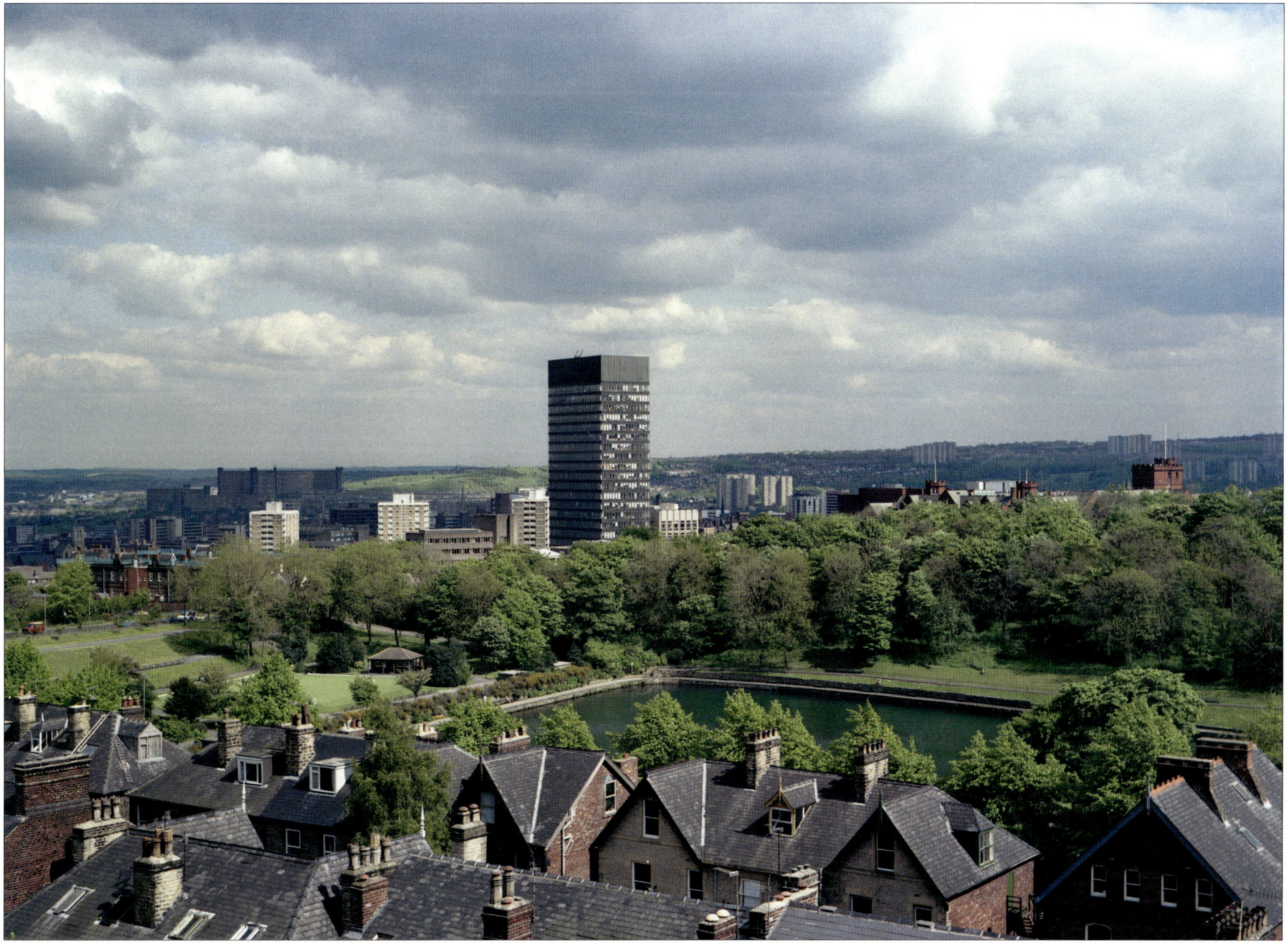

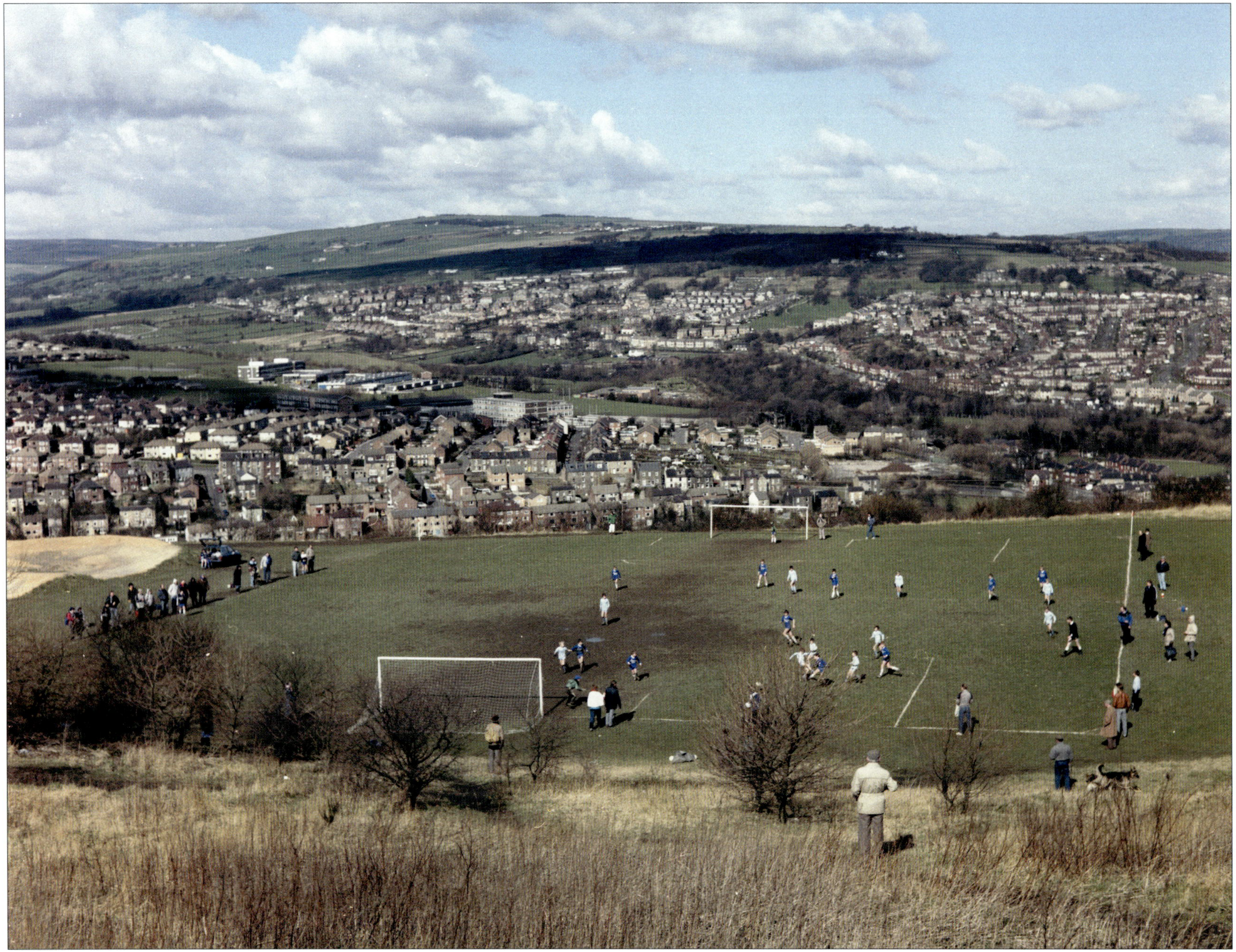

Bole Hills, Walkley, 1985. Looking over Malin Bridge to Wisewood.

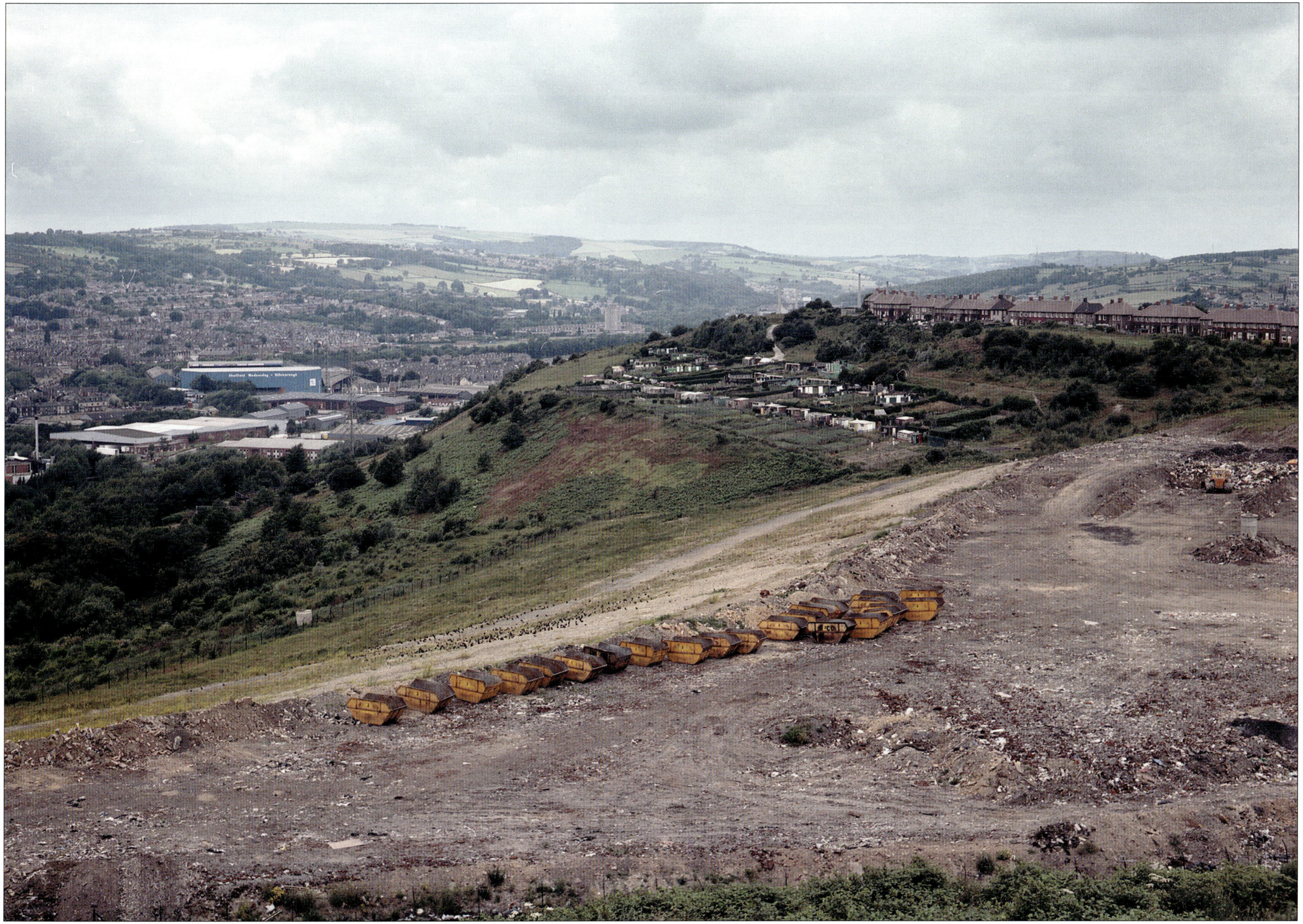

Parkwood landfill site, 1988.

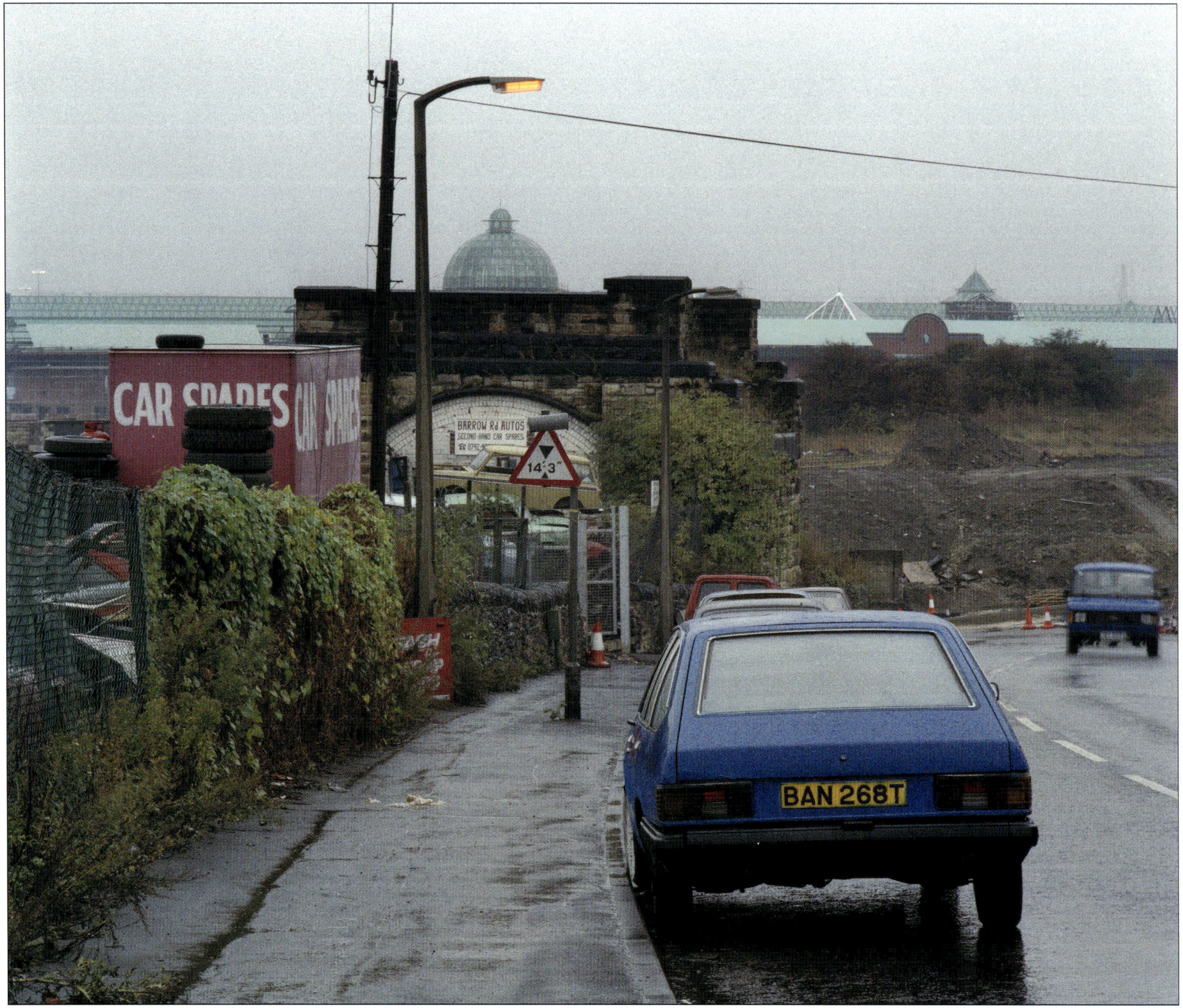

Barrow Road, 1990.

Sidney Street, 1992.

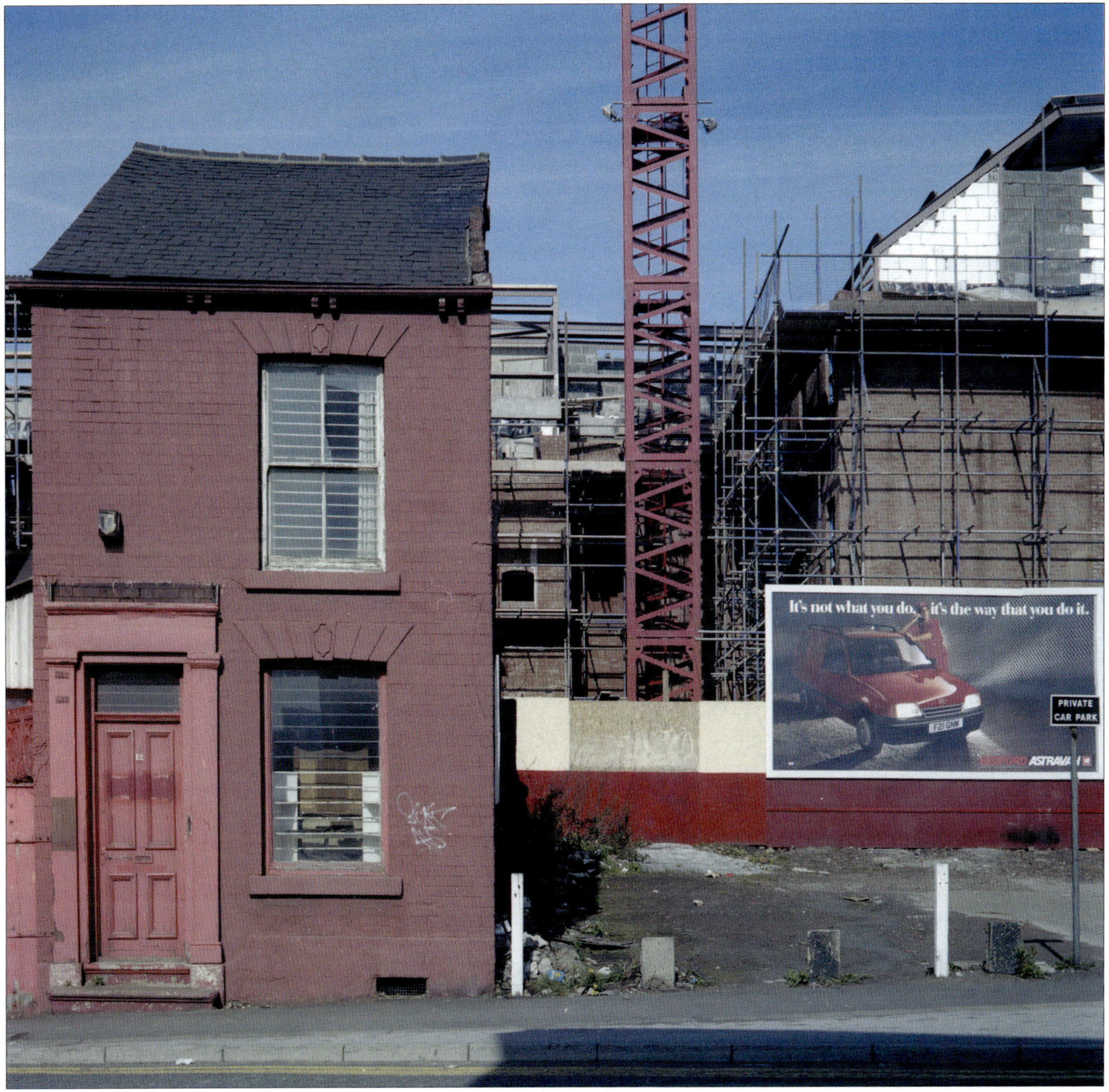

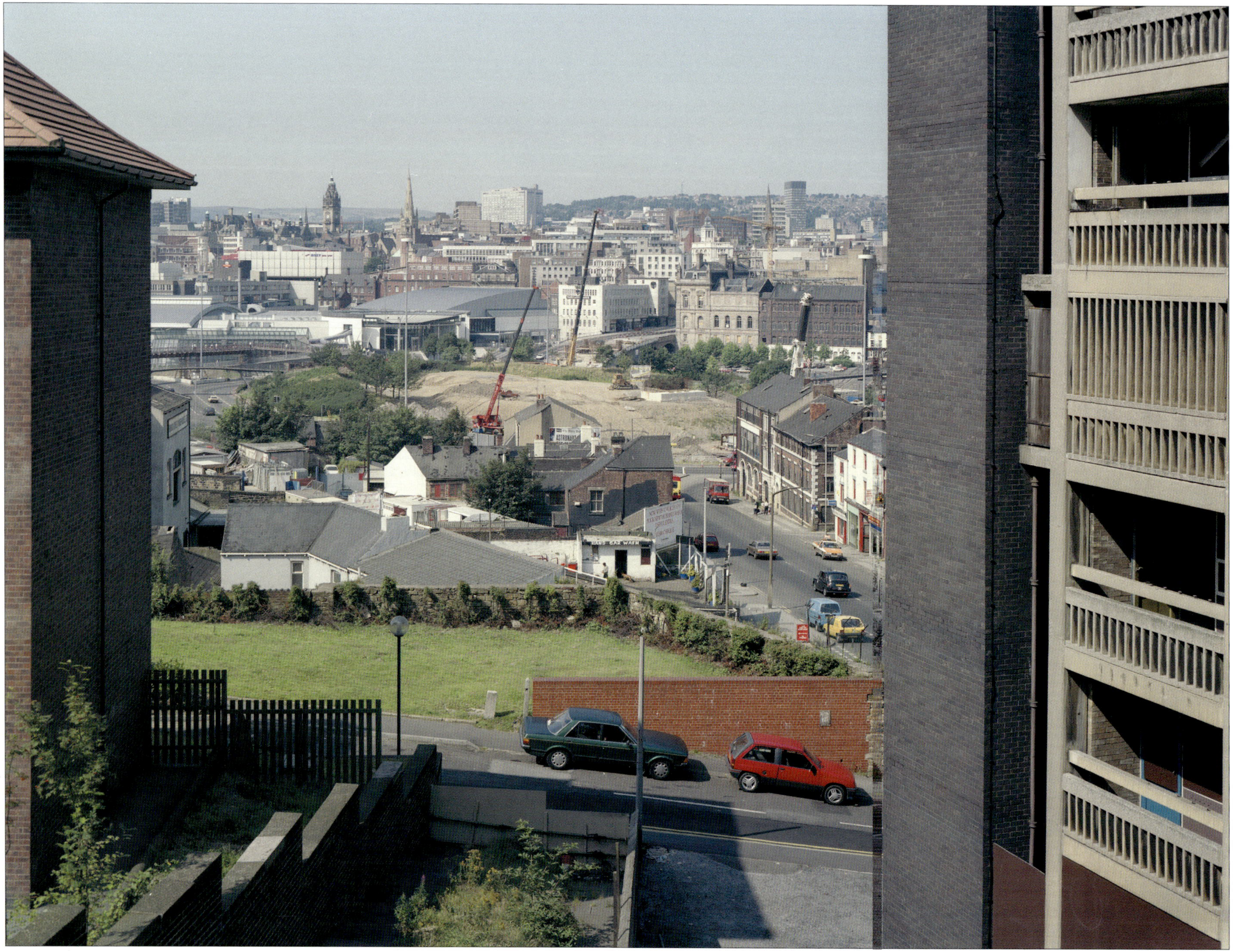

Park Square, 1992.

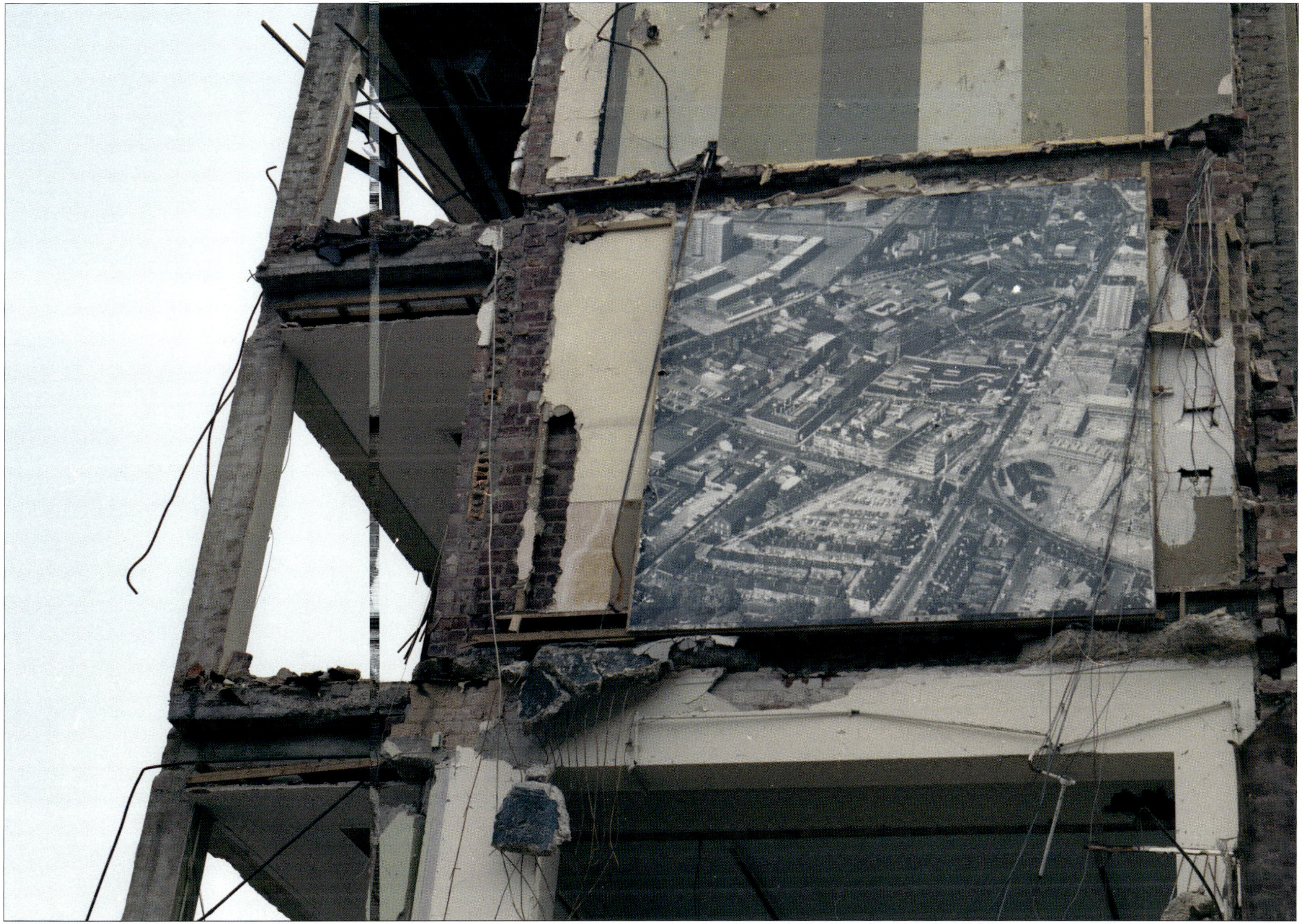

Napier Street, 1987. The photograph on the wall dates from the 1960's

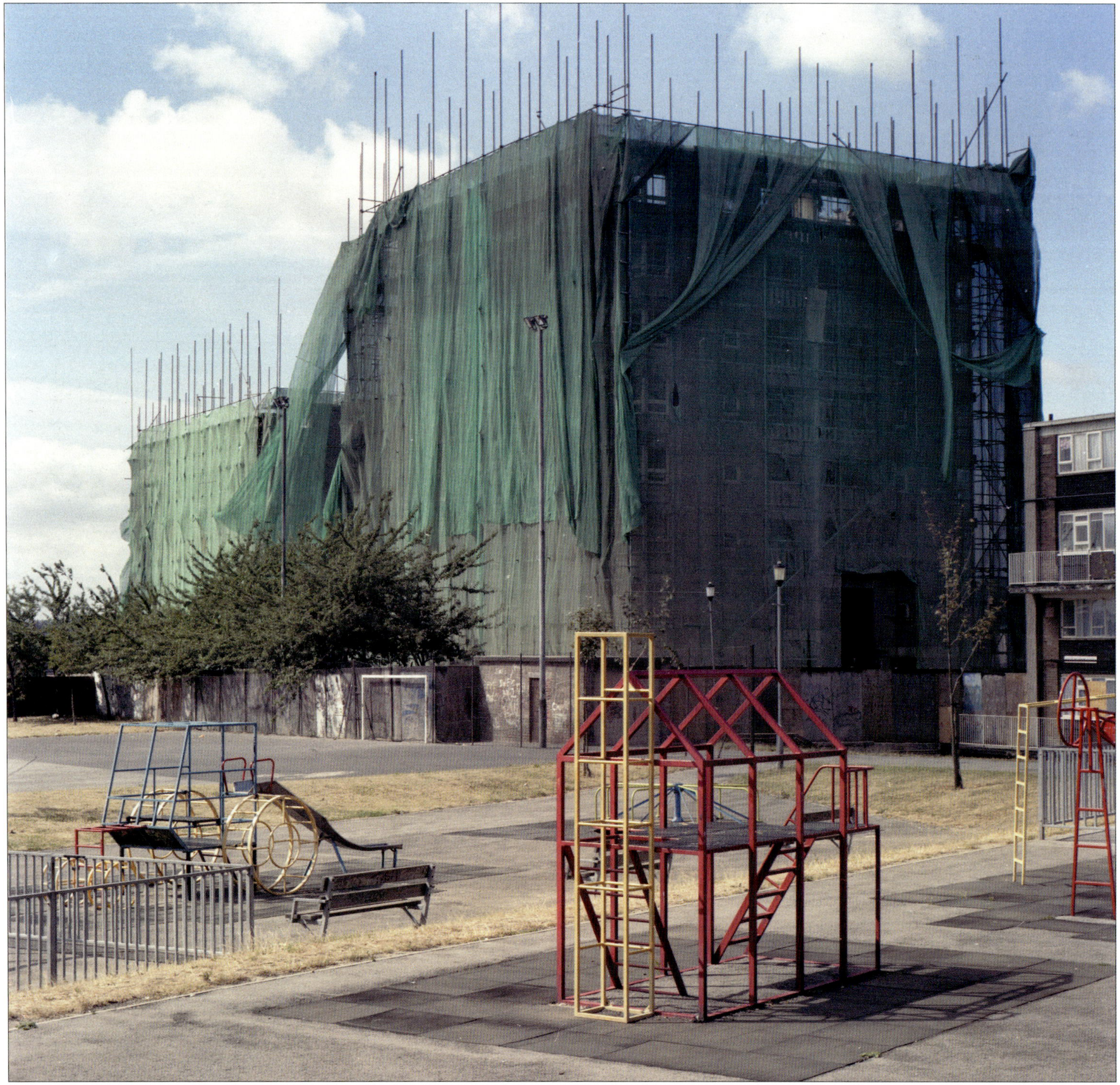

Pye Bank, 1990.

Pye Bank, 1990.

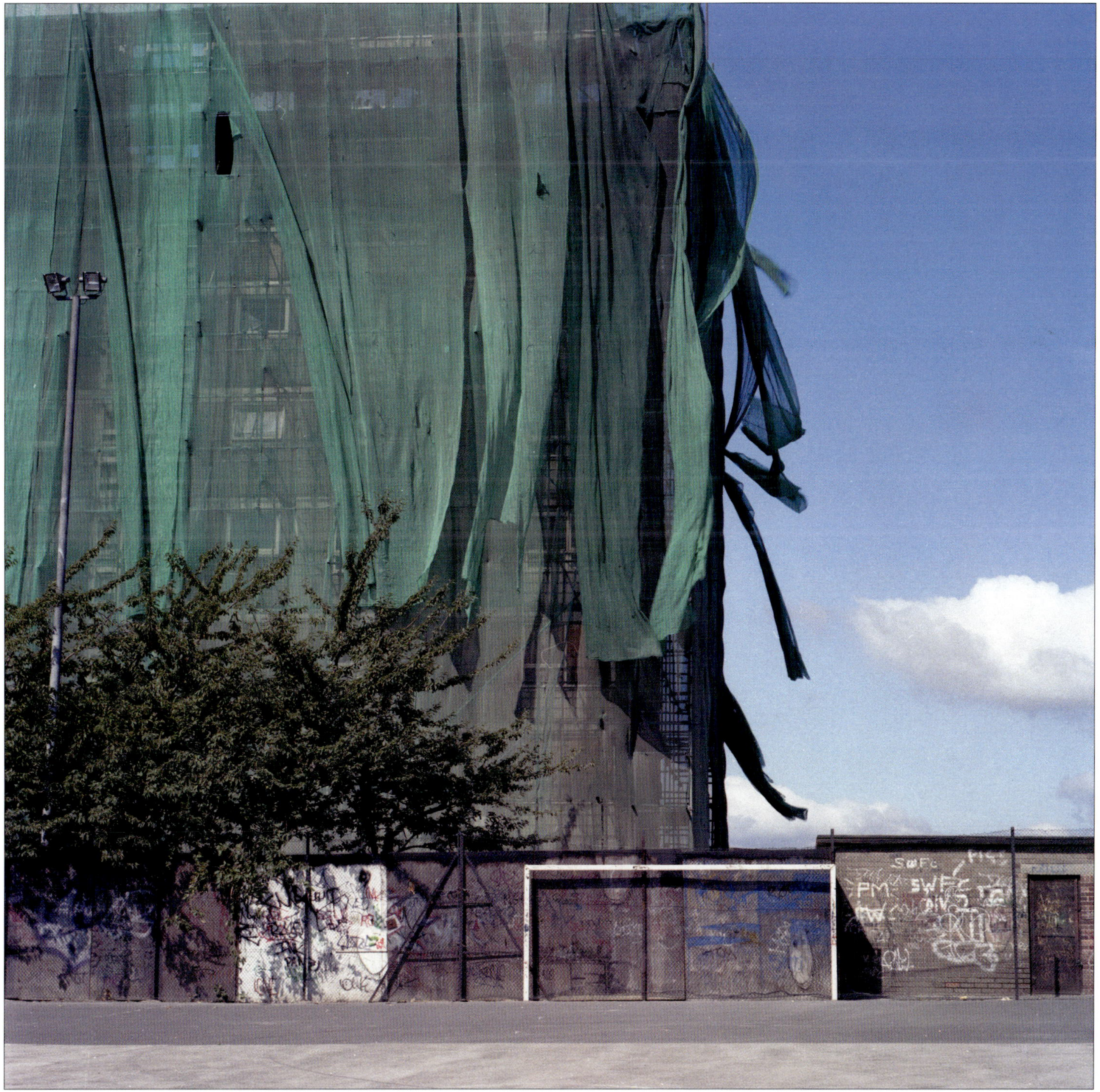

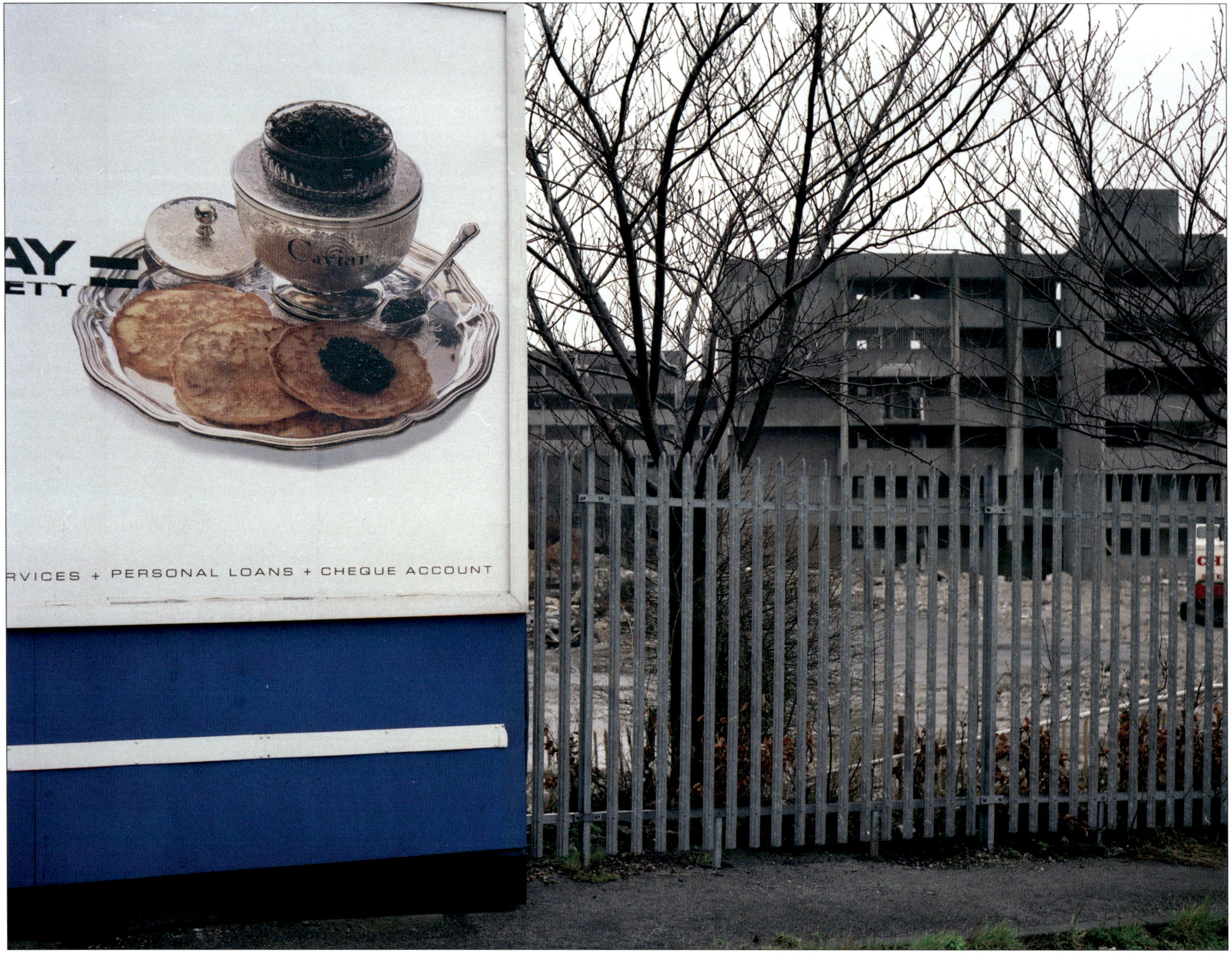

Broomhall flats, 1988.
The corner of
Broomspring Lane and
Hanover Street.

Beighton 1987.
Most new house building at this time took place in the south east of the city.

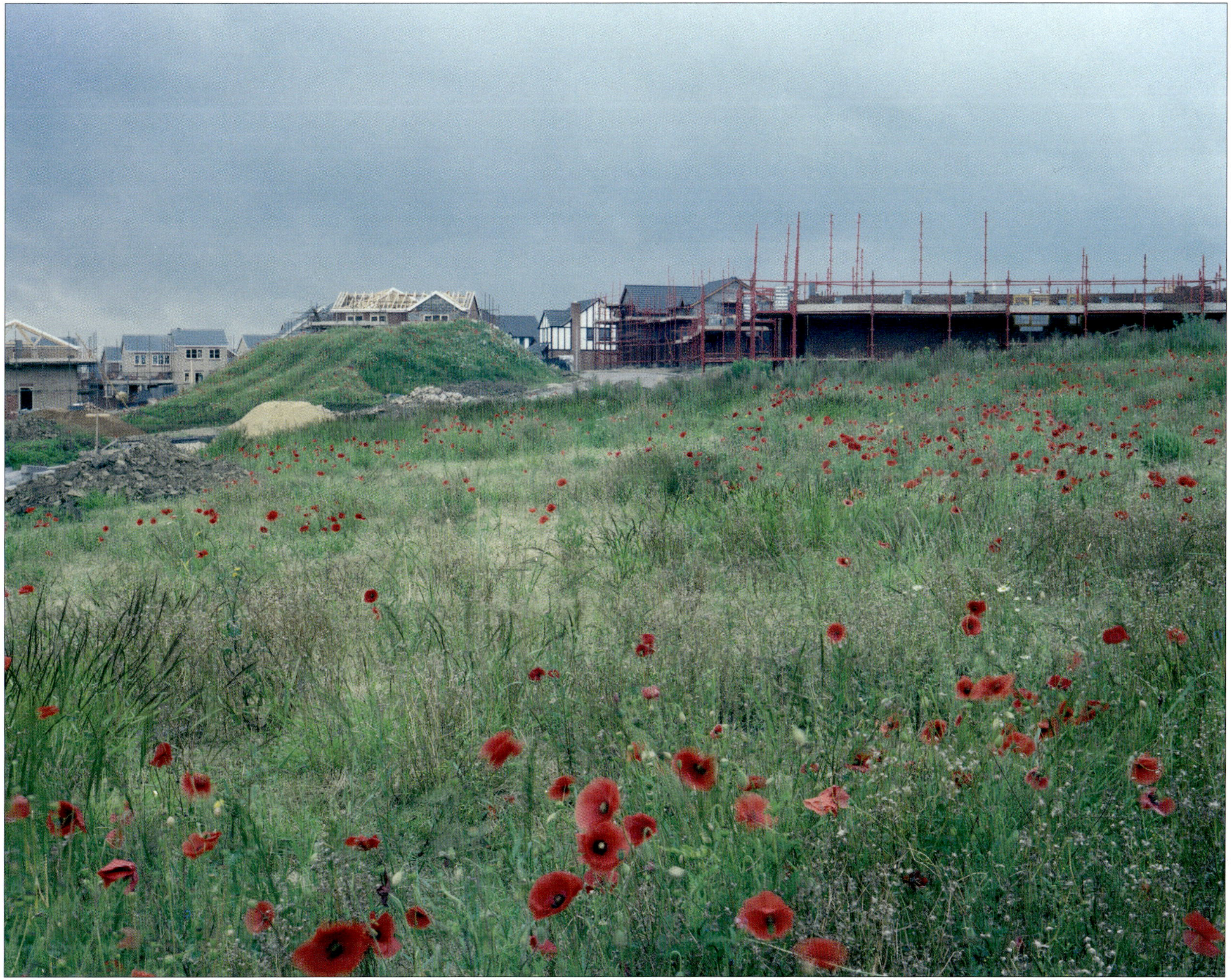

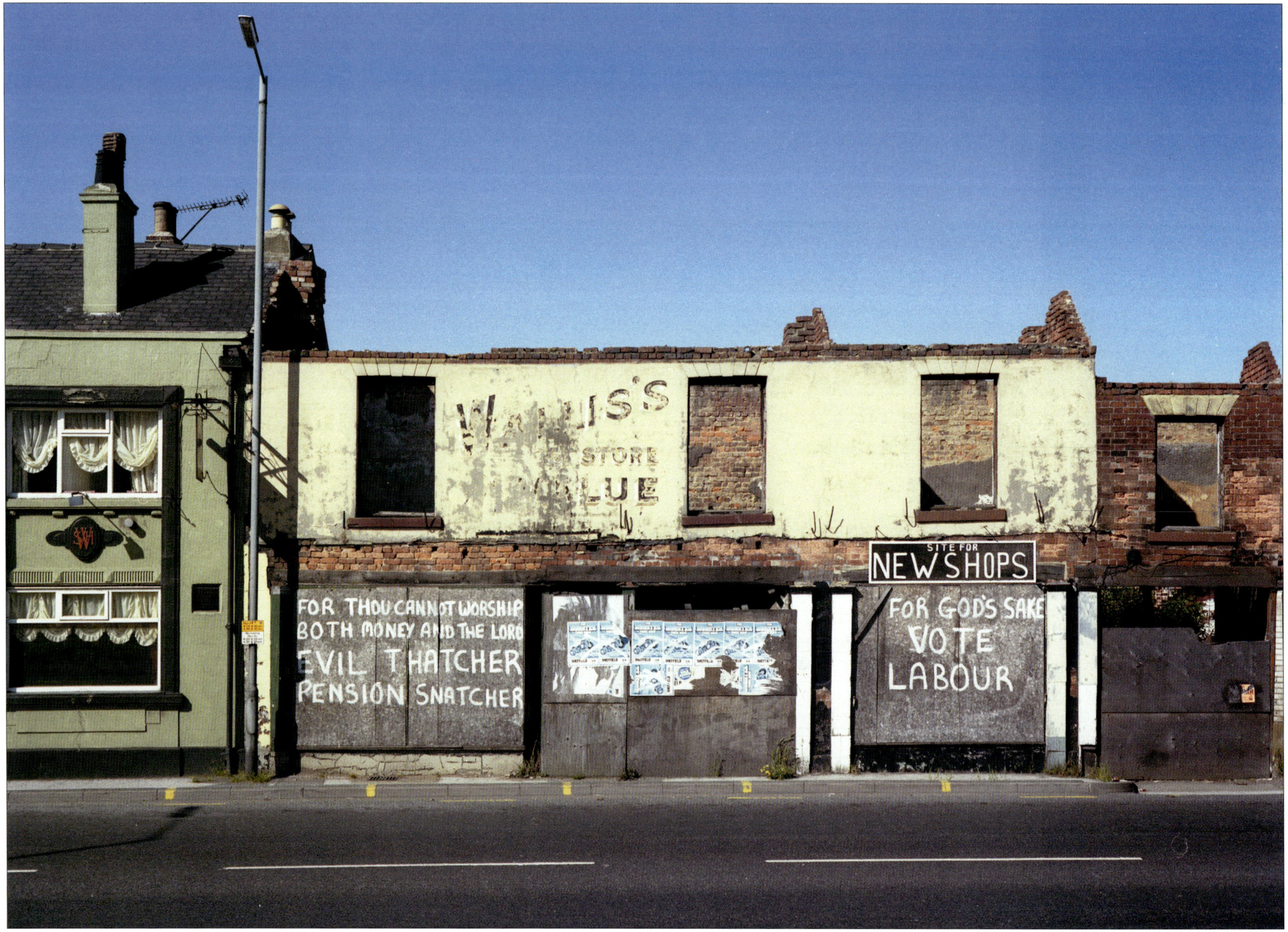

Langsett Road, 1990.

Hoyle Street, 1990.

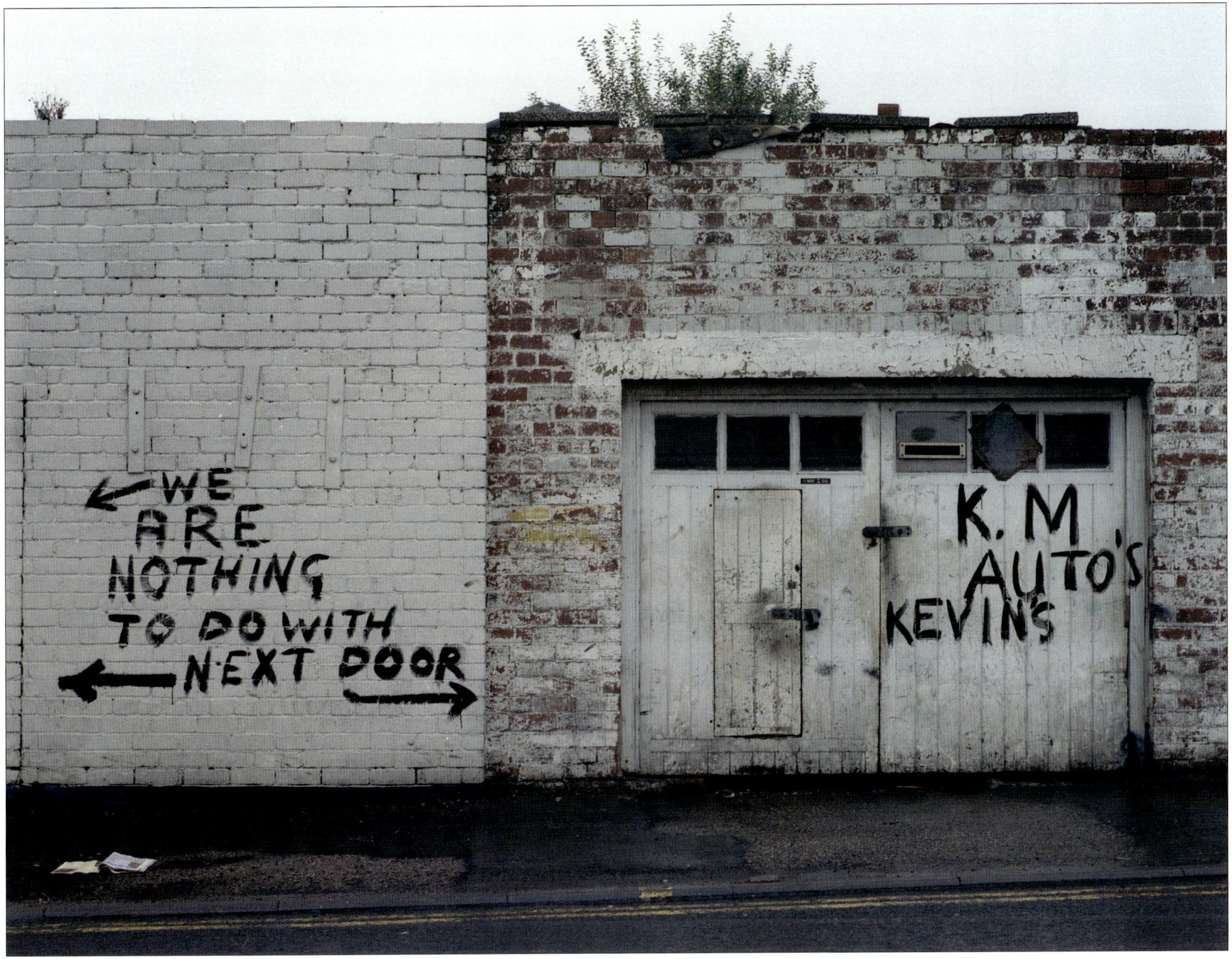

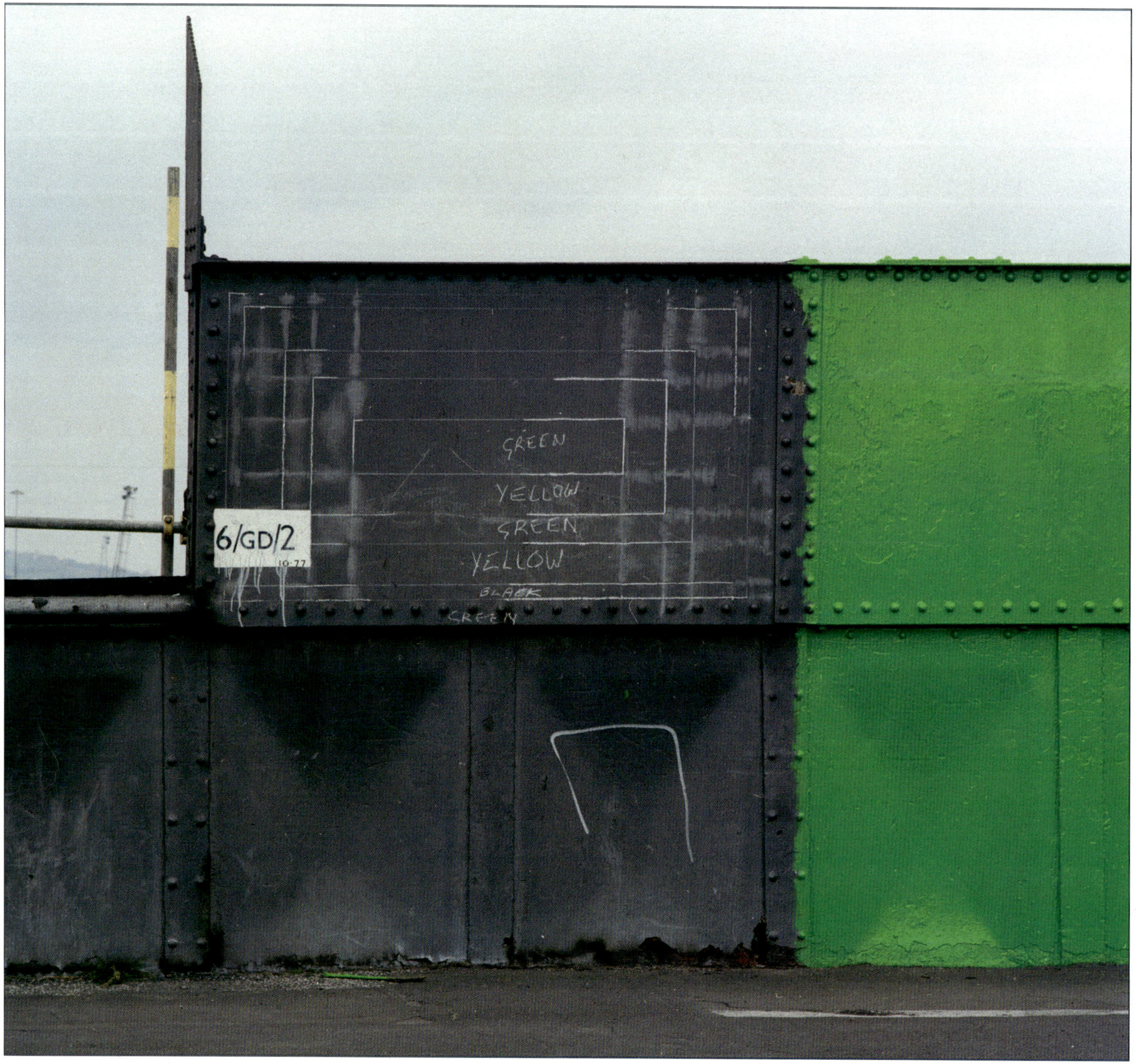

Railway bridge, Carbrook Road, 1990.
Hosting the 1991 World Student Games involved the construction of new sports facilities at huge expense, but inevitably some of the changes were cosmetic.

Canal Basin, 1991.
Fly posting during construction
of a new car park.

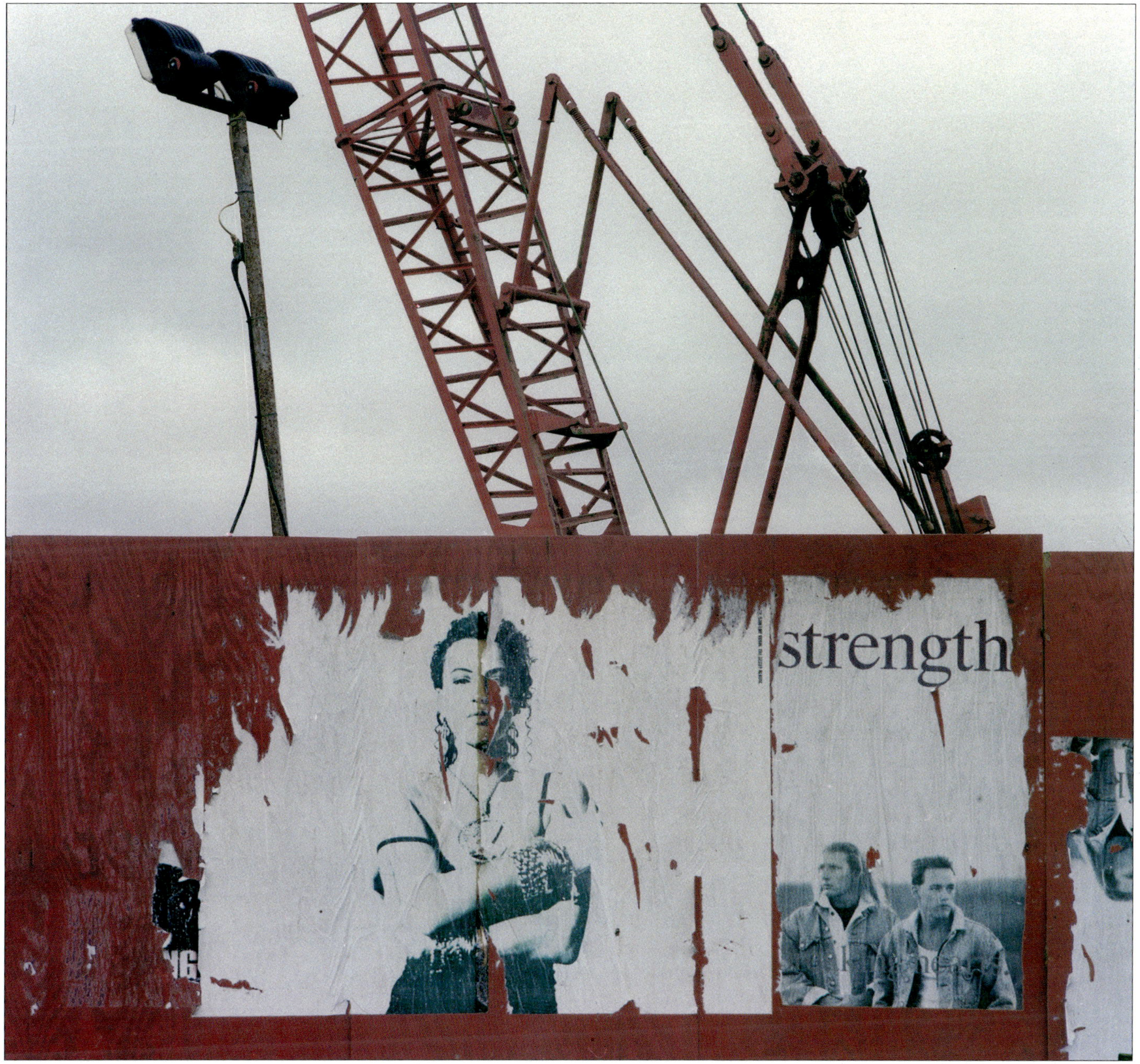

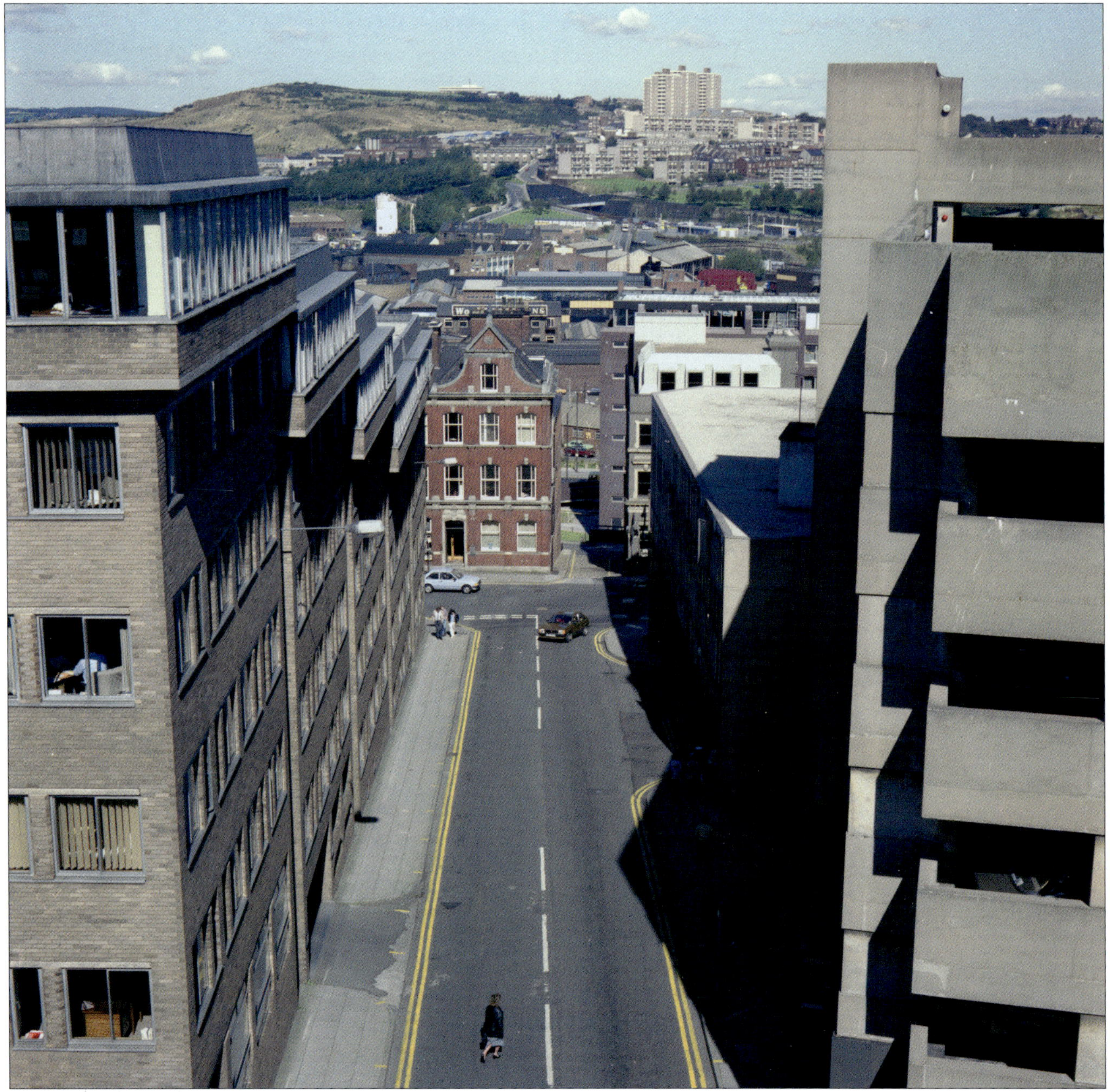

Meetinghouse Lane, 1984.
Looking over the Upper Don to Pye Bank flats.

The Don Valley from Crookes, 1988.

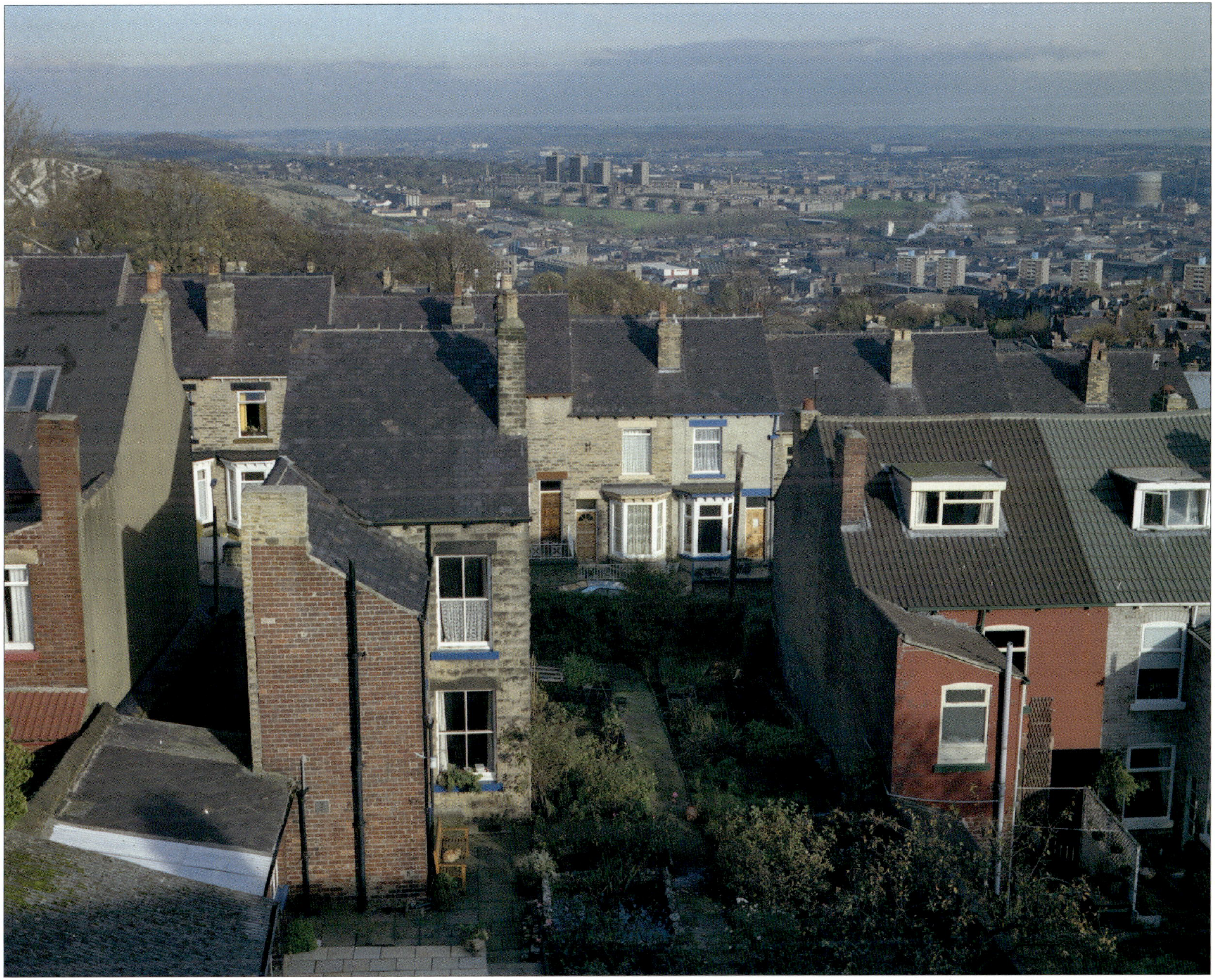

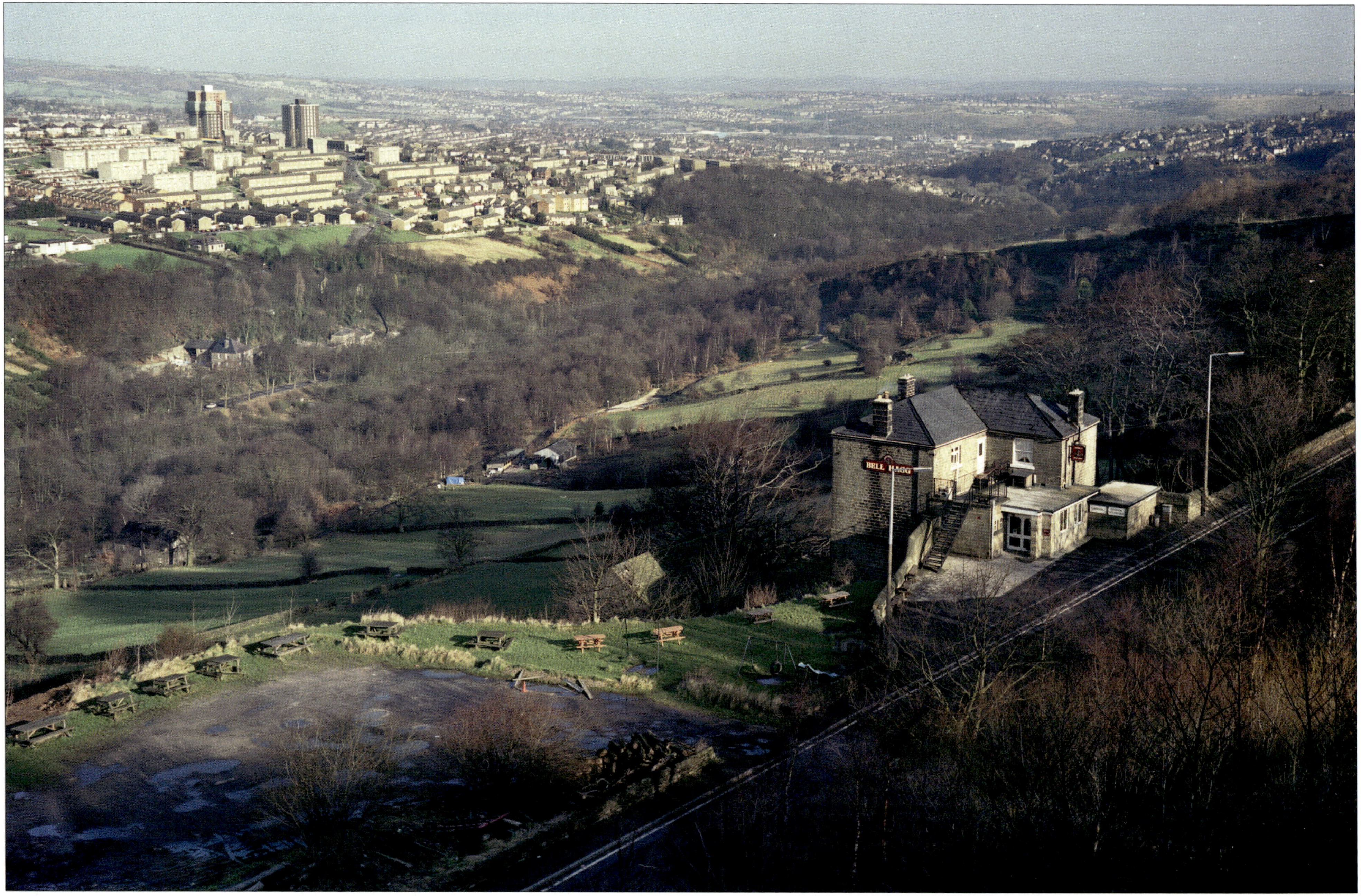

The Rivelin valley, 1987. The “Bell Hagg” public house, now closed, is on the A57 Manchester Road

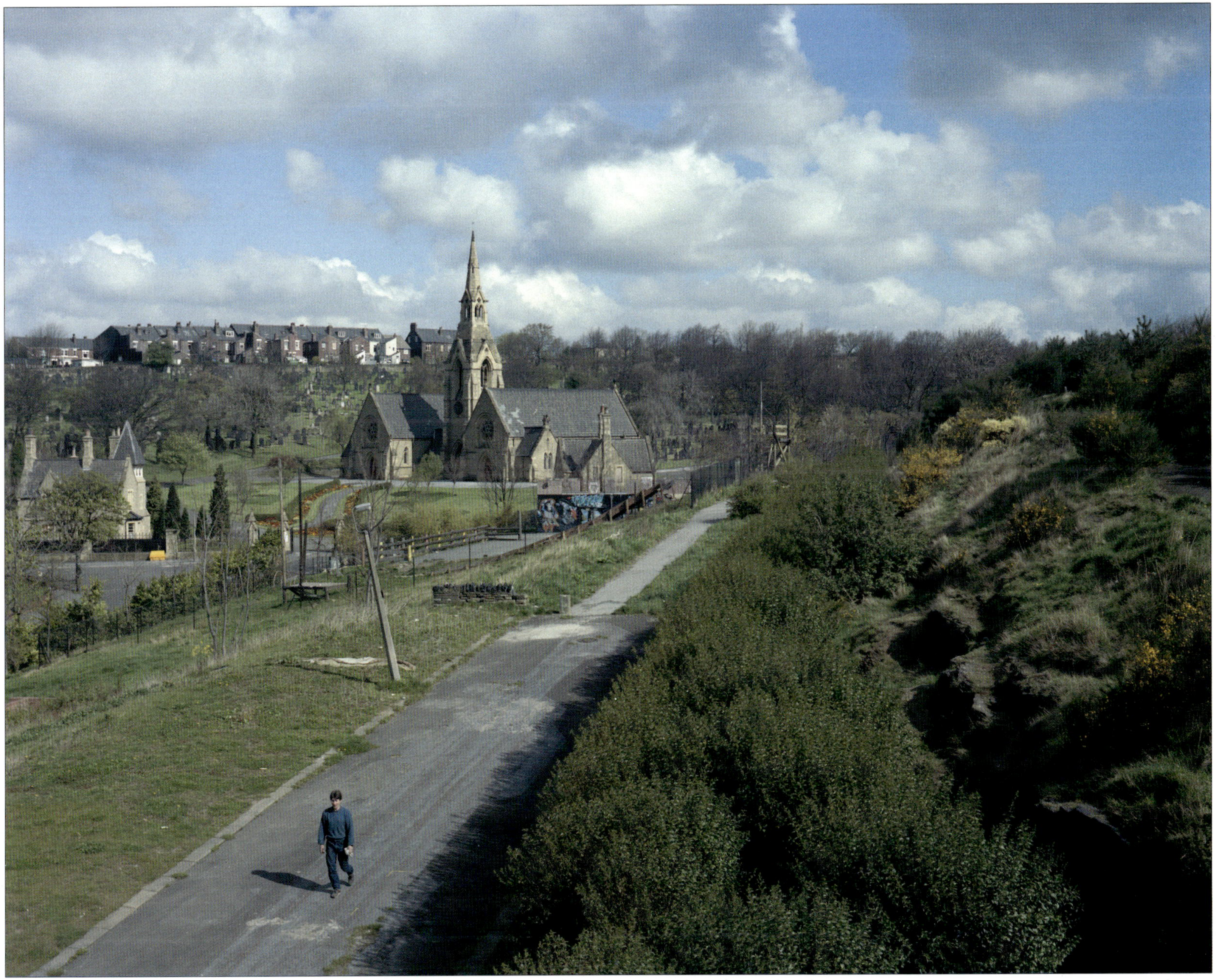

Burngreave Cemetery chapel, 1988. The picture was taken from Burngreave Bank, where the houses at the end of the street had recently been demolished.

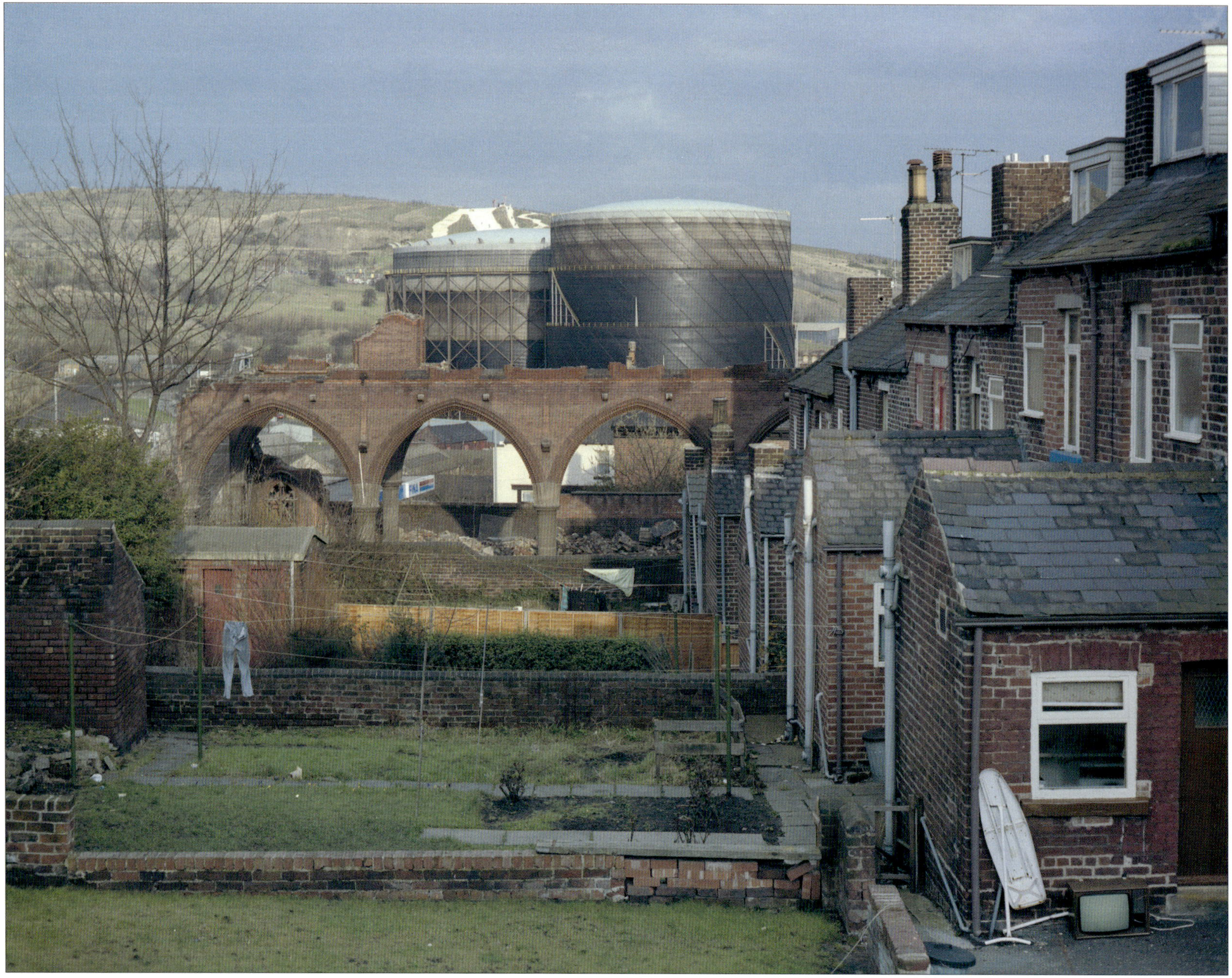

Burgoyne Road, 1989.
St.Bartholomew's
church in the process
of being demolished.

St.John's church, 1991.The church stands amid the part refurbished, part demolished Hyde Park flats

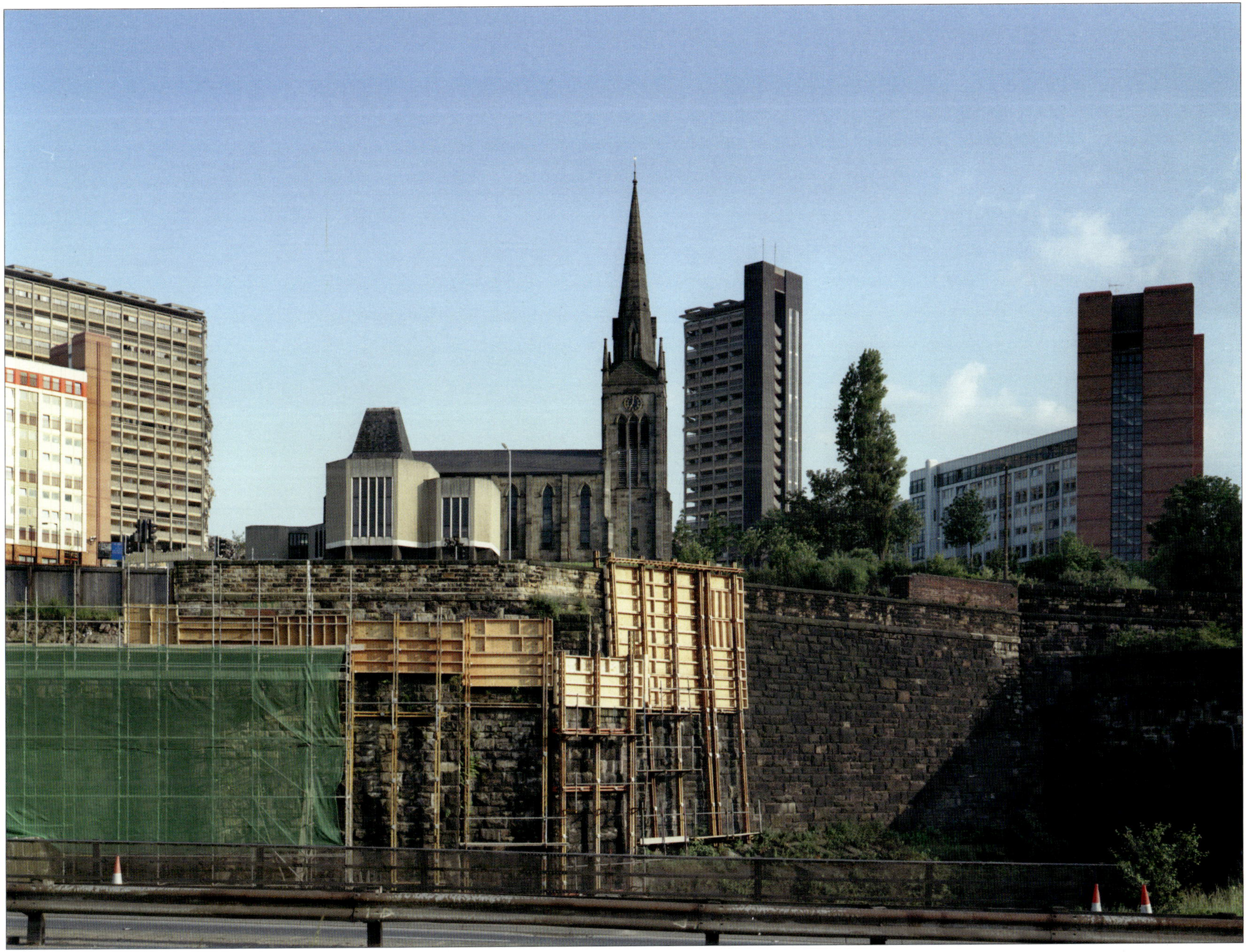

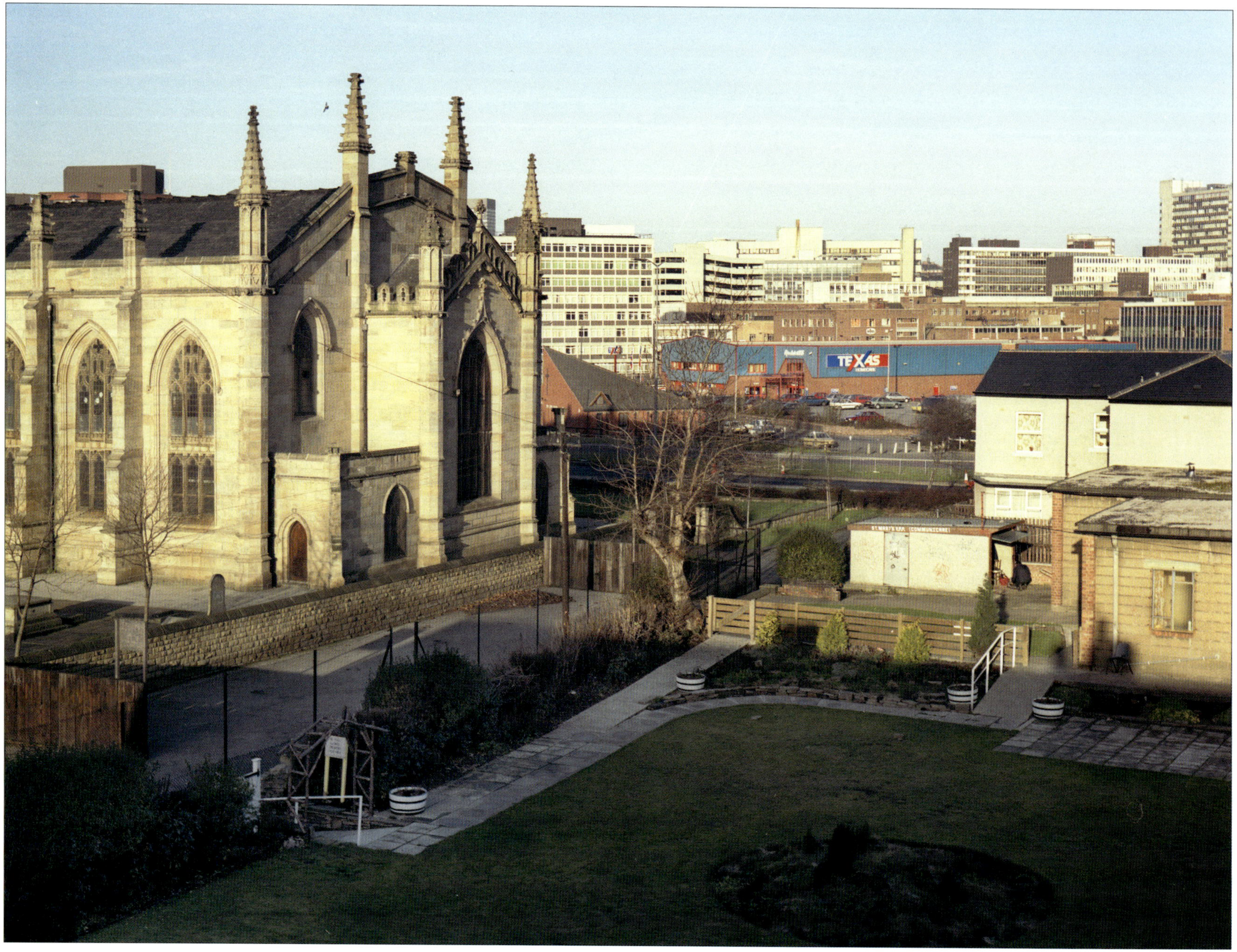

St.Mary's,
Bramall Lane.
1988.

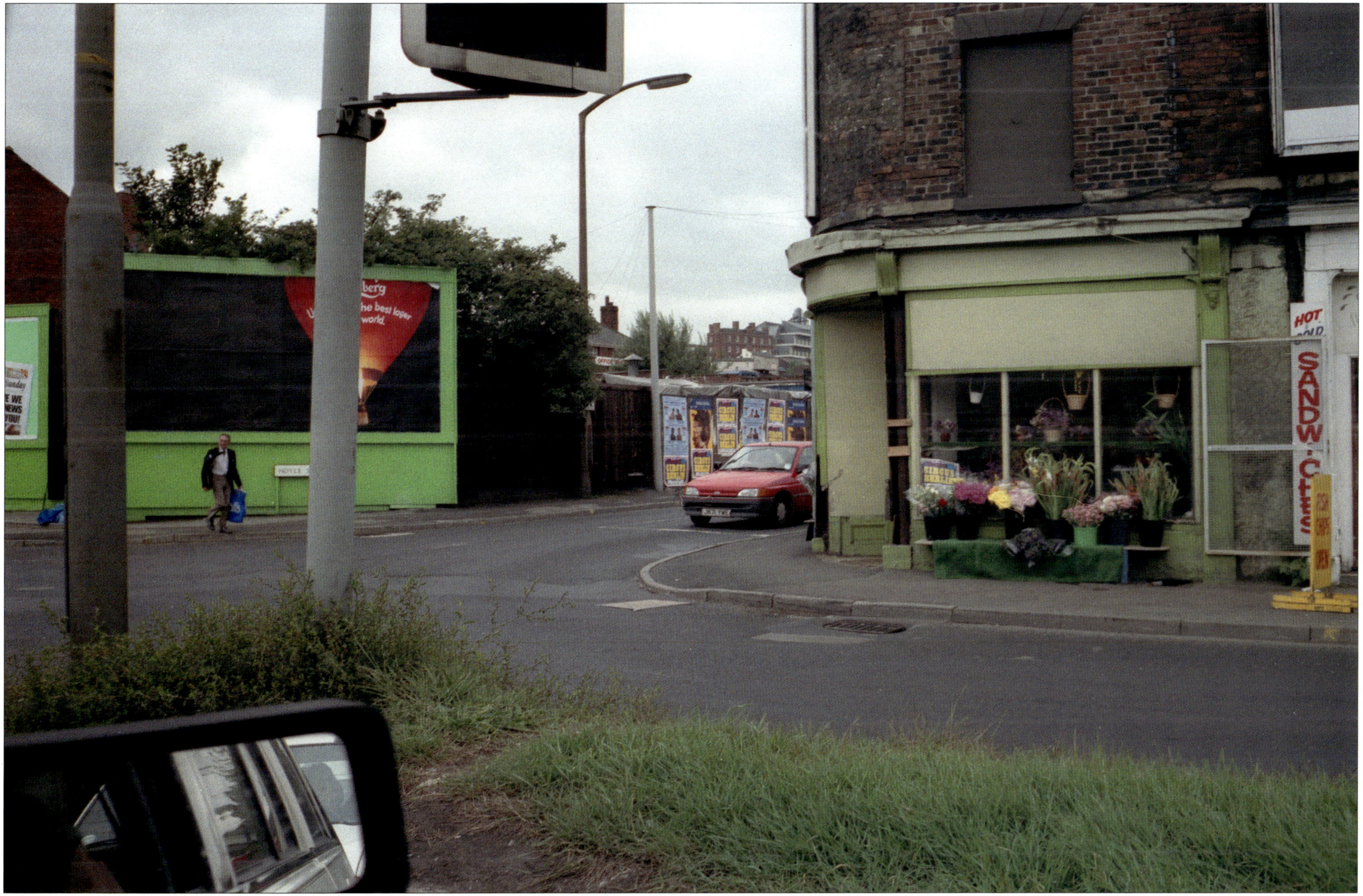

Hoyle Street/Infirmary Road. 1992

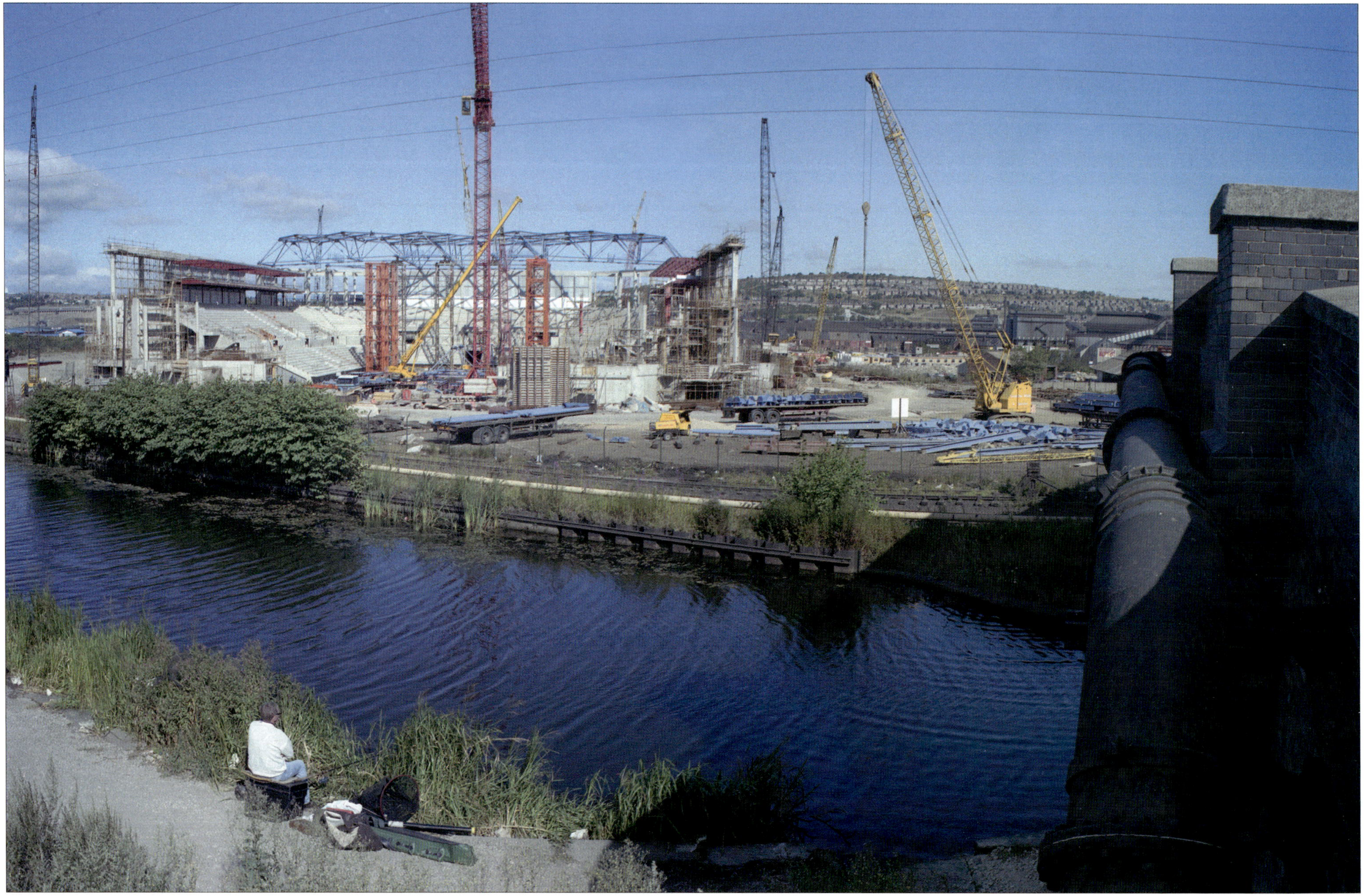

Sheffield Arena, 1991. Broughton Lane bridge was later demolished as part of a road improvement scheme.

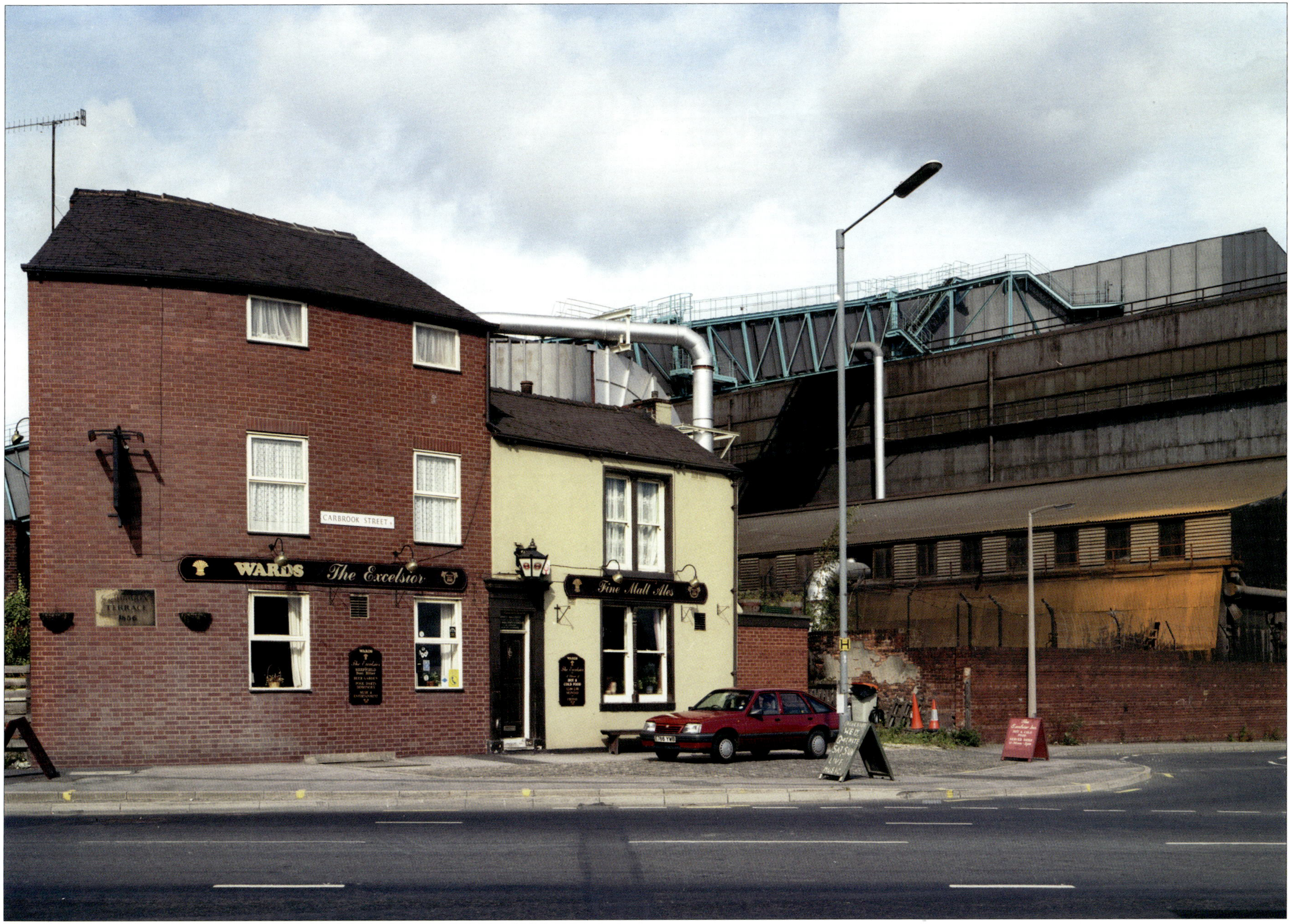

The "Excelsior", Attercliffe Common.1992

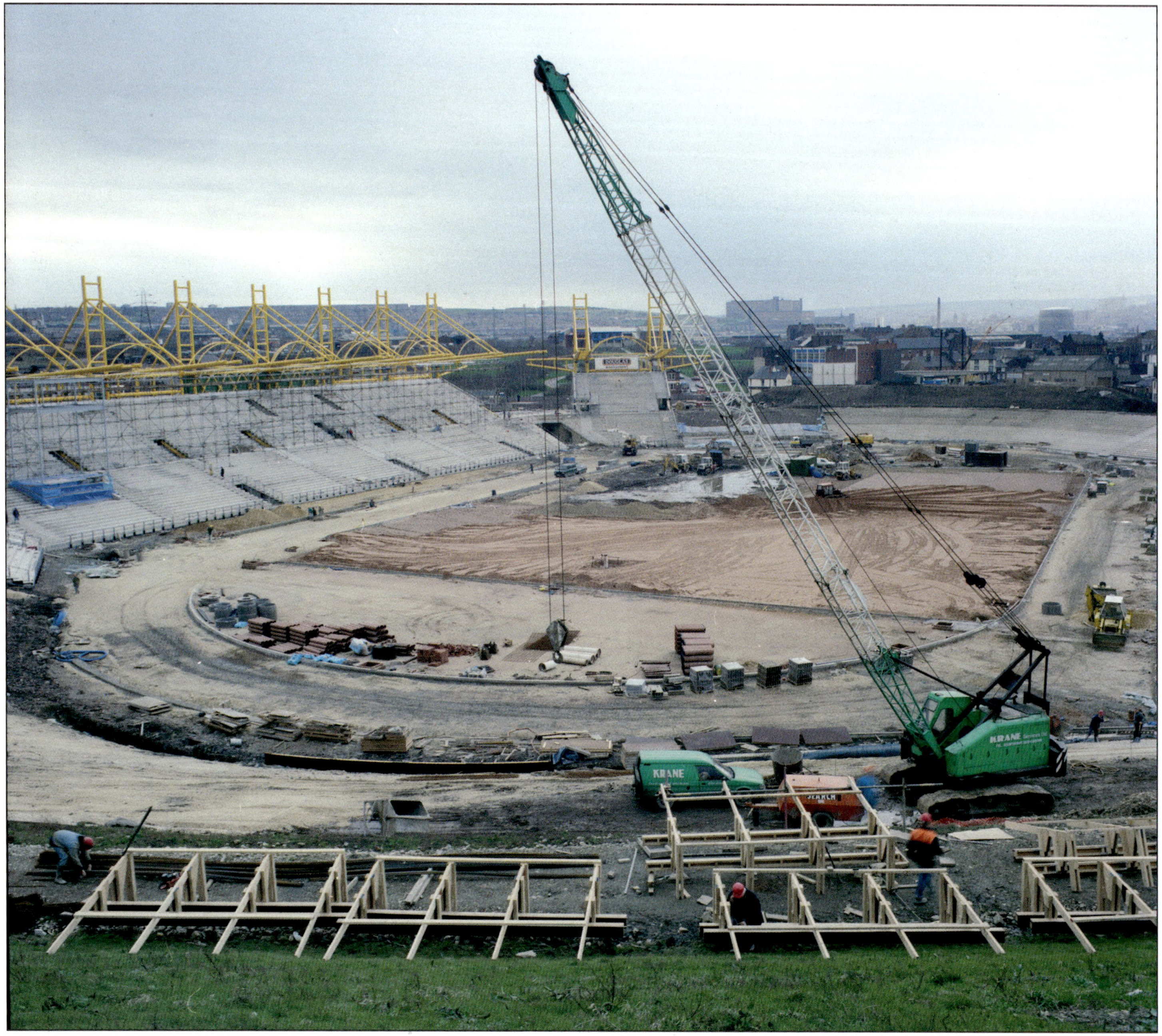

Construction of the
Don Valley Stadium, 1990.

Tinsley opencast, 1991.
As part of the construction of the Sheffield Airport JJB mining first opencast mined the site. In doing so they revealed the pillars that the miners who worked the seam in the 19th century had left in as supports, and these can be seen in the background of the picture.

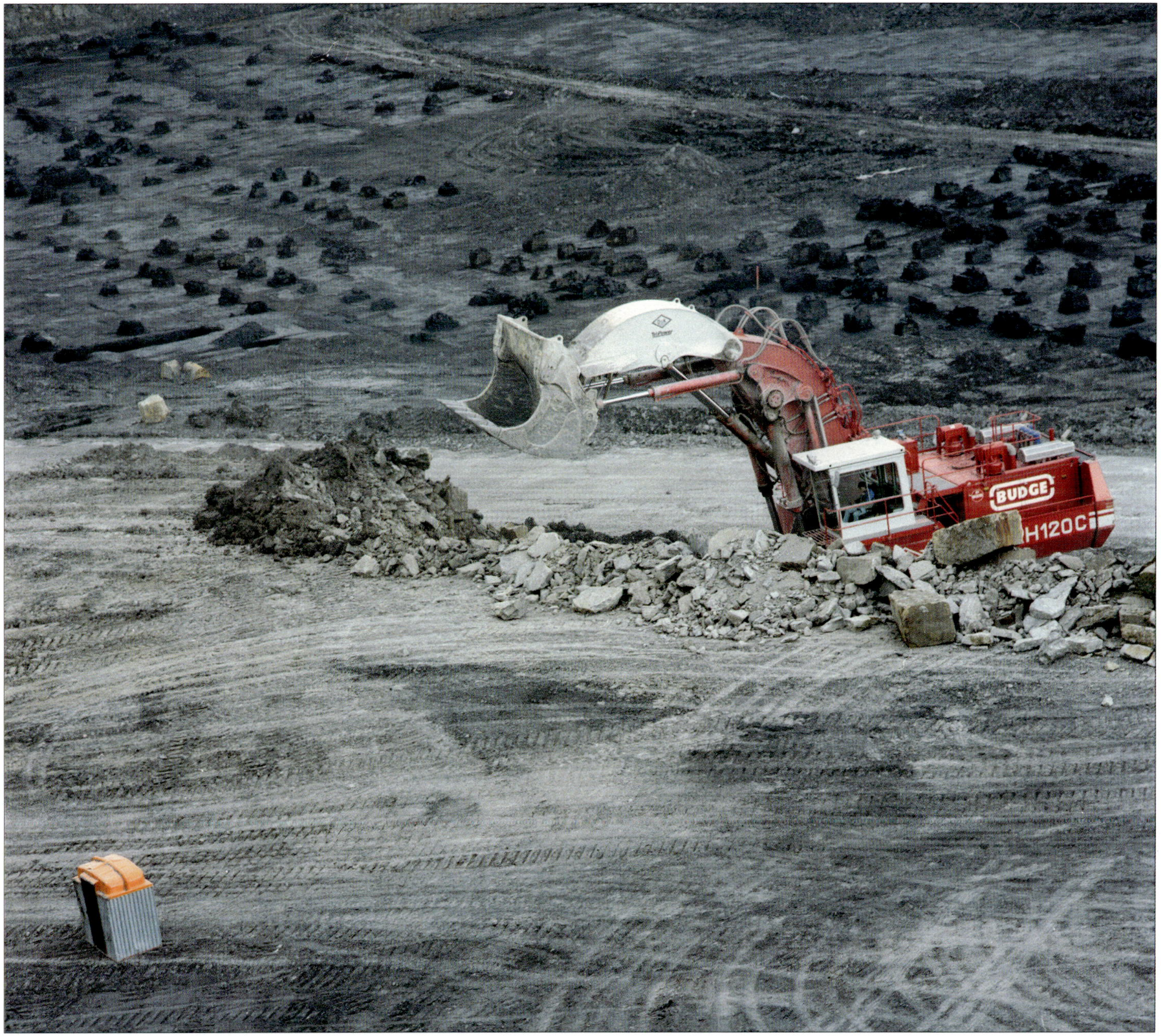

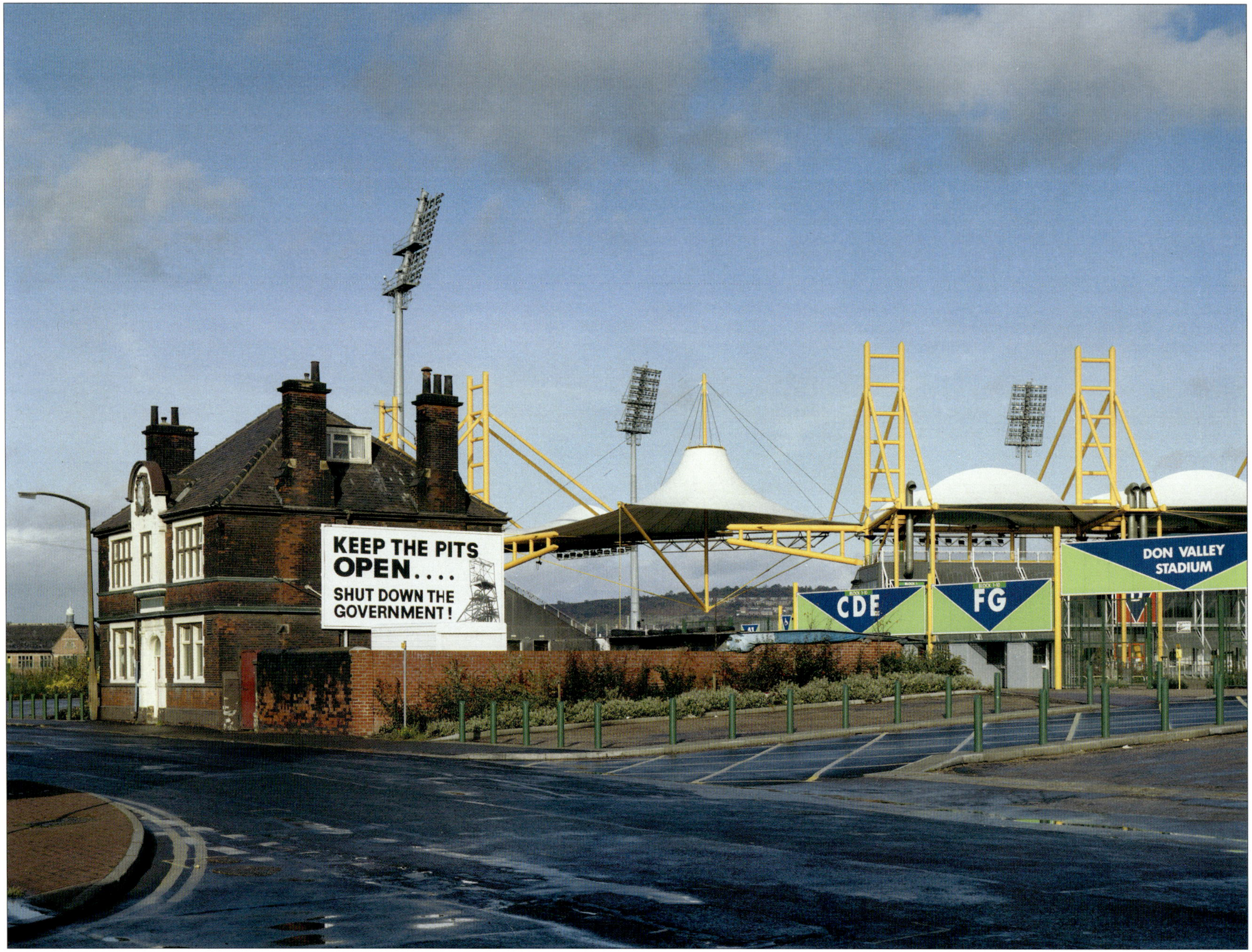

The Don Valley Stadium, 1992.
In October 1992 the government announced the closure of 31 coal mines. The NUM supported by the Daily Mirror newspaper ran a campaign of opposition.

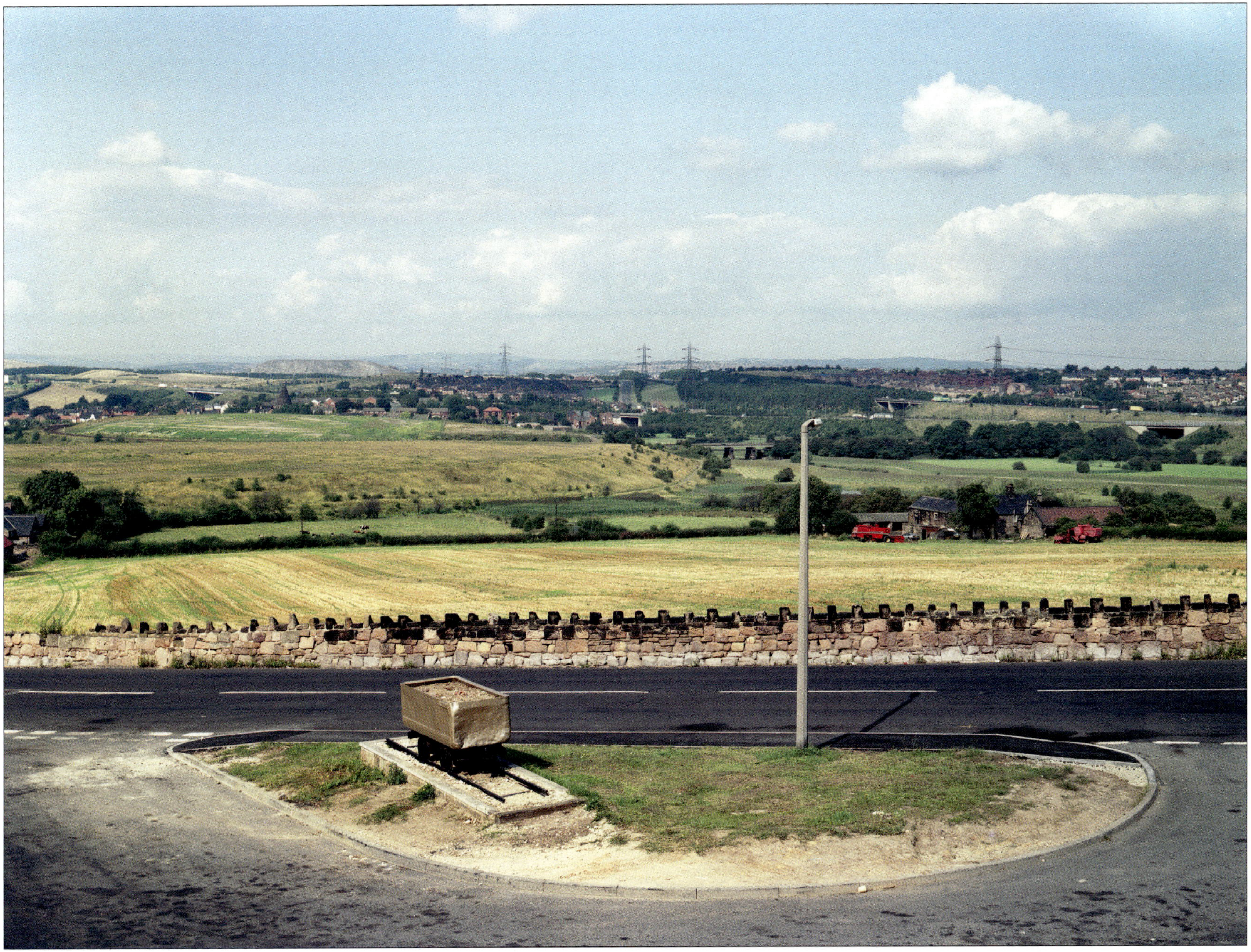

The site of
Treeton pit, 1992.

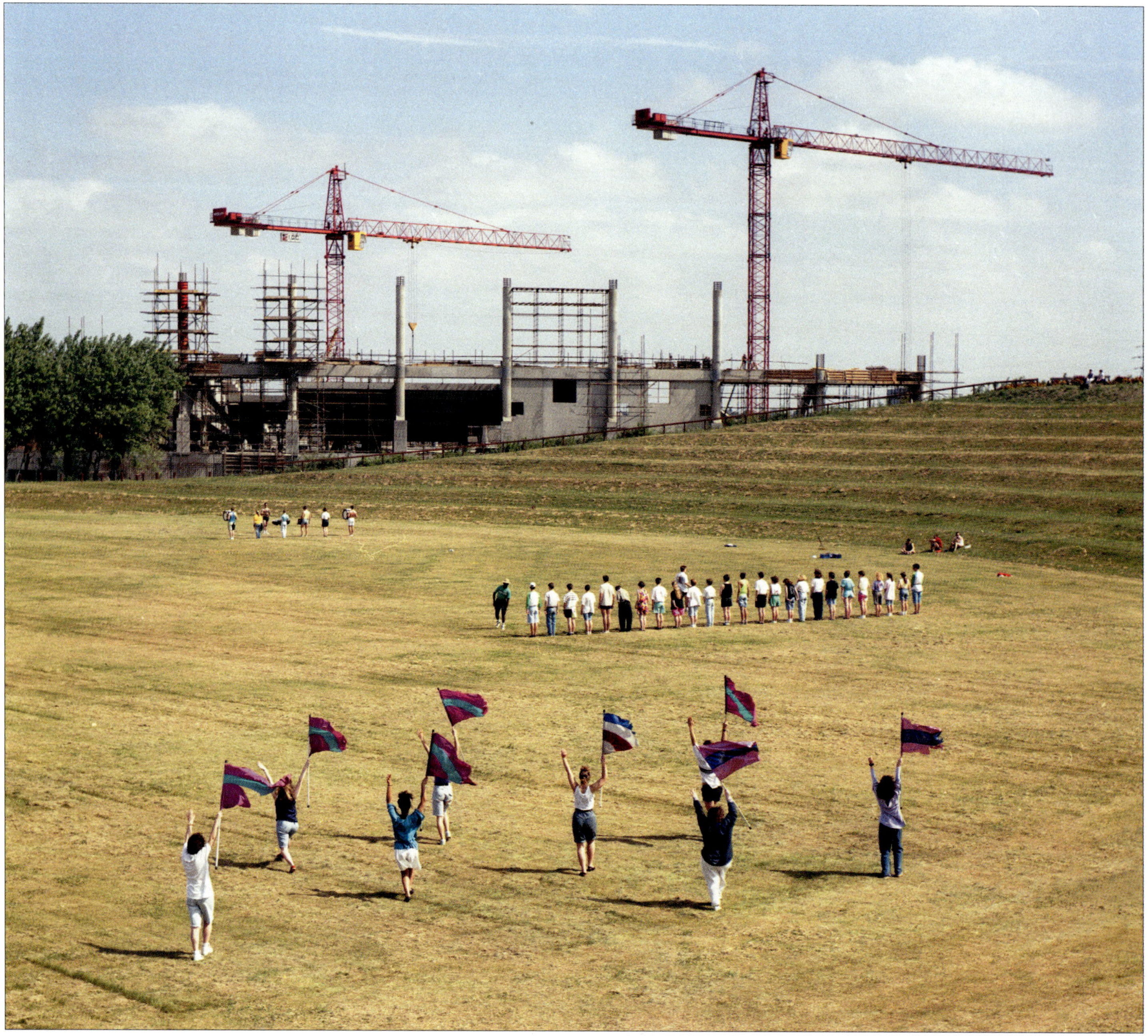

The Don Valley Bowl, 1990. Practising for the World Student Games opening ceremony.

Hanover Street, 1983.
Broomhall carnival.

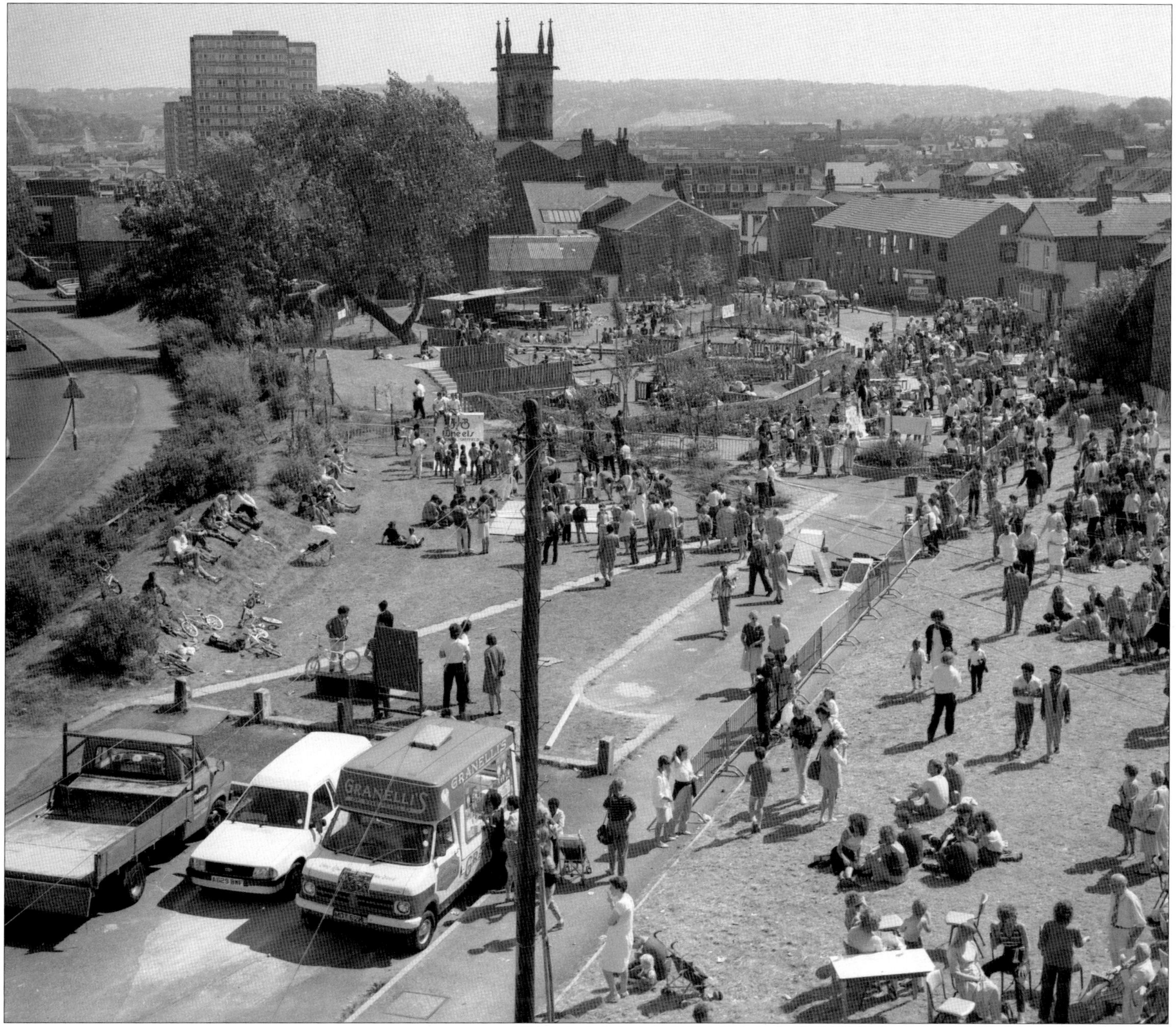

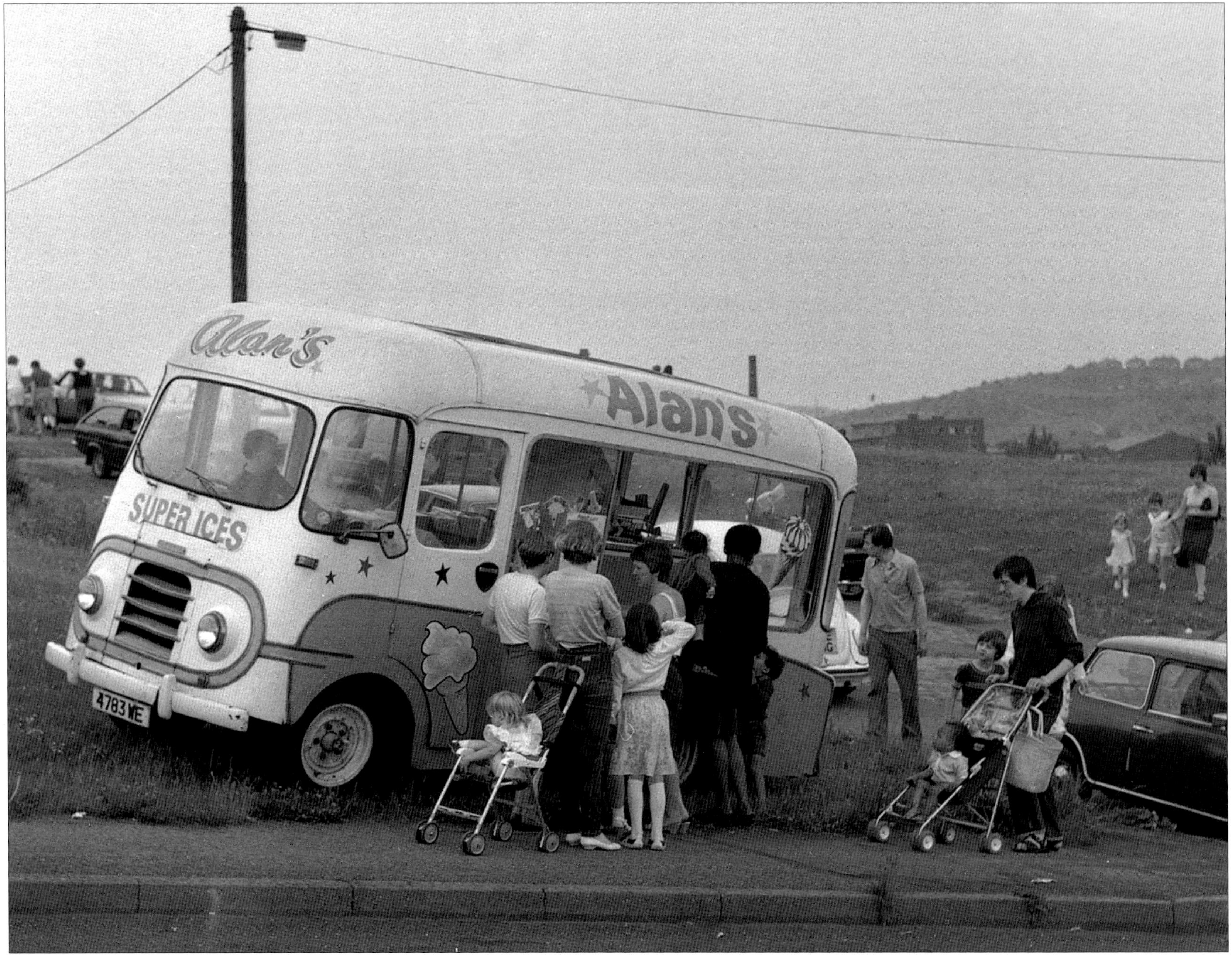

Wood Street, 1982.
The large number of people wanting ice cream are spectators of the first Sheffield marathon passing along nearby Neepsend Lane.

The "Earl Grey",
Ecclesall Road,
1984.

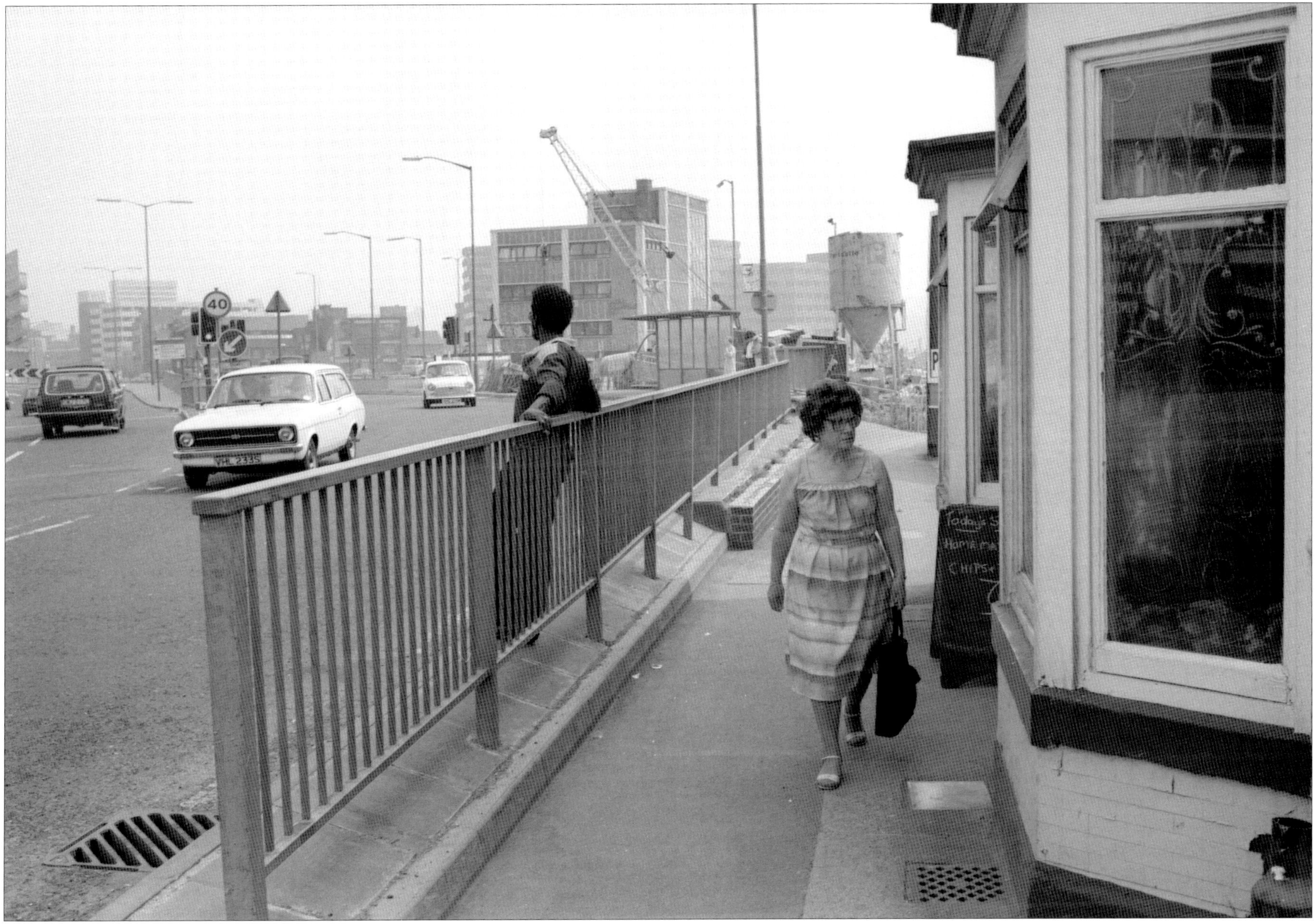

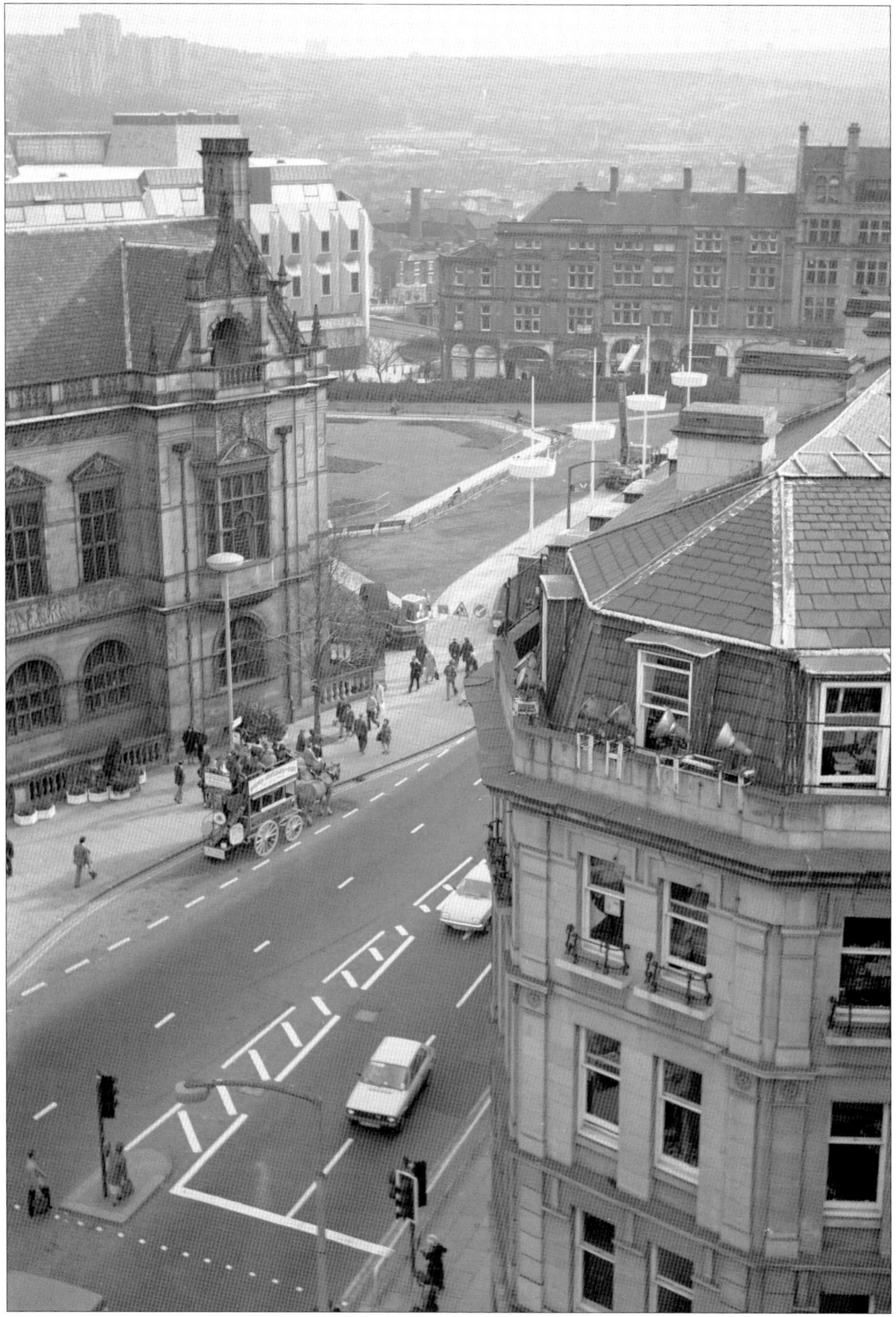

Pinstone Street, 1985

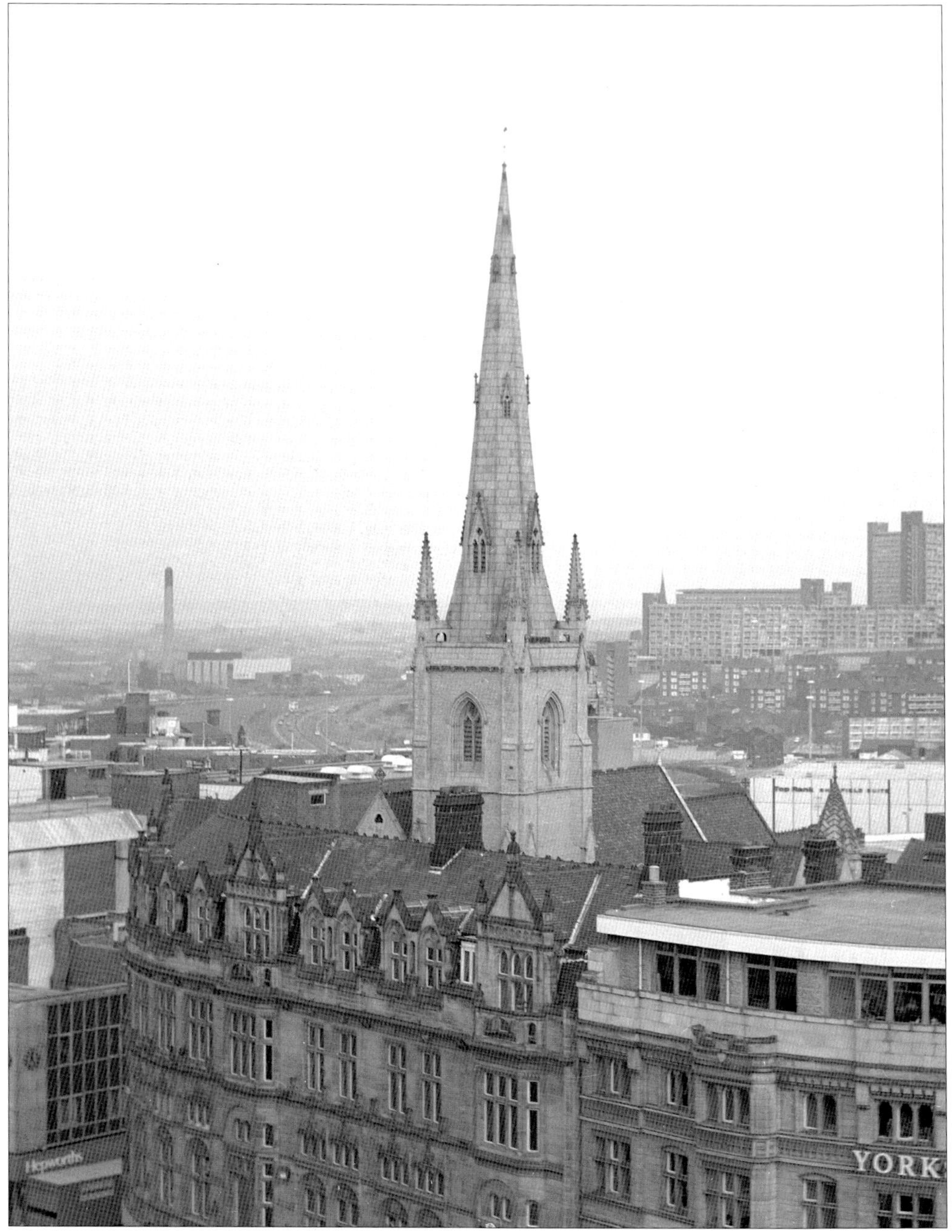

Fargate, 1983

Tinsley, 1983.

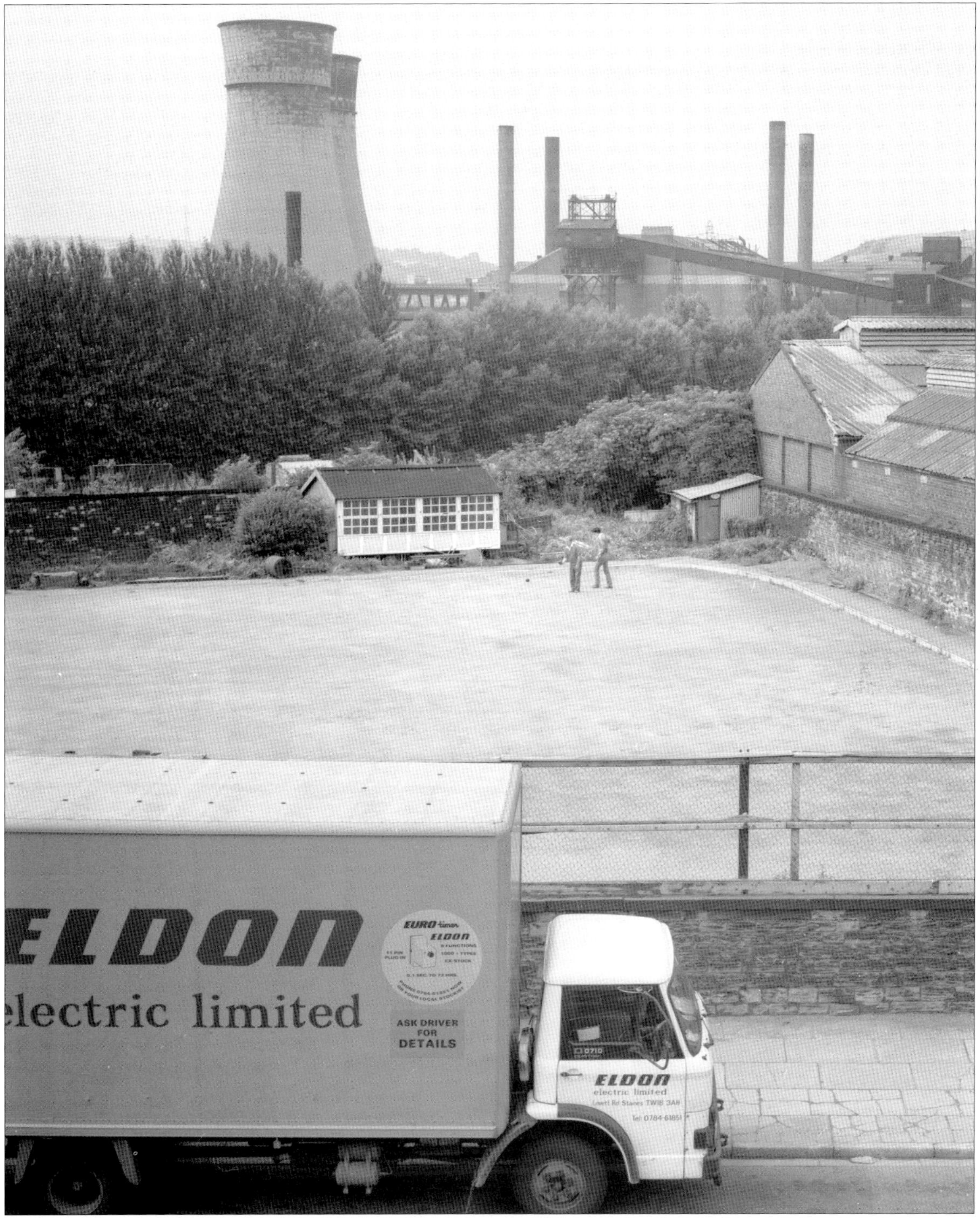

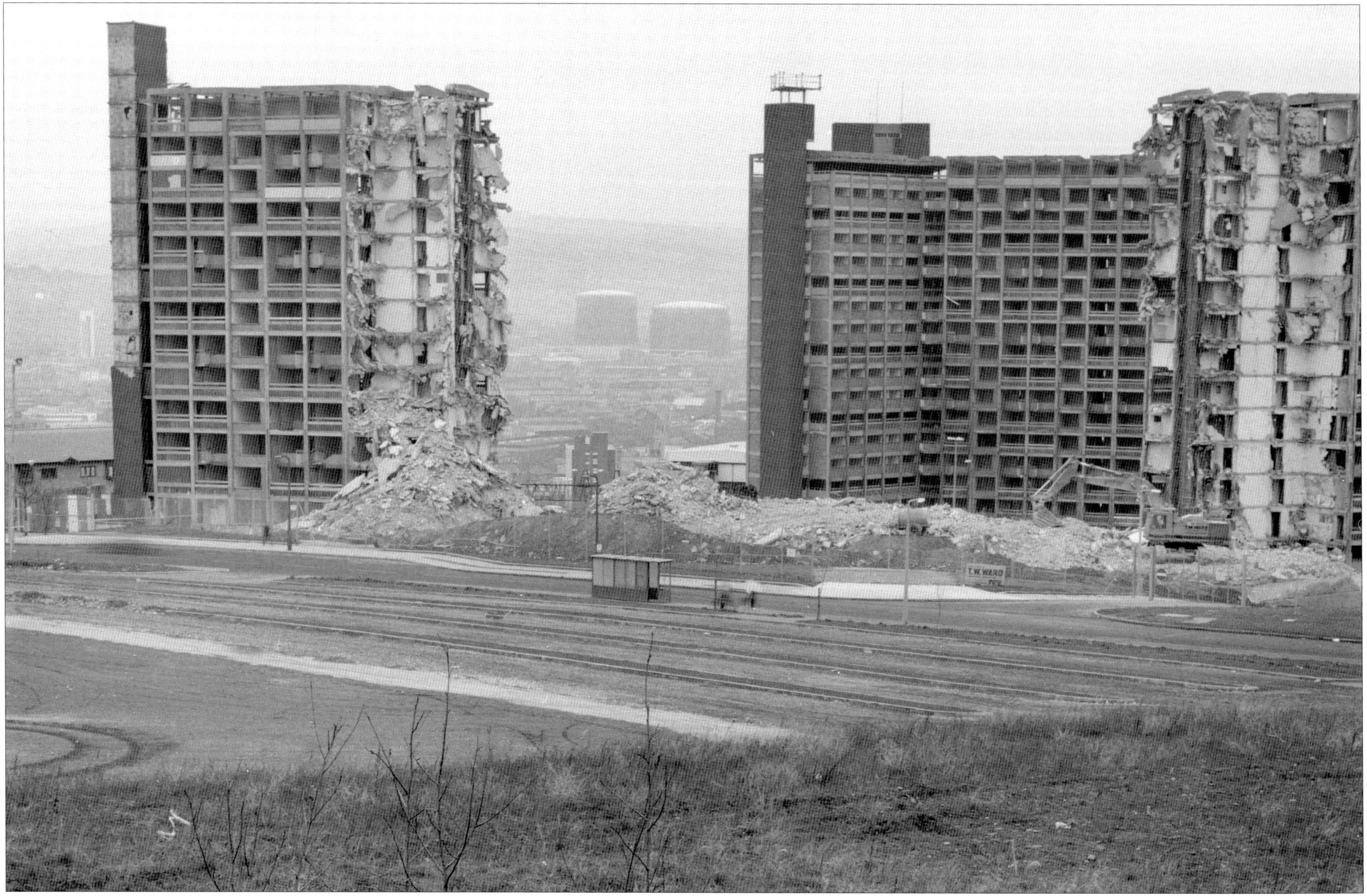

Hyde Park flats, 1990. Seen through the gap in the building are Neepsend gasworks and the Upper Don valley.

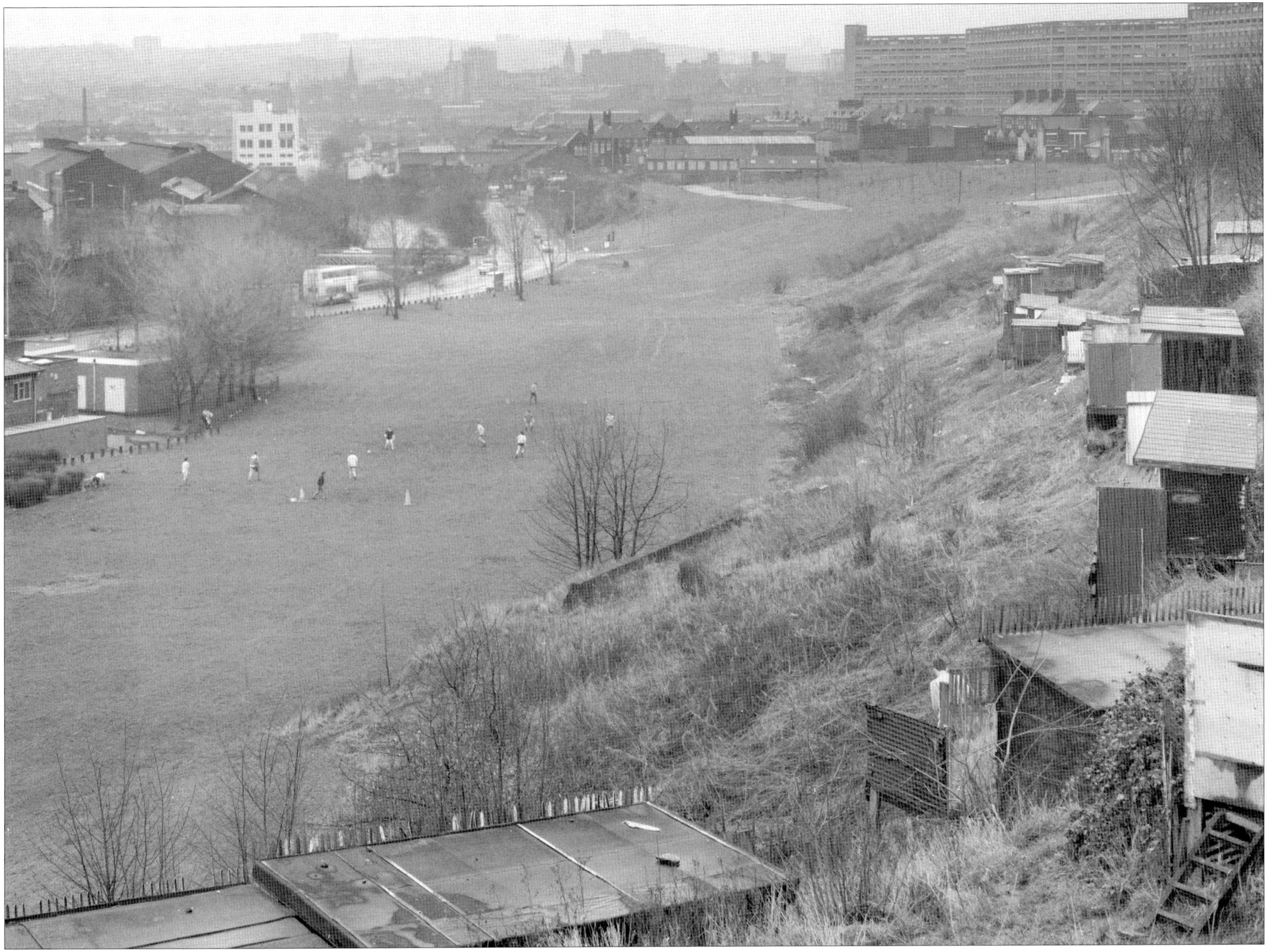

Cuthbert Bank, 1988. Looking towards the city centre.

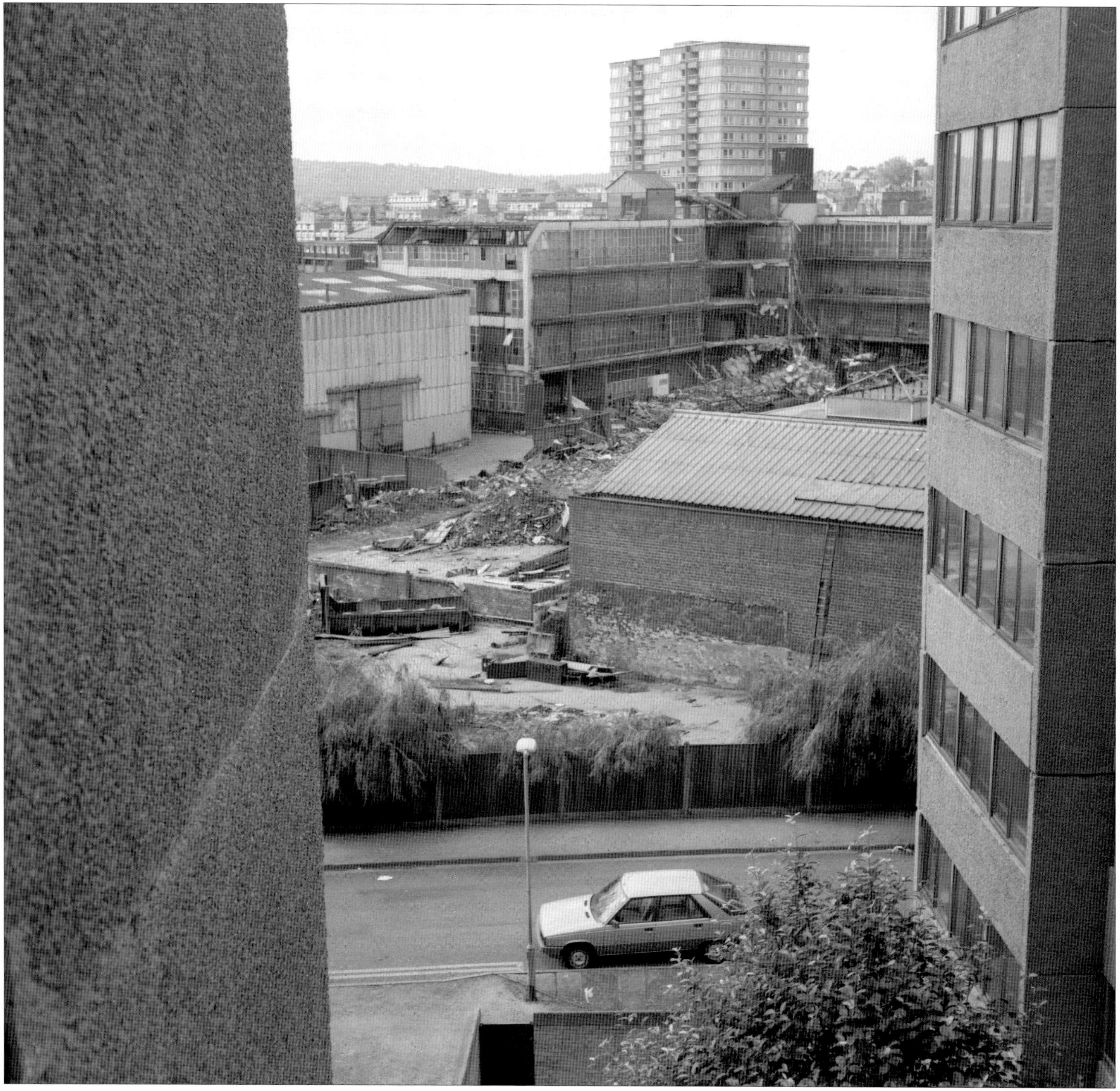

From Broomhall flats, 1988.
Looking towards Sharrow
as the Viners cutlery factory
is demolished.

Viners factory,
Hanover Way, 1988.

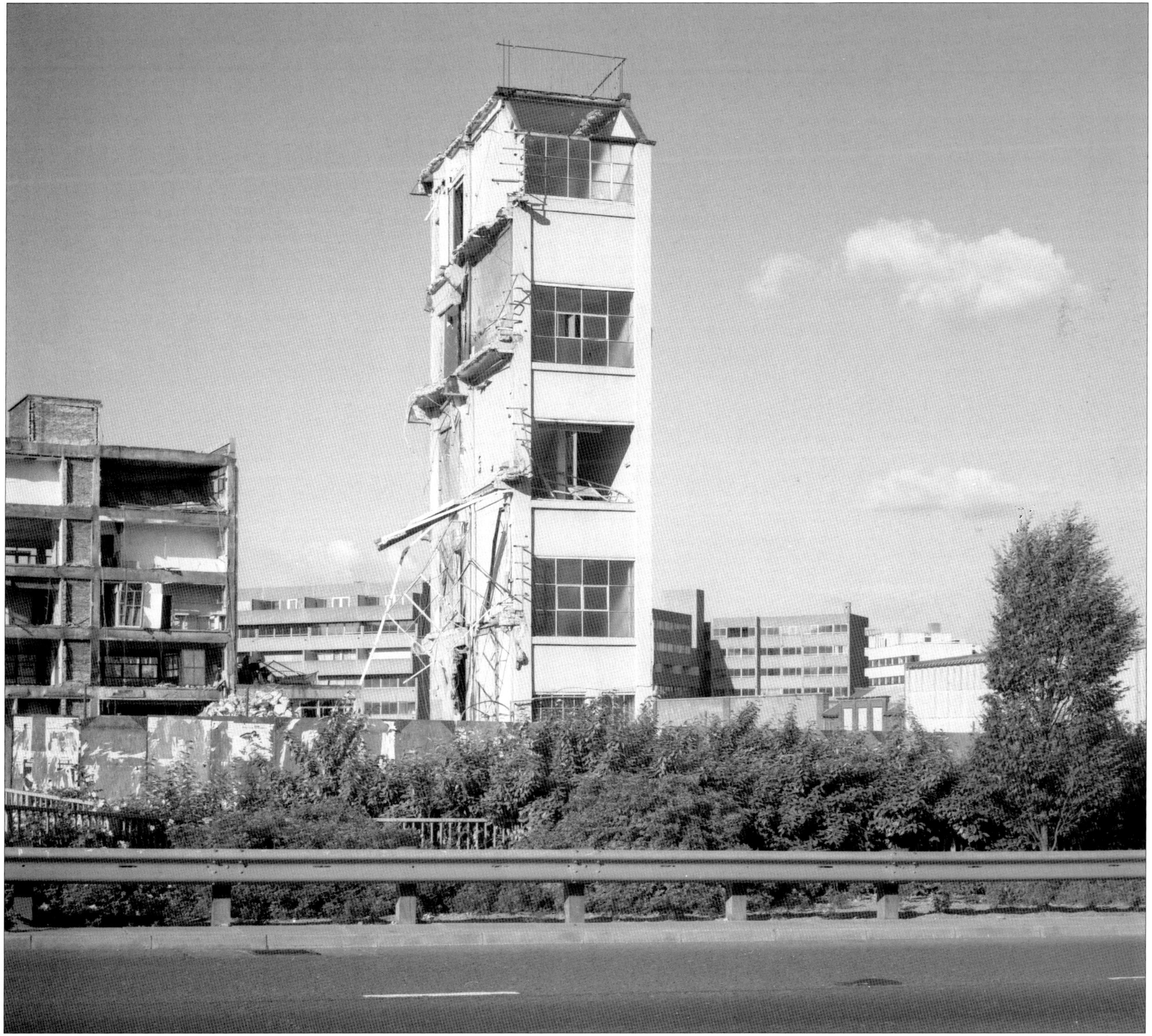

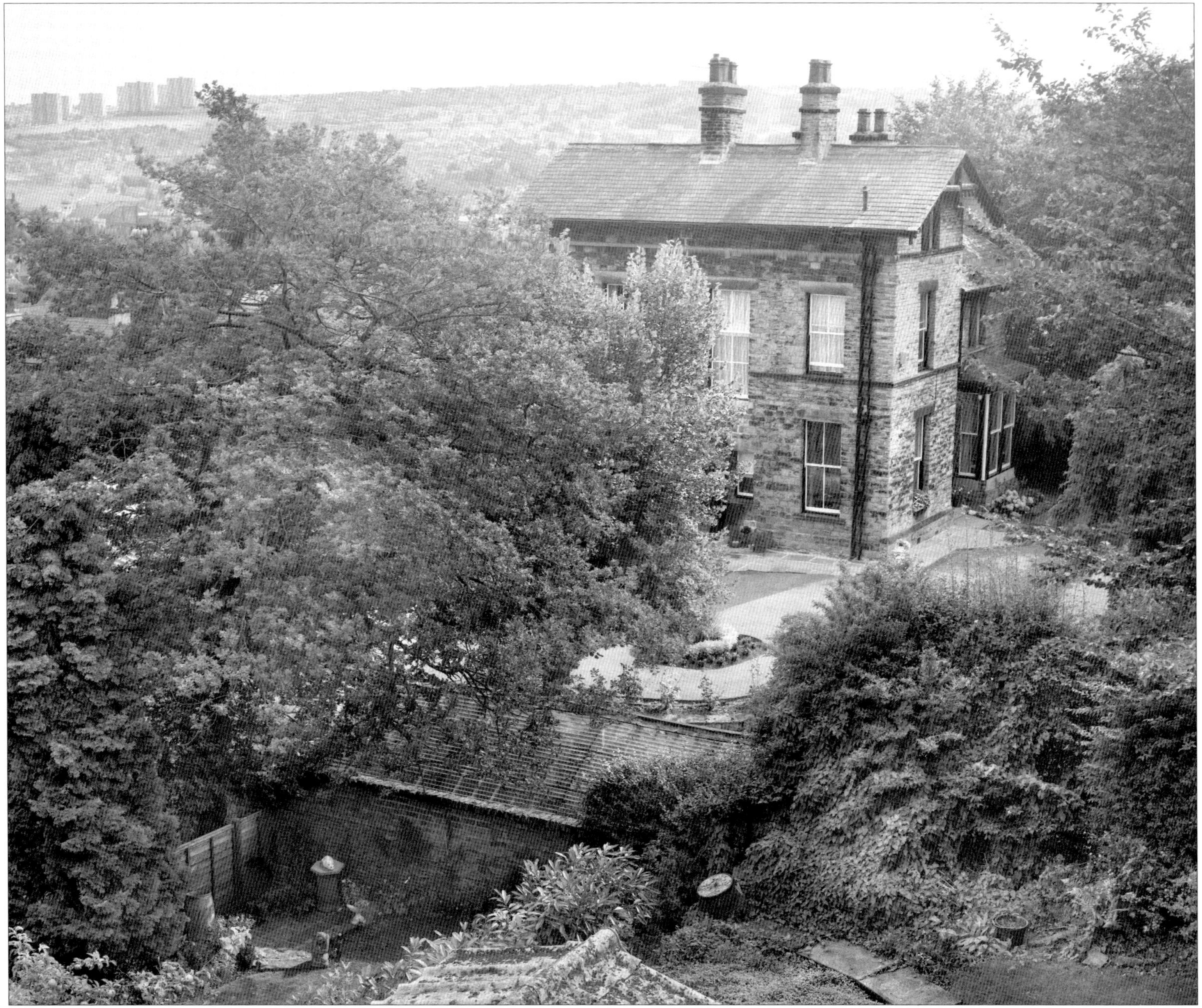

Brincliffe Edge, 1983.

Nether Edge, 1986. Norfolk Park flats are on the horizon.

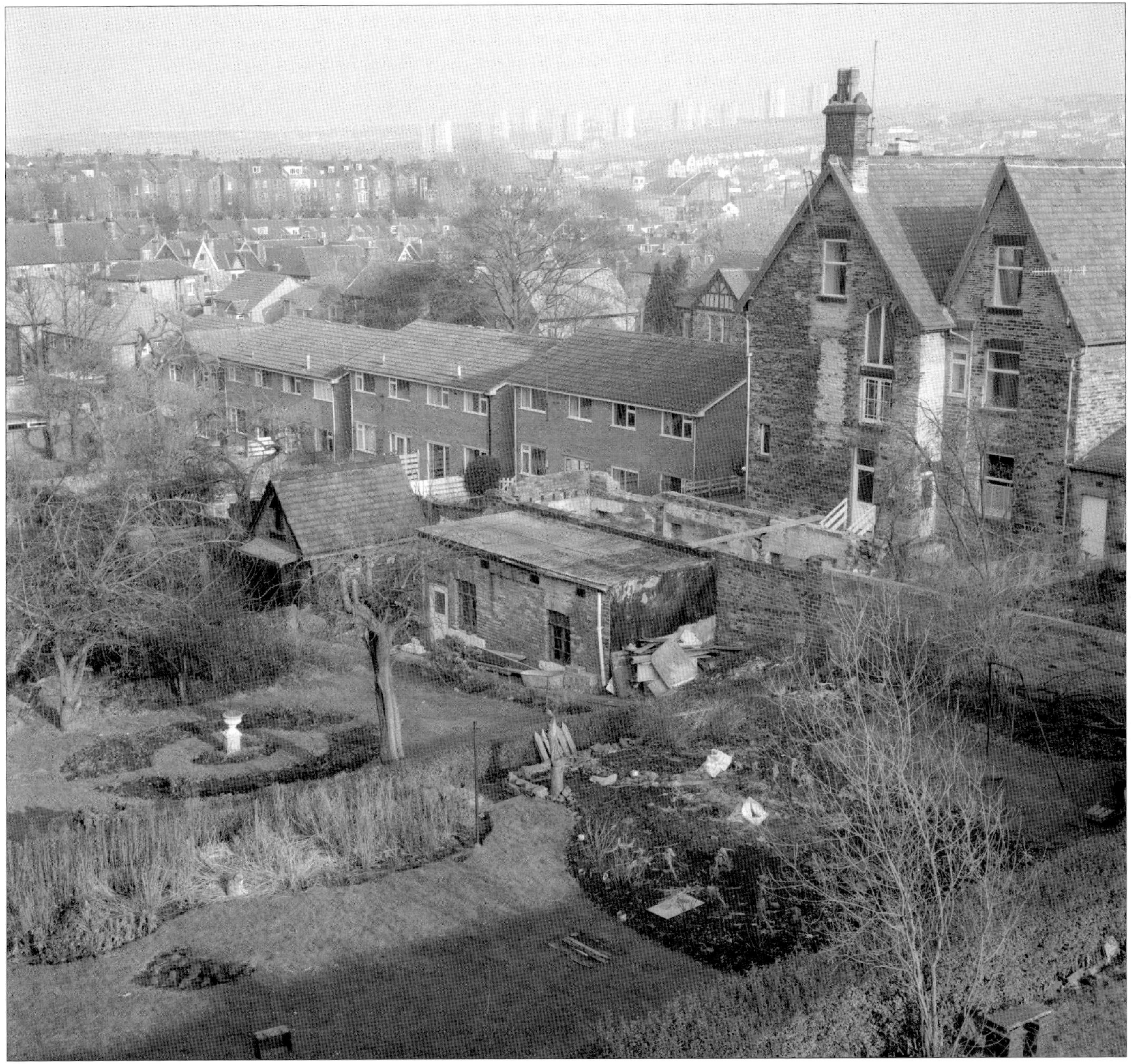

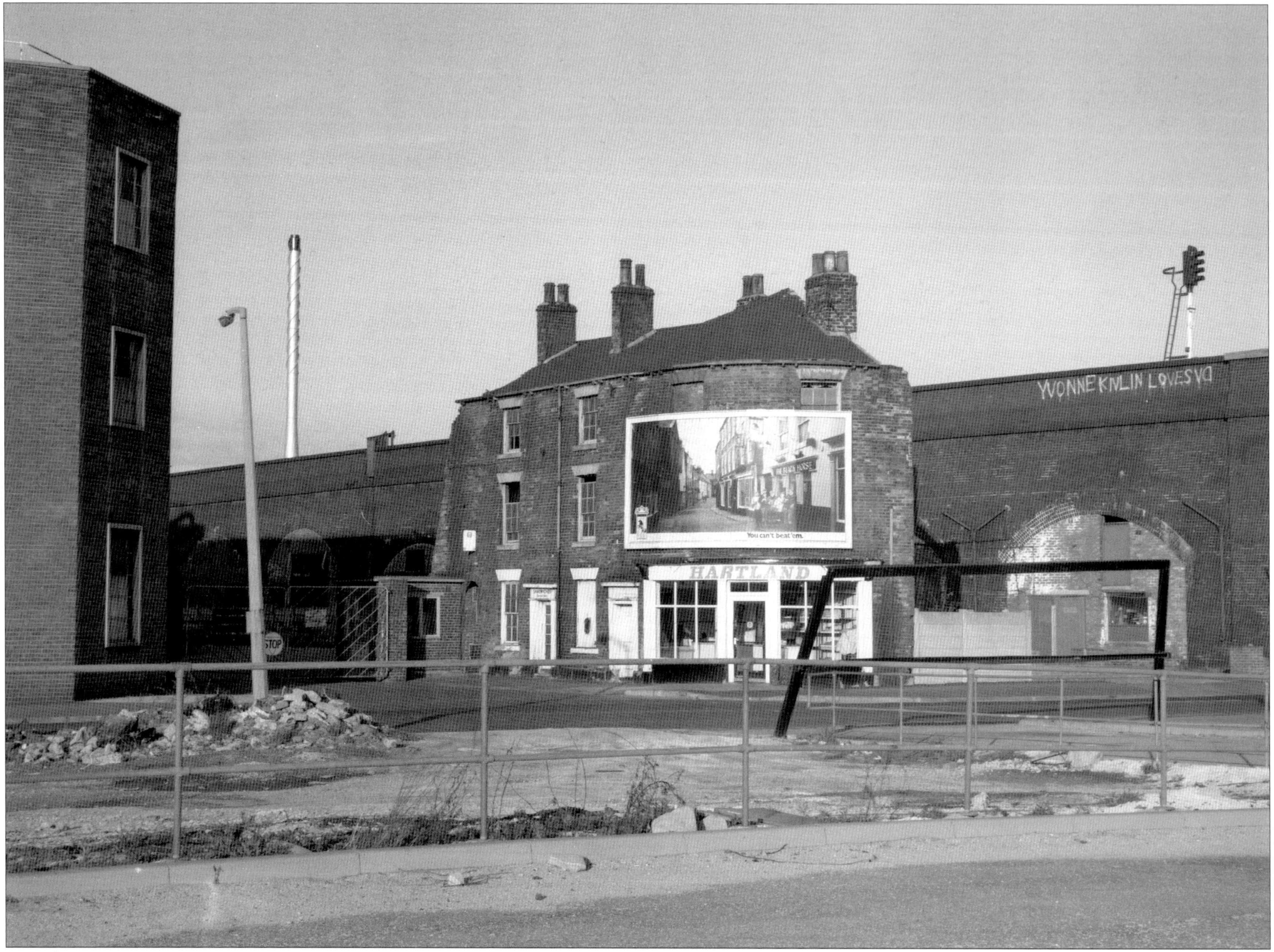

Sutherland Road
1985.

Burnaby Street 1982.

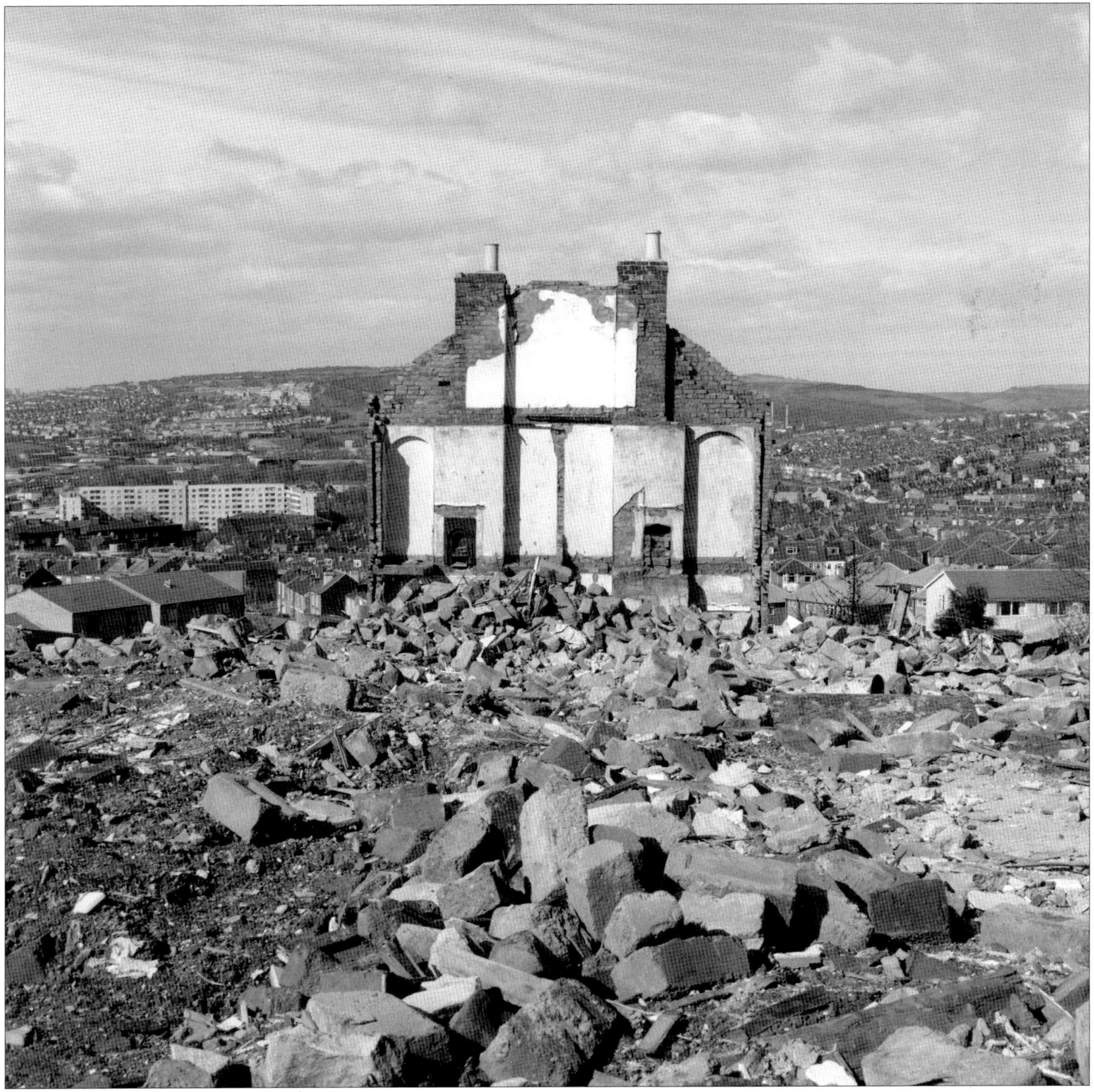

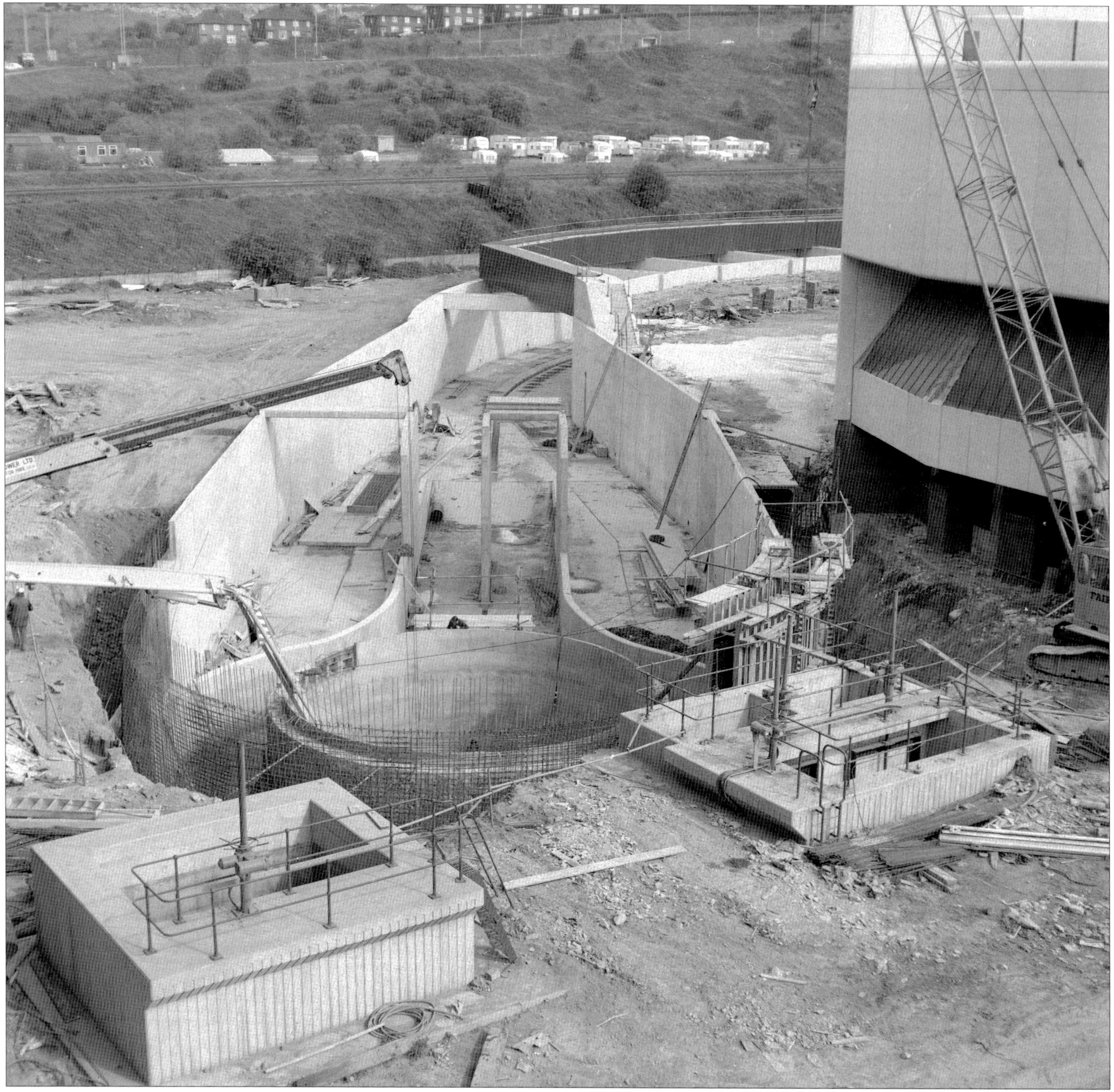

Blackburn Meadows
sewage works.1982

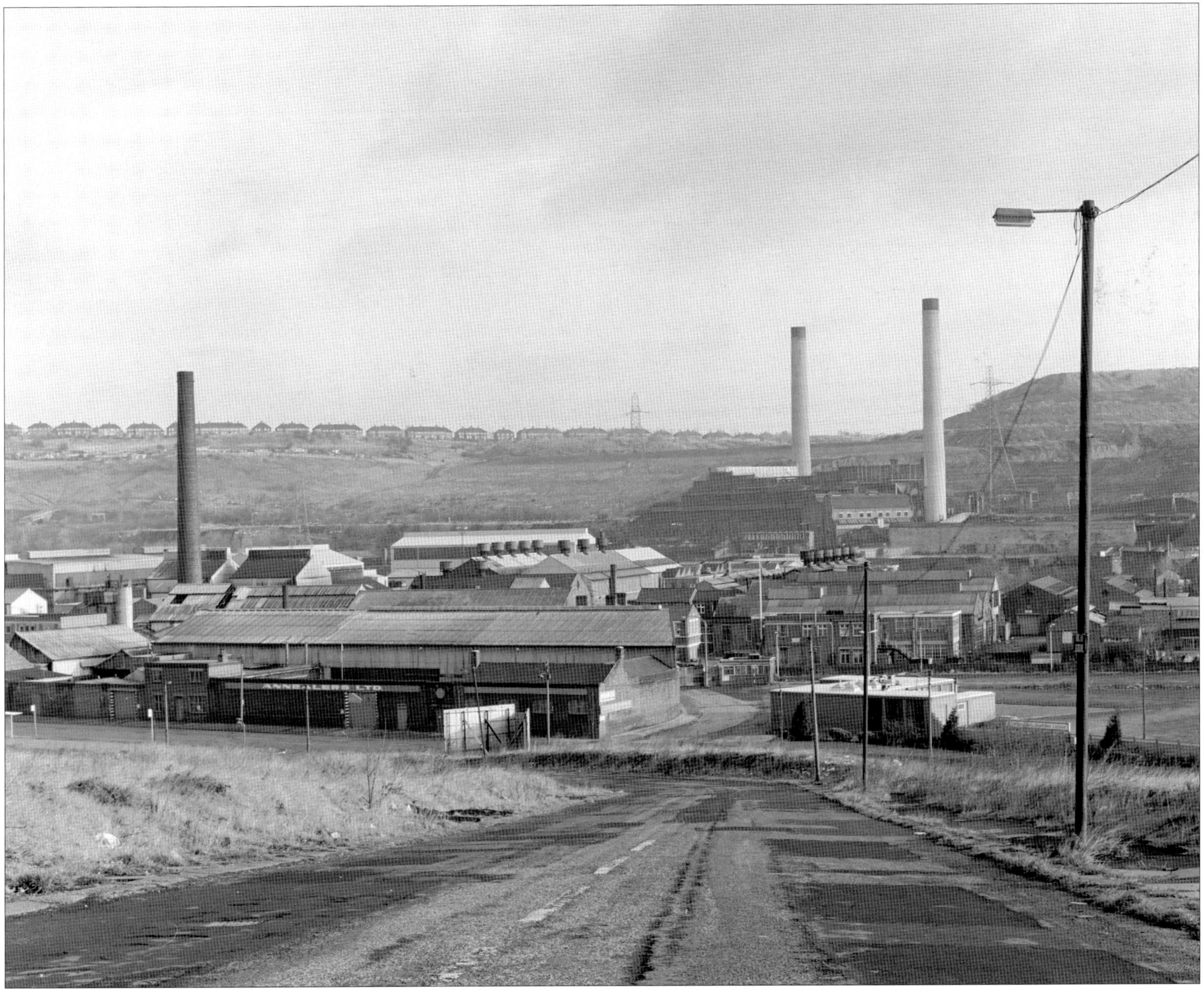

High House Road. 1982.

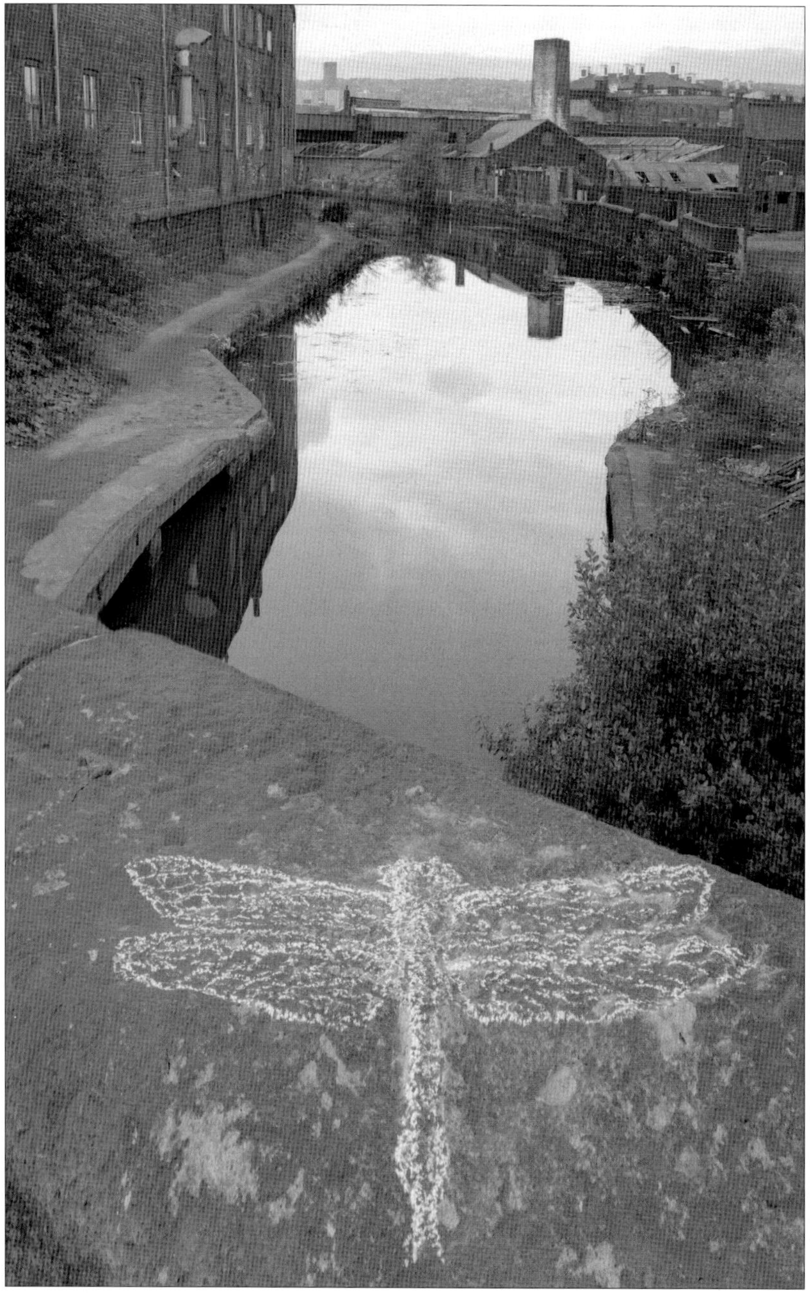

Cadman Street canal bridge, 1985. A dragonfly has been chalked on the parapet

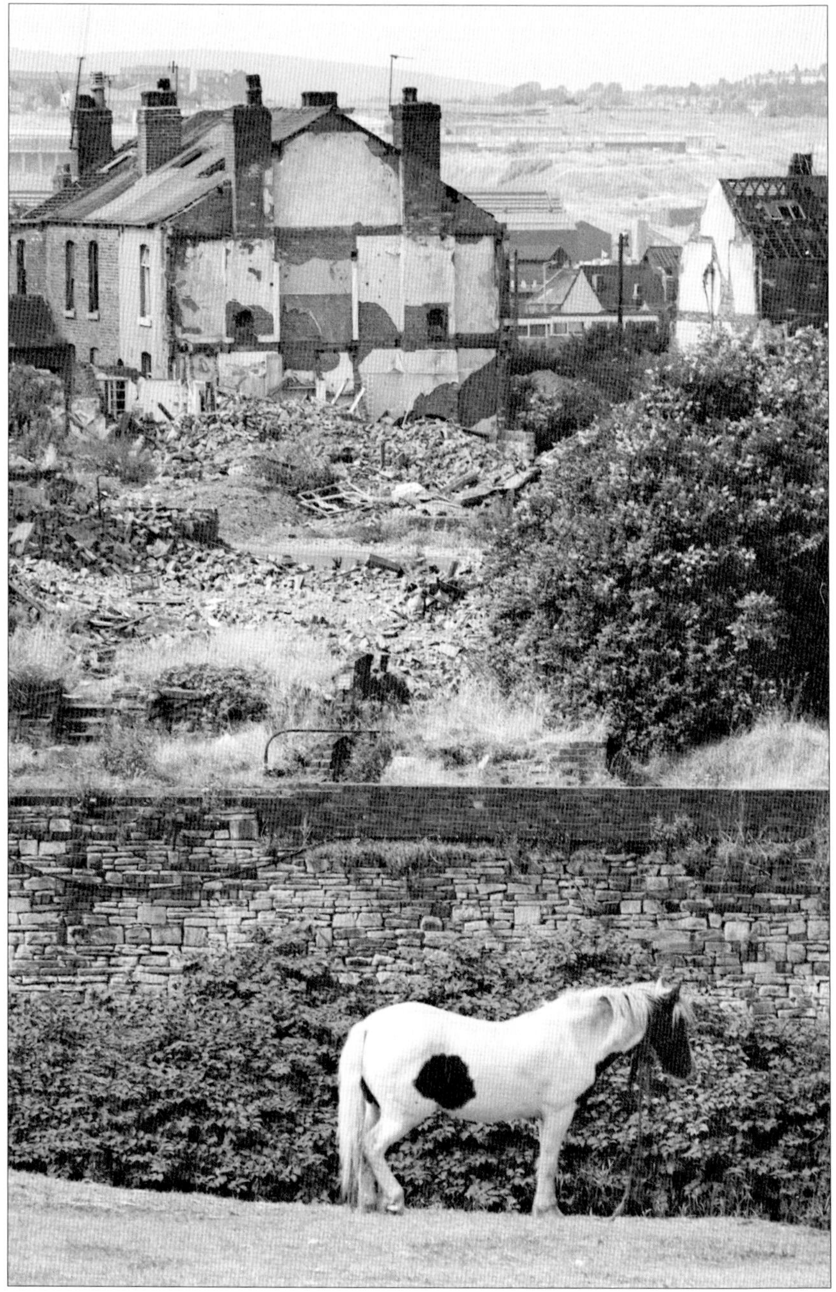

Canal Bank, Attercliffe, 1982

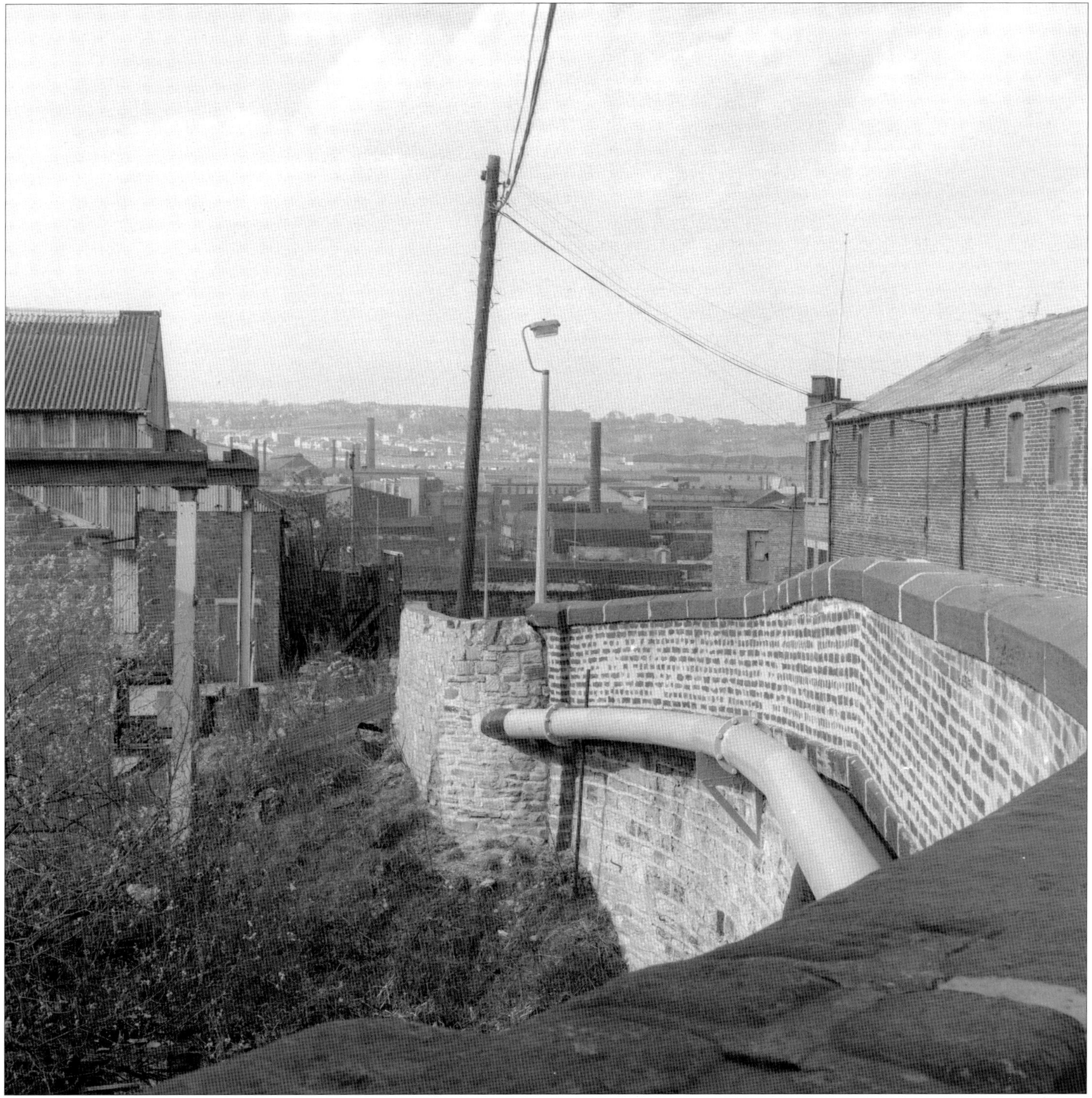

Bacon Lane
canal bridge,
1982.

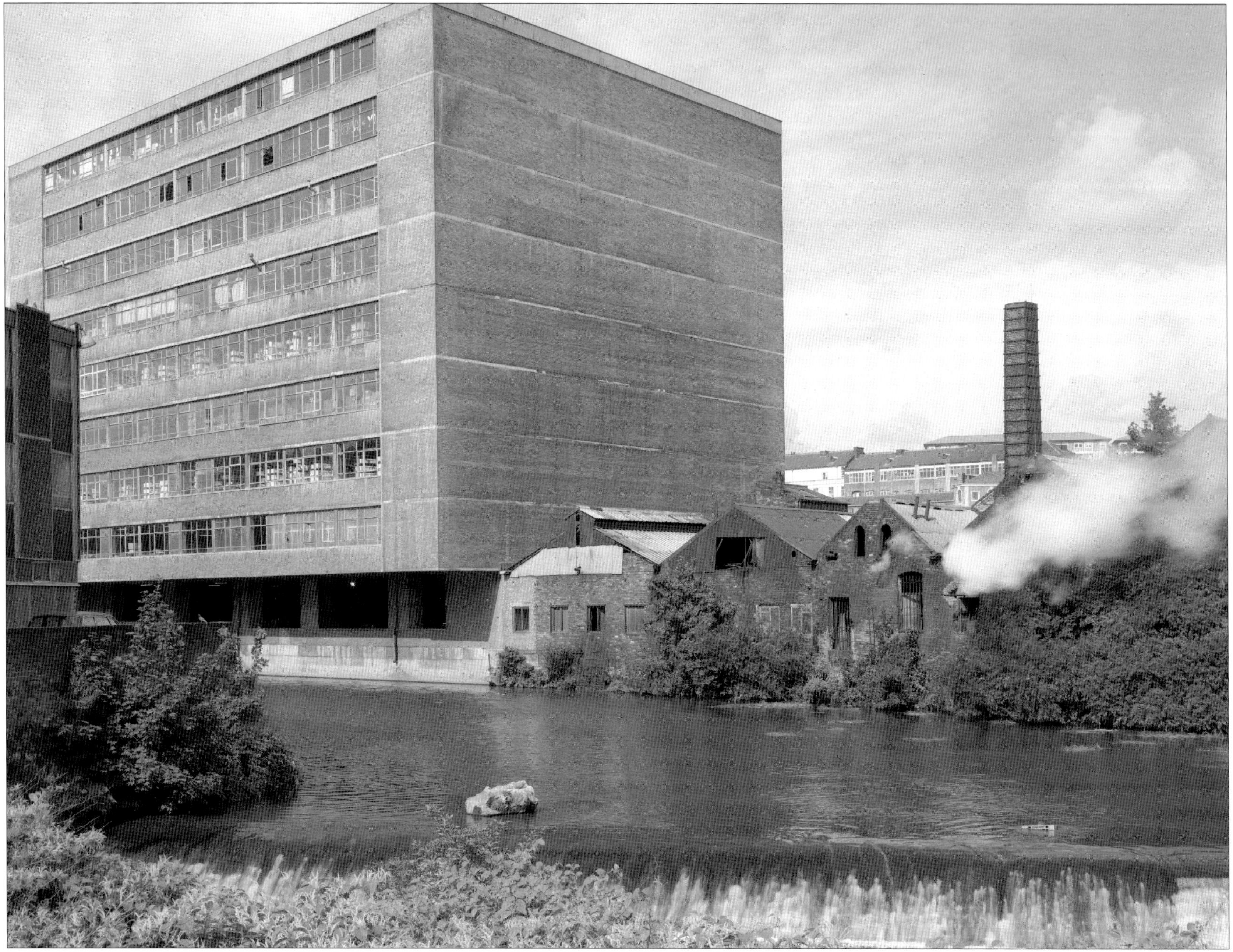

Walk Mill weir,
River Don. 1992.

Wigfall's warehouse,
Wicker Lane 1982.

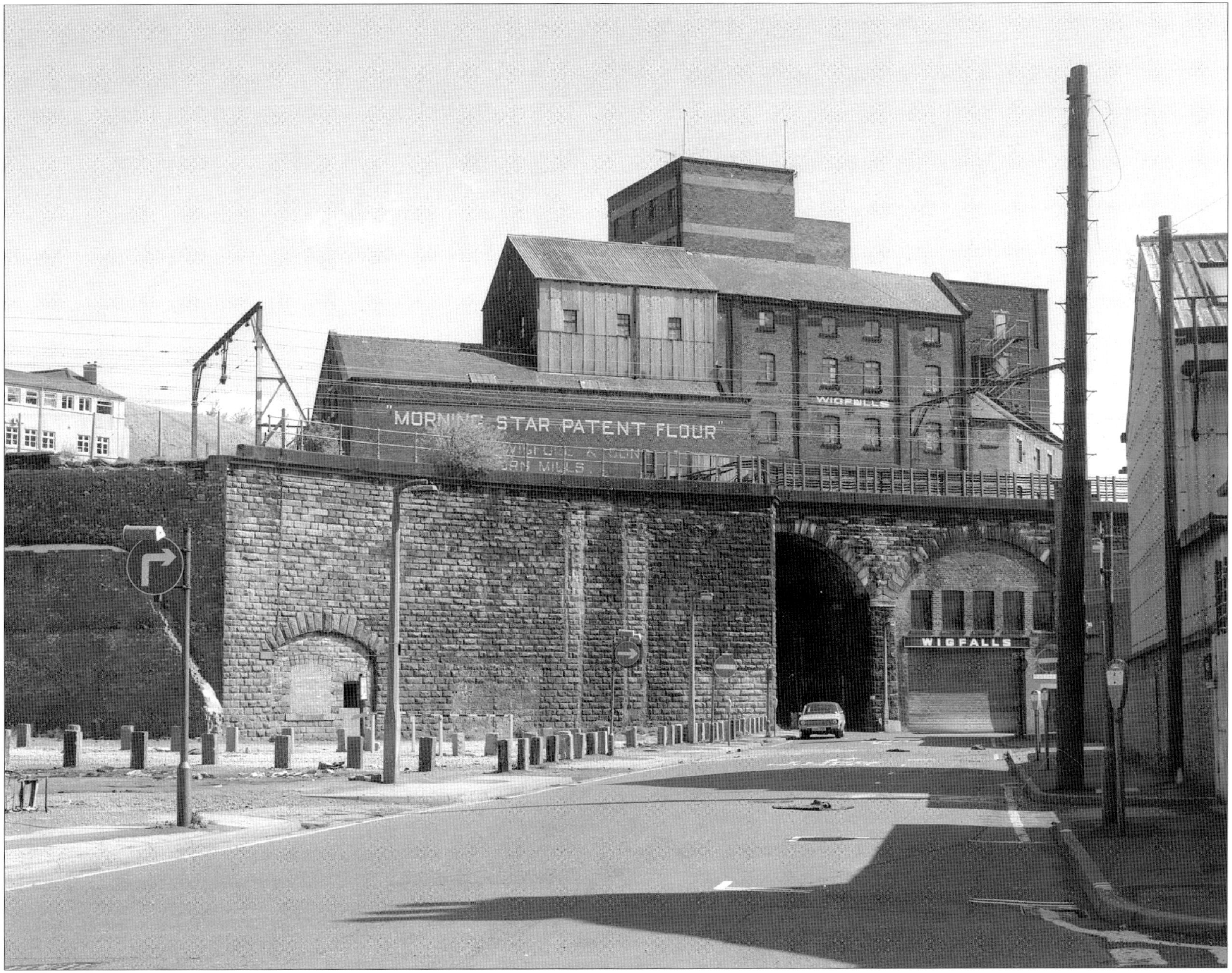

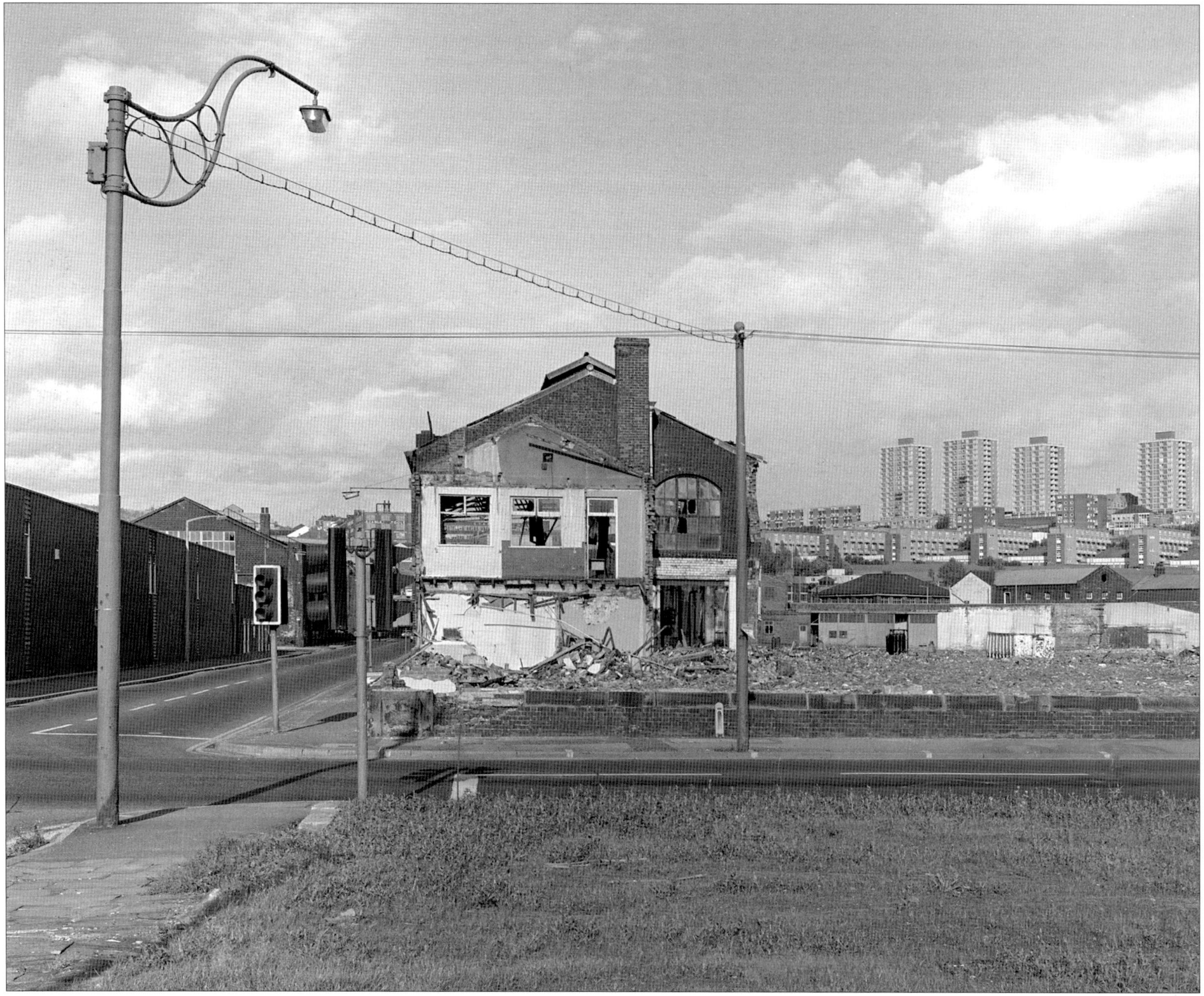

Regent Works,
Neepsend. 1982

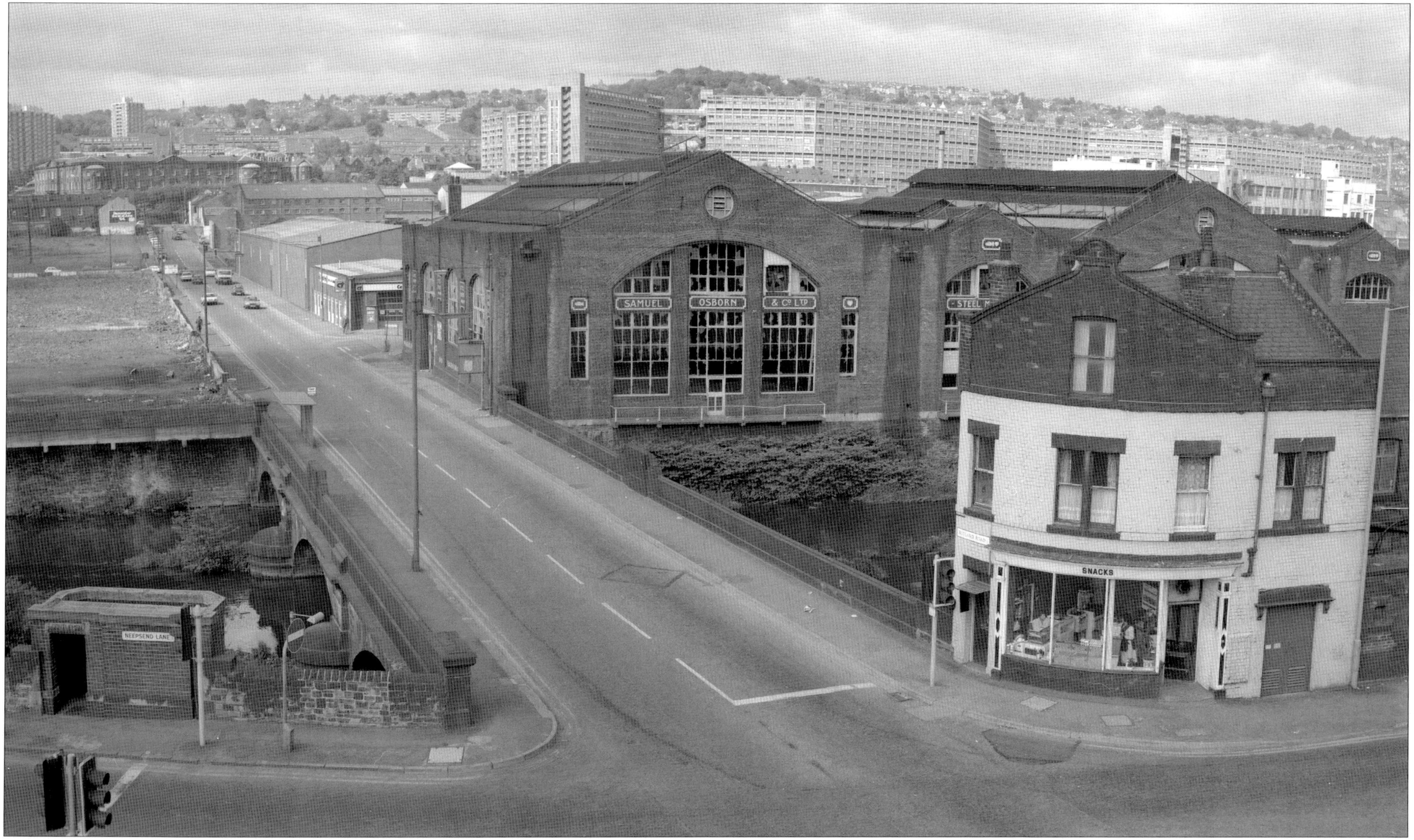

Neepsend Lane/Rutland Road junction, 1984.

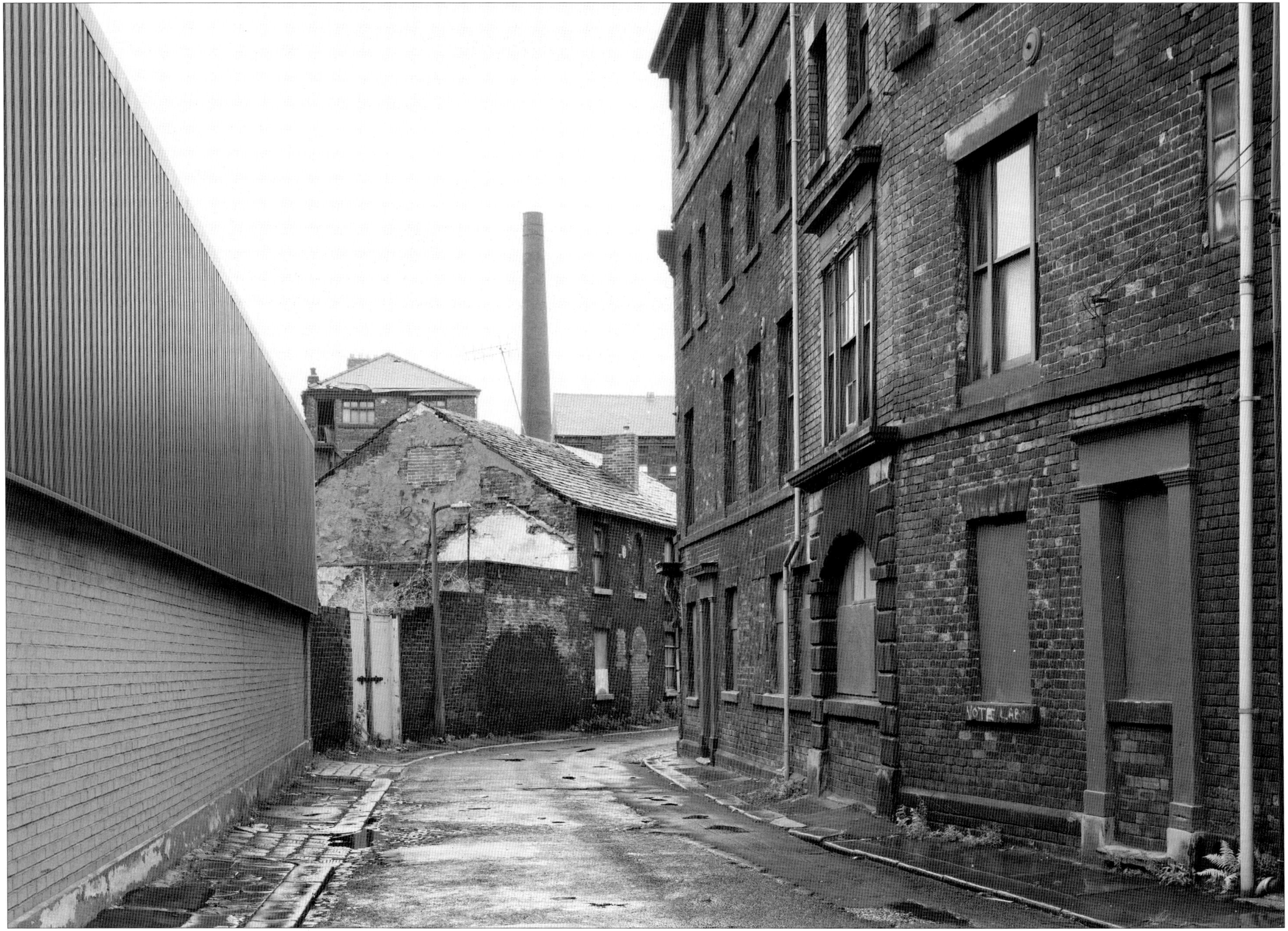

Cornish Street, Neepsend, 1992.

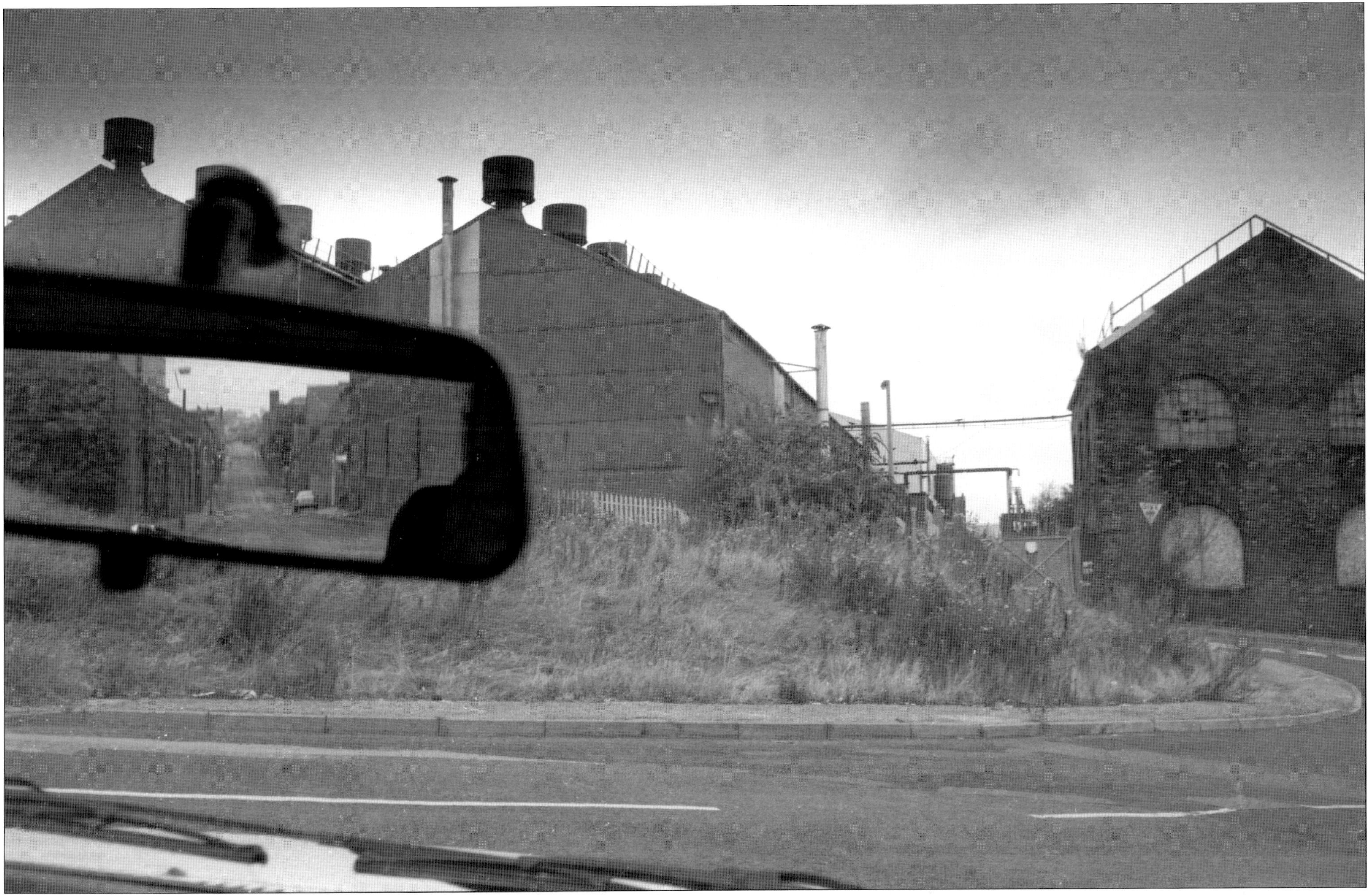

Lyons Street/Carwood Road junction, 1992.

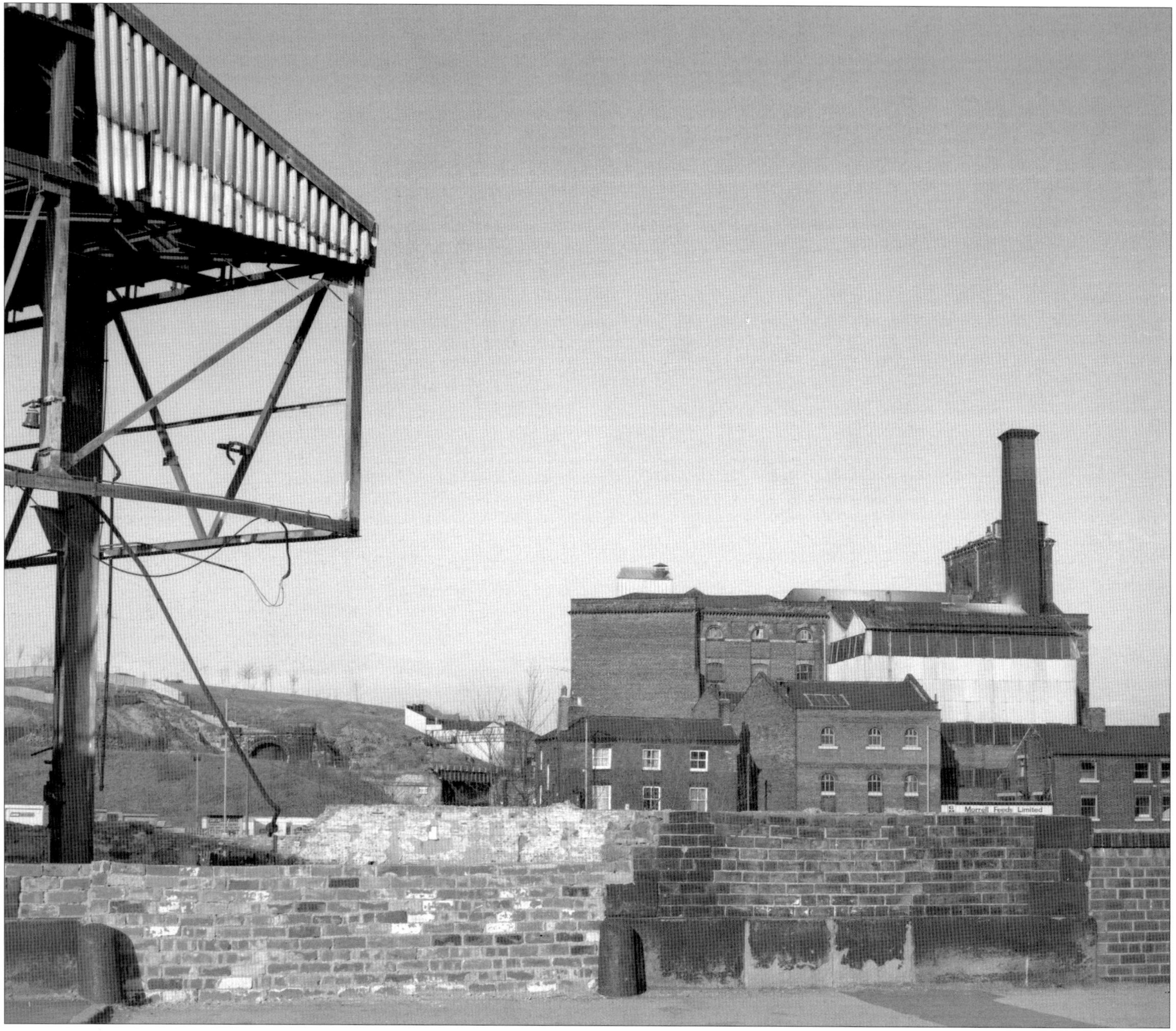

Millsands, 1986 Looking towards Mowbray Street and Aizlewood's Mill.

Attercliffe Common, 1989.

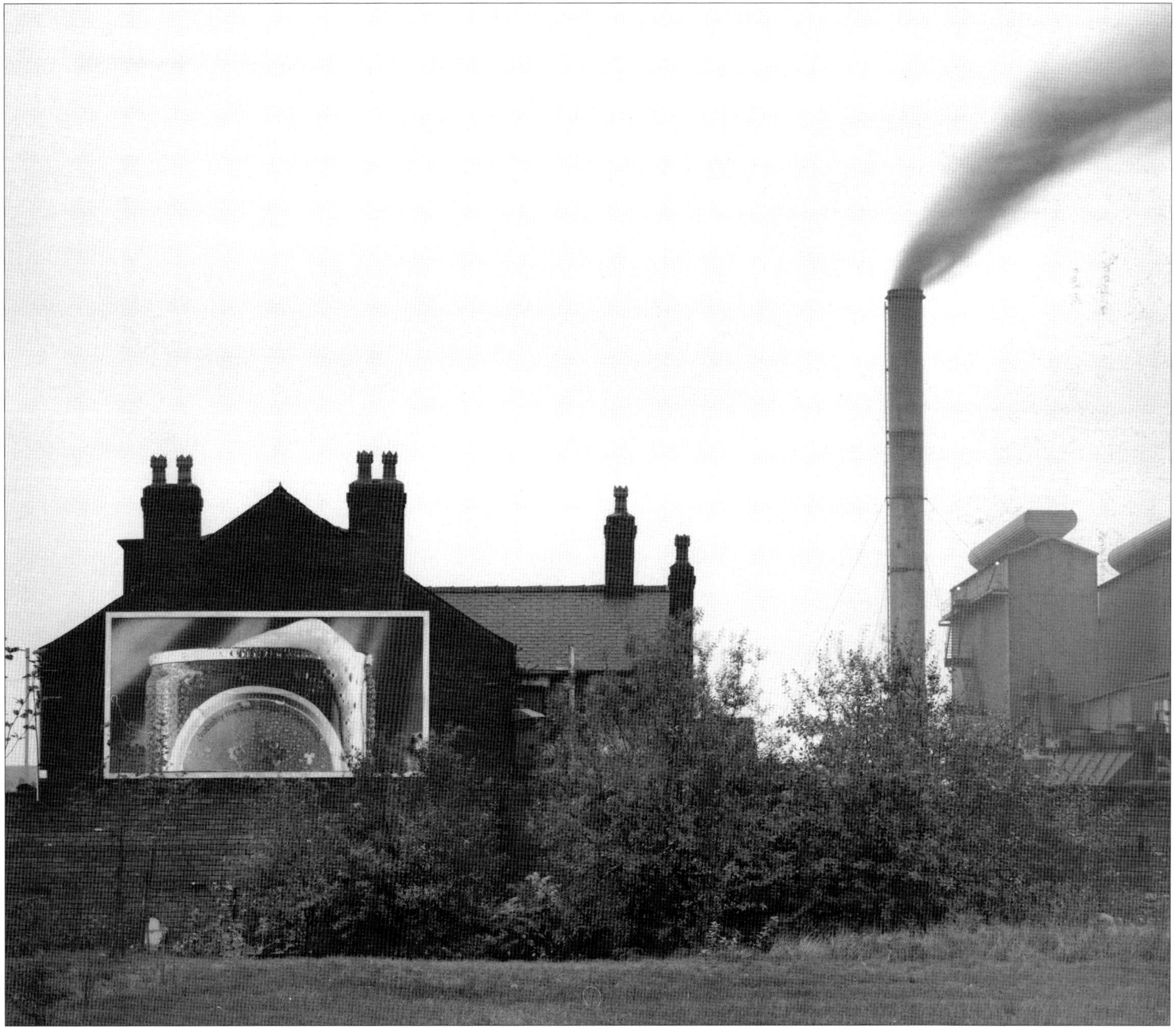

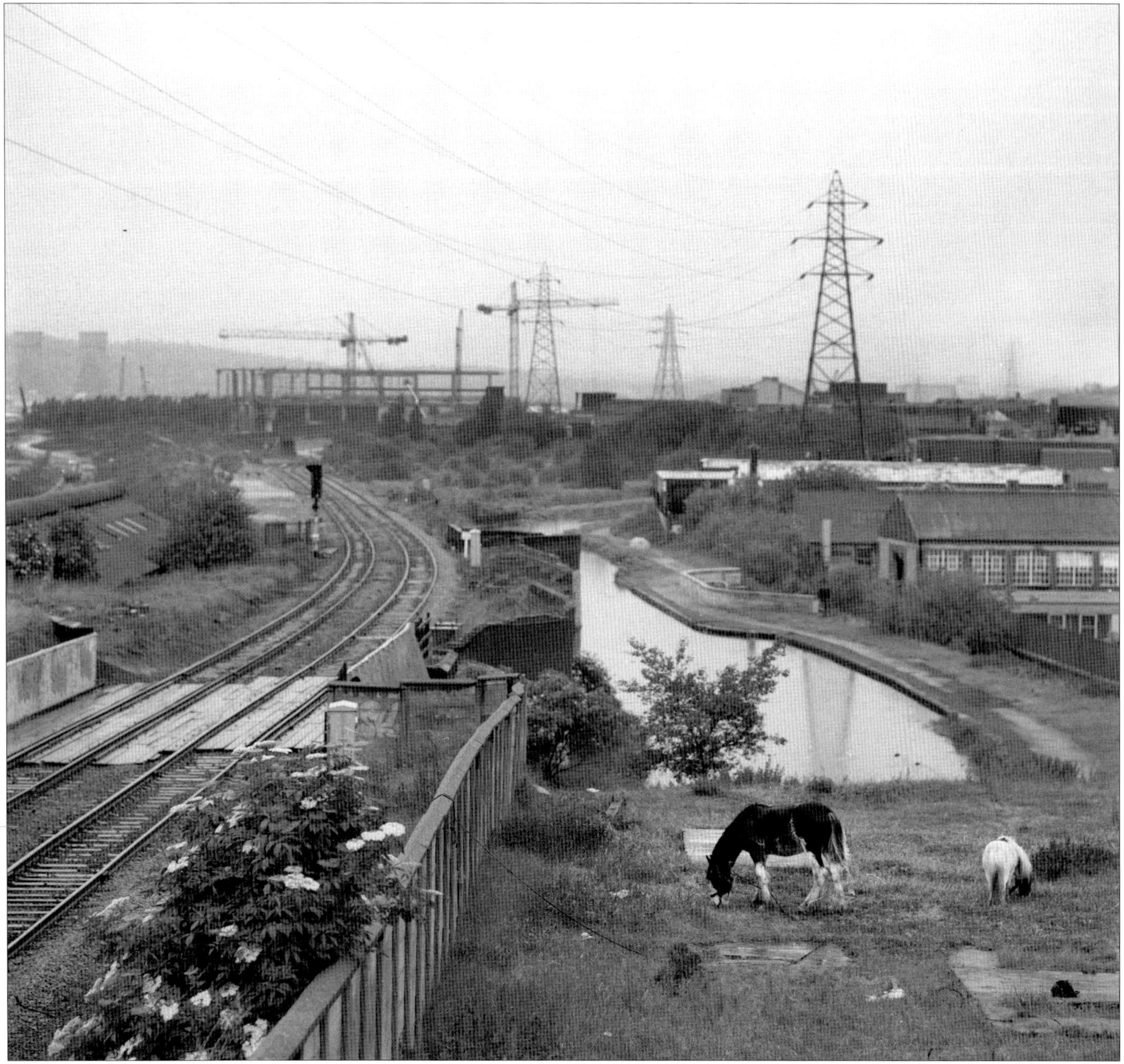

Worksop Road aqueduct.1990.